EDUCATION
ON TRIAL

EDUCATION ON TRIAL

STRATEGIES FOR THE FUTURE

Edited by

WILLIAM J. JOHNSTON

ICS PRESS

Institute for Contemporary Studies
San Francisco, California

CONTENTS

II
Standards for Various Grade Levels

III

The California Reform Movement

IV

The Teaching Profession: Problems and Prospects

VI

Special Problems

VII

Conclusions

PREFACE

Much has been written about education, especially since publication of the federal report, *A Nation at Risk*. A number of major studies have appeared, and the nation's press has been filled with reports of attempted reform from across the country.

In light of this broad concern about American educational quality, the Institute assembled a galaxy of experts to examine progress in efforts to implement reforms, but also to step back and reexamine the essential problem. As an interim report, this volume, unlike other studies, takes the problem to include all major levels in our educational system—K–12 through professional school.

In approaching the problem, we decided it would be valuable to organize the project in the form of a dialogue between theoreticians and practitioners; and because we knew the study inevitably would include more of the former, we chose an eminent practitioner as editor. William J. Johnston was for a decade superintendent of one of the largest public school systems in the nation, the Los Angeles Unified School District, with 700 schools and 540,000 pupils. We also thought his experience managing an urban school system valuable for this study because of the special educational problems that exist in the inner city.

It is important to note also that because California is often at the leading edge of educational innovation—both good and bad—we encouraged Dr. Johnston to emphasize the California experience both in examinations of specific problems and in considering the state's own particular response to the educational reform movement. The reform movement has had an especially energetic champion in California since the election of Bill Honig as State

Superintendent of Schools. Honig also contributed a chapter to this study.

In reexamining the essential problem of educational "standards," we were especially anxious to ventilate deep conflicts of opinion that exist within the educational community and the public at large regarding the nature of those standards. However, the fact that not all contributors to this book agree with each other is very much in keeping with the Institute's past practice of encouraging debates on major public policy issues.

Public concern about this subject is widespread. Although most consider themselves natural-born experts on education, many people are groping for solutions. We hope this volume will provide intelligent guidance and make an important contribution to the ongoing debate.

We want to extend our special thanks to the Exxon Educational Foundation and the Weingart Foundation for their support in financing this important study.

Finally, our gratitude to the Institute staff, which has contributed in many ways to move the book from idea to reality.

Glenn Dumke
President

San Francisco, California
June 1985

FOREWORD

William J. Johnston has gathered together in this volume an impressive array of distinguished contributors. The writers present a lucid discussion of one of the nation's seemingly insoluble problems: how to educate all students to a level approaching their potential. In the chapters of this text are found many constructive recommendations proposed by some of the nation's most widely known educators. School administrators, school board members, legislators, and other policy makers, as well as concerned parents, will find this book to be a rich resource.

If American education is to survive the current storm of criticism and meet the expectations of a nation that is now aroused and worried about our schools, many of the recommendations in this volume must be implemented. The mandate for excellence in education will require action based upon the best thinking from those who know and care the most about learning. Many such experts are authors of chapters in this book.

In a world that has shrunk to one global village of international commerce and trade, the future will belong to the intelligent. This means, in no uncertain terms, that the leading nations will be those that make the most effective use of their schools and colleges to develop the intellectual potential of their citizens to the outer limits of their abilities. Our immediate past history has been one of benign neglect of our schools. This text defines our problems and points to some new directions.

The reform and renewal of American education has been under way for only a short time. The question on many minds relates to its continuation with the intensity and commitment necessary to result in meaningful and lasting change. The outcome rests upon those with leadership and policy-making responsibility. They, most of all, should read this highly stimulating volume, for it is written to enlighten, motivate, and strengthen the decision makers.

Terrell H. Bell
Professor, Department of
    Educational Administration
University of Utah
Secretary of Education, 1981–1985

I

Education on Trial

1

WILLIAM J. JOHNSTON

Introduction

Concern about the crisis in education intensified in 1983 with the publication of the Gardner Commission Report, which began with its now famous statement: "The educational foundations of our society are presently being eroded by a rising tide of mediocrity." Entitled *A Nation at Risk: The Imperative for Educational Reform,* the Gardner Report—named after its chairman David Gardner, who is now President of the University of California—has been followed by a number of other studies, which have examined various dimensions of the continuing decline at all levels of achievement in our nation's schools.[1] *The New York Review of Books* summarized these studies with a simple and succinct headline: "The schools flunk out."

States and school districts around the country have responded to the calls for reform. A *San Francisco Chronicle* editorial captured the sense of dedication in the following words: "[T]he educational pendulum is starting to swing again. This time, it is likely to move back toward traditional educational values, and that would be beneficial to the whole society as well as the students."

Gardner himself captured a sense of urgency people feel, when in 1984 he observed that current efforts to improve education in the United States are "more intense, and of a larger scale, than anything we have seen for twenty-five years." He emphasized the importance of continuing these efforts because such commitment tends to be infrequent. If we falter, he concluded, and do not sustain our commitment, "The threat to the quality of education in our schools is serious enough to constitute a threat to the nation itself."

One year after *A Nation at Risk* was published, pressed by grassroots concern, 275 task forces had been formed in every state to study the problem and present proposals for reform. In their turn, state legislatures in thirty-five states raised high school graduation requirements, and thirteen other states were advancing plans to do the same. Twenty states raised college admission standards, and fifteen more were considering similar actions. And twenty-four states were studying merit pay proposals and other incentives to attract and keep good teachers.

Individual school districts were also very active in seeking out ways to improve. Some districts have experimented with barring students from extracurricular activities until they brought their grades up to a certain grade average. One school superintendent, recognizing that parents are an essential component in educational achievement, visits them at home and requests from them written pledges to spend at least some time each day supervising work on the three Rs and to talk to their children about school. Another district has enlisted the business community in an "Adopt-the-School" program, with executives tutoring, arranging company visits, and making financial contributions. A sampling of this nationwide trend at the grass roots is presented in Appendix A.

Despite this response, the problem persists. Prodded by the extensive media coverage of these reports and books, educational reform and the need for excellence in education continue to hold our attention.

Although professional educators have long been aware of the problems that set off the wave of reform, real improvement has nevertheless proved to be extremely difficult. One reason for that goes to the most basic questions of what we want the education reform movement to achieve. Without more serious attention to this issue—on which there is far from perfect agreement—inaction or even conflicting reforms can result. In his chapter in this book, James Likens reveals the extent of this problem, when he states the *potpourri* of things we want schools to do and be. "At a minimum," he writes, "the schools should advance upward social mobility, achieve racial integration, assimilate immigrants, prepare future scientists and engineers for national defense, provide child care for working parents, compensate for the breakup of the nuclear family, and train a labor force which can compete in the international economy."

Wanting so much, it is hardly surprising that schools often seem to fail so completely.

This study brings together a national group of educators and scholars to examine the contemporary educational reform initiatives, reexamining its essential purposes, assessing progress, and exploring the continuing dilemmas and difficulties. Among the questions they ask are: At a time when demands are everywhere for high educational "standards," what standards should govern our educational system? How should we measure achievement at various educational levels? What measurements of achievement are realistic? What problems arise from influences on the criteria for educational standards from various sources—political (legislature, courts, school boards, etc.), professional (teachers, educational administrators), and personal (parents, children)? In light of enormous differences in social, cultural, and intellectual backgrounds among students, how should we measure the success of individual schools?

More specific questions are: How should we approach the reality that we cannot educate all children in large urban, multi-cultural, multi-ethnic settings to the same degree of competence? Can we nevertheless avoid a "two class" educational system in America? Can we establish the discipline and rigor that are necessary to encourage high academic achievement in our schools and universities? What problems result when local expectations and values conflict with our national educational objectives?

Finally, what are the gains, the risks, the consequences of a real commitment to high educational standards in the United States?

Perhaps the first issue in any discussion of standards is what

standards? And this question leads naturally to the dilemma of
choice. To what extent do we want *society* to determine the mix of
values in education, and to what extent are we willing to permit
individuals—parents and children—to choose their own mix of
values and institutions? The issue is important because some
people agree with a recent editorial in the *Wall Street Journal* that
public schools are a "sluggish monopoly," which can be made accountable only by introducing choice into education.

This is still a hotly debated topic, which arises in discussion of
educational vouchers (which include everything from full
vouchers for use at both public and private schools to vouchers
that limit the behavior of either parents or schools to vouchers for
special purposes such as aiding children who have special learning
problems), tuition tax credits, and even magnet schools. The complexity of these matters is such that they deserve a study of their
own. However, James Likens does review the basic concerns associated with choice in chapter ten.

EDUCATION ON TRIAL begins with a discussion of broad issues.
In Part I Philip Marcus reviews our current condition, and Francis Keppel then considers the problem of what standards we want
to use in judging educational performance. Ruth Love follows with
a view from an urban school district (Chicago) on problems related
to reform.

Part II focuses on problems associated with individual grade
levels and institutional settings. Most educators agree with
Madeline Hunter's view that elementary school, reaching children
at the beginning of their educational lives, requires a broad series
of concerns and must attend, beyond academic rigor, to development of the whole child. Paul Possemato addresses the problem of
secondary schools—which are widely thought to be the central
problem in education. Here the focus is more narrowly academic,
concentrating on what skills and competences should we expect
students graduating from high school to have attained? Hobert
Burns and Sally Kilgore then address problems of higher education and special features of private versus public schooling.

Because of its size and demographic complexity, and also
because it has often been at the forefront of experiments in educational reform, California and the California Reform Movement

under recently elected State Superintendent of Schools Bill Honig has been a special subject of interest in this book. Although reference to California is evident throughout the book, Part III presents two chapters focused entirely on the state's experiment. The first, by Honig, presents his view of the need for reform and the outlines of his widely acclaimed program for reform. The second, by James Likens, summarizes a major research project by the Southern California Research Council and presents an evaluation of progress in the state.

Part IV looks at the teaching profession, which is surely the central concern of much of this book. Bernard Gifford and Trish Stoddart lead off with a critique of teacher training, which is an important element in the drive for educational excellence. Robert Doherty analyzes teacher bargaining from the standpoint of an academic expert on labor relations, and Albert Shanker comments on the responsibilities of teacher unions and school boards in the educational process as seen by a union leader. Shanker stresses the need to weed out incompetent teachers or, better yet, keep them from entering the educational process in the first place. The next two chapters (forming Part V) address problems of education and technology. The first, by Richard Simonds and James Wiebe, tackles the place technological innovation may play in our educational future (answer: as yet, not as much as was hoped); and the second, by George Bugliarello, addresses the special responsibility of technical universities, specializing in technical education, to reach beyond specialization to integrate such studies with elements of a liberal education.

Part VI presents Glenn Dumke on accreditation, which deals with the issue of institutional self-policing; and then Kenneth Sirotnik and John Goodlad argue the importance of improving rather than testing our schools. In the final section, Ernest Boyer offers an overview of our educational problem, and Glenn Dumke comments on some of the issues analyzed by the other authors.

There are other matters of importance that, while not chapters in their own right, appear at various places in these pages. The problem of incentives, for instance, is one such item—the question of overall pay scales, and what they reflect about the nation's commitment to quality education. (For the striking disparity in teacher salaries by states, see Appendix B.) And then there is the issue of differential incentives to encourage good teaching. This latter aspect is, of course, raised most prominently in the debate about merit pay.

In selecting a mixture of contributors to this volume, our intention was to combine the perspective of the academy—of those researching and analyzing educational problems—and practitioners who run school districts while coping with practical problems and dealing with the complex political realities and limitations that surround education. The result is a balance of theory and practice.

In sum, EDUCATION ON TRIAL is an interim report which reflects on the mounting demands for educational reform at all levels and examines problems and opportunities. The stakes in this debate could hardly be greater. Our educational institutions have played and continue to play an important and dynamic role in the American social and political experiment. They have been instruments of social stability as well as innovation, repositories of the finest ideas and ideals from our past, as well as testing grounds for the future.

Our problems are anything but insoluble; they do not come from external forces. "The decline of educational standards," David Gardner said in 1984, "stems more from weakness of purpose, confusion of values, underuse of talent and lack of leadership than from conditions beyond our control."

Our problem is one of will—summoning the energy and sense of purpose to create a system of public and private education that is worthy of a great nation.

2

PHILIP N. MARCUS

Evidence of Decline in Educational Standards

Schools preoccupy America. The teacher-student relationship has a reverential place in the public's mind, as well it should in a new nation dedicated to bettering itself and all whom it has welcomed. But as America grew, that little schoolhouse became the small center around which growing layers of administrators and public officials gathered to observe, judge, and direct what goes on in the classroom.

"America's public school system is confronted with the most serious crisis in its history," Benjamin Fine, the *New York Times'* education writer, proclaimed in 1947. By this reminder of the perennial crisis in education, Diane Ravitch launched her masterful history of the last generation, *The Troubled Crusade.*[1] Echoing that charge, the 1980s began with dozens of public commissions, foundation studies, and public statements by citizens and educators, with many more yet to come. It is "the rising tide of mediocrity" as described by the National Commission on Excellence in Education that is causing these new waves of concern with the quality of our education.

Education's newest crises began in the late 1970s when America's most broad-based grass-roots movement began to assemble, a collection of angry and even desperate parents determined to save their children from the sorry state of education. It is the public's determined effort to ensure their children's future that fuels the present campaign to restore the faded quality of the public school system.

In short order parents and concerned citizens forced onto the public agenda their concern for reestablishing a commitment to excellence in education. Joined quickly by responsive politicians at the local and state levels, nearly forty states, in a span of about seven years, passed minimum competency tests to ensure that high school graduates of public schools could, at least, do the arithmetic needed to balance a checkbook and fill out a job application. In the 1980s nearly twenty states, in addition, have tightened the standards for teacher certification. When the U.S. Department of Education received *A Nation at Risk* in 1983 it was the educational establishment that was shocked, but not by facts or the urgent style of reporting the sorry state of American schools. The shock occurred in the report's aftermath when public opinion galvanized politics and media into action. The pedagogical folly behind these dismal facts, finally trumpeted at the highest levels of public opinion, is causing a real crisis within educational circles. A bandwagon has been set in motion toward the one least mentioned but oldest goal of American education—an open, accessible, mass educational system striving for excellence.

This latest war about the purposes of education is being carried to the public arena by valiant forces bravely arguing for an idea that had seemingly been subdued for generations, an apparent cost of our having created the largest, most accessible system of education in the modern world. The small but growing number of intellectuals who champion excellence in education, a rump group in the twentieth century owing to the intellectual fashion for utilitarian measures, had seemingly turned the tables on much that the democratic impulse for equalitarian education had achieved. Finally, in modern America we have a most serious examination of just what it is that schools *do.*

It is not the nation's teachers who must act as defenders of the massive and flawed educational enterprise whose results are so appalling. What had been an unspoken national conspiracy to ignore in public had, when it suddenly appeared, a wider circle of blame on which to focus attention. And it was not yet teachers themselves who should be singled out for criticism.[2] In Diane Ravitch's catalog, colleges and universities had created massive remedial programs to cope with hordes of semi-literate students, but kept silent about how their own lowered admission standards had undermined high school graduation requirements. Businesses and employers had established private educational programs of huge size to teach basic skills to those leaving schools unable to perform minimal tasks of arithmetic, spelling, and writing simple sentences, but in silence they repaired the flaws in their employee's educations. Federal and state legislatures, ever ready to answer the strident demands of special interest groups and the self-serving proclamations of professional educationists, had cut away the ground for basic education courses while heaping extraneous curricular requirements on the schools. Even the courts, eager to defend alleged rights of children, joined in the emasculation of education by whittling away the school's abilities to maintain order and discipline. And finally, the publishing world, together with the press, justified "dumbed down" text books and other barbarities of lapsed taste by using so-called balanced panels of professional educators to assure themselves of meeting market acceptability.

In answer to this barrage of criticisms and widening circle of blame, bureaucrats of education have been testy, aggressive, and desperate to counter-attack with what Gilbert Sewall calls the "good news" about our educational system. For example, College Board President George Hanford tried to herald a rise of *four* points in the 1983 Scholastic Achievement Test scores as a trend upwards, reversing nearly two decades of declining performance by high school students. (And the Secretary of Education pointed to *A Nation at Risk* as if it were a cause of the rise, implying that the President achieved what parents, teachers, and students had failed to gain.) Beginning in the early 1960s, but unremarked upon until the early 1970s, the median scores on both the quantitative and verbal portions of the SAT declined, and declined still further until hitting the present bottom in 1981. More worrisome, the number of students scoring at top end, the truly bright, continued to shrink despite the leveling off in median scores.

The bottoming out of median scores, sadly, may result from the leveling down of the performance of superior students. Today, higher achieving students do significantly less well, and in smaller percentages, than they did a decade ago. From 1972 to 1982 the proportion of students scoring on the verbal tests above 750 (very high) declined 47 percent; those scoring above 650 (relatively high) declined 45 percent. Yet the number of test-takers declined only 3 percent. The equivalent declines on the math portion of the tests were, for over 750, 23 percent, and for over 650, 16 percent. It is the best students—or those who could do best—whose performance has slipped most. While there may be continuing opportunities to satisfy "high-tech" interests (teenaged computer whizzes do exist), there may be few left to do all the rest of society's work. Even accepting the last two year's data as signaling a trend upward, at this rate of recovery Hanford cautioned that "it would take until the year 2000 for the national math average to reach the level of 1963 . . . we should be well into the next century before the verbal average reached its 1963 level."

"The tide of mediocrity" is creating the shocking prospect, for the first time in the nation's existence, of a generation of students *less* well educated than its predecessor.

The Clash of Lyres

> *Thou shalt not be on friendly terms*
> *With guys in advertising firms,*
>   *Nor speak with such*
> *As read the Bible for its prose,*
> *Nor, above all, make love to those*
>   *Who wash too much.*

Excerpts from "Under Which Lyre," *W. H. Auden: Collected Poems,* edited by Edward Mendelson. Copyright © 1976 by Random House, Inc. Reprinted by permission.

Thou shalt not live within thy means
Nor on plain water and raw greens.
   If thou must choose
Between the chances, choose the odd;
Read The New Yorker, *trust in God;*
   And take short views.

"Under Which Lyre" was W.H. Auden's poetic address to the Phi Beta Kappa chapter at Harvard College. Though we recognize these sentiments as having been celebrated in vulgar, raucous tones throughout the academy in the 1960s, Auden's address, delivered in 1946, prefigures those radicalized cries. How this elegant anticipation of counterculture, "doing your own thing," and quiche-eating present-centeredness could have as its subtitle, "A Reactionary Tract for the Times," a generation before the popular appearance on the other side of the political scale requires reflection.

Because the Harvard class of 1946 included members of the first wave of returning veterans, their dilemma anticipated the plight of the great number of new students soon to be brought into higher education by the G.I. Bill. The poem addresses their dilemma of having escaped the battlefield of World War II only to be cast into another, more ephemeral, but equally fateful battle. Auden portrays in classical terms "the brutal dialectic" occurring in minds newly recruited to higher education as the contest between Apollo and Hermes (or Mercury). The first is the god of light; the second is messenger of the dead, god of luck, and the original hustler living by his native wit. Though Auden presents these two mythical figures as antitheses in the soul between which there is no compromise, he sees native common sense at risk due to Apollo's strengths.

And when he occupies a college,
Truth is replaced by Useful Knowledge;
   He pays particular
Attention to Commercial Thought,
Public Relations, Hygiene, Sport,
   In his curricula.

Athletic, extrovert and crude,
For him, to work in solitude
  Is the offense,
The goal a populous Nirvana:
His shield bears this device: Mens sana
  qui mal y pense.

Auden's heart is with the academic innocents for whom he
devises a strategy for routing Apollo's battalions, the Hermetic
Decalogue, the last lines of which appear above. Yet if the poem's
closing lines look backwards to the 1960s, the first command-
ments are equally prophetic of today's battle lines:

Thou shalt not do as the dean pleases,
Thou shalt not write thy doctor's thesis
  On education,
Thou shalt not worship projects nor
Shalt thou or thine bow down before
  Administration.

Thou shalt not answer questionnaires
Or quizzes upon World-Affairs,
  nor with compliance
Take any test. Thou shalt not sit
With statisticians nor commit
  A social science.

It is a "Reactionary Tract" that continues to resonate today
because it is squarely aimed at the heart of the progressive educational agenda. Auden evokes an even earlier time when the purpose of higher education was to create gentlemen or scholars, but
not citizens or productive members of a prosperous society. This
conflict must be acknowledged and its grounds examined because
these are fundamental choices about the purpose of education in
our nation that Auden evokes.

A more recognizable form of this classical battle familiar to
Americans are the characters of Huck Finn and Tom Sawyer, the
choice between them driving the American character. Should we
strive to be the solitary romantic dreamer or the sober industrious
achiever? These models are poles of our consciousness. Their
elaborated versions in educational theory lie beneath today's

intellectual battle between what progressivism created and its stubborn alternatives, newly transformed into what is known as the "excellence movement."

That choice of lives for Americans, with all it entails for morality and character, is intrinsic. It is alive today in the battle between educational theories in a society more democratic, more prosperous, and more advantaged in most all means—save clarity of purpose—than it has ever been. And our familiarity with Auden's closing advice to "take short views" introduces the greatest dimension of that basic choice—the choice at bottom between excellence and equality. We shrink from recognizing that choice because not only have we lived through the 1960s and all that it brought to education and intellectual life, but we have also accepted what Allan Bloom identifies as a "routinization of the passions of the sixties that is the core of what is going on now, just as the sixties were merely a radicalization of earlier tendencies."[3]

But that enlargement of the impulse to "do your own thing" has come by undermining the claims of any moral or political authorities to regulate self-expression, which has, in some schools of thought, been made identical to education itself. The freedoms that have been bestowed evermore on Americans in the 1980s seem to be in danger of curtailment by concern for the poor results of that very excess of freedom. The educational and political critics of the excellence movement, which, like Auden's Apollo, do control colleges and educational establishments of all sorts, have powerful weapons in their great argument against the current tide of public opinion. Chief among these are the results of the last generation's work and money and the weight of the symbol in whose name all that work was done, educational equity. Owing to the small number of intellectuals ready and able to listen and articulate the sometimes inchoate public criticism of today's schools, they are in grave danger of having their advice assimilated by what Saul Bellow has called America's belief in "easy virtue," a mixture of egotism and high-minded acceptance of every lifestyle, which together denies the very possibility of excellence. The comfortable American belief in moderation is yet another threat to this opportunity to improve the educational results of our handsome investments in education. That popular instinct to blur and absorb truly unlike things, however conducive to tranquility, encourages a facile comparison between the collapse of educational standards in the 1960s and the resurgent interest in the results of education in the 1980s. In this comparison, if the pendulum is allowed to swing back (some marginal curricular changes, some more money, and more research into the use of new learning techniques), all will be put right. But this soft, easy answer ignores the problems and necessary steps to rectify the causes of the educational failure we are surely experiencing. It also obscures what has happened, good and bad, in education. In order to focus the issues raised by concern for the poor results of our schools, let me summarize the best of the "good news" about American education—the massive size and quantitative changes achieved in our school systems over the last several decades.

The Good News of Education

Ben Wattenberg, ever the cheerful advocate of democratic progress, has put the quantitative expansions of American education in clear view in *The Good News is the Bad News is Wrong.*[4] He takes us on a quick march through the levels of education to show what we have achieved.

Preschool education in 1970 was used by little over one-third (38 percent) of American children aged 3–5; by 1982 that advantage was enjoyed by 52 percent of preschoolers. Included in this educational benefit was the black female-headed household, whose children participated in preschool programs at the national rate. Attendance in elementary and junior high school retains its (compulsory) rate—98 percent.

High school graduation has now become a national norm with 86 percent of adults, 25–29 years old, holding this degree, up from 50 percent in 1950. Turning those figures around, only 14 percent of young adults lack a high school degree, while in 1960 nearly forty percent (39 percent) of young adults had not finished high school.

Wattenberg notes that in college attendance, "the typical American young person (almost) completes his or her freshman year of college. Or, stated another way, *well more than half of our youngsters go to college."* The percentage of young adults attending college rose from about 18 percent to nearly 34 percent; the percentage of young adults completing four years or more of college rose from 11 percent to 22 percent. Even more dramatic is the changed composition of the student body, with the percentage of women attending college rising from one-third to one-half, and the number of blacks attending college rising from 95,000 to 814,000. Between 1950 and 1982 the raw numbers of young adults enrolled in colleges went from 2.7 million (up from the prewar, 1940 level of 1.5 million) to 12.3 million.

Since the democratization of higher education began with the G.I. Bill, college enrollments have quadrupled, and the number of college graduates has nearly tripled. To handle this influx, the number of college faculty rose from 266,000 to 633,000 in 1974. The number of masters degrees conferred in 1982 was 296,000, a 42 percent increase over 1970. The number of Ph.D.'s conferred rose from 8,800 in 1955 to 33,000 in 1982 (and it has held around the level of 30,000 for about a dozen years).

Adult higher education has been stimulated and provided in a quantity hardly imaginable fifteen years ago. During the late 1960s a new community college was opening *every* week. Since 1969 the number of people taking part-time courses or participating in some other form of organized, accredited higher education went from 13 to 21 million. A recently noticed expansion of higher education is in the corporate world, where IBM is reported to be spending $700 million on education for its employees.

Corporate spending on higher education programs run by businesses has become, also, a "booming industry." According to first accounts of a report by the Carnegie Foundation for the Advancement of Teaching, "Corporate Classrooms: The Learning Business," an estimated $60 billion a year is spent on corporate-run education. This heretofore little noticed educational system involves about 8 million people, approaching the total enrollment at the nation's four-year colleges, public and private. The budgets for these programs is similar to the cost of the nation's colleges.

Discovering an uncontrolled educational system of this size in the midst of our huge and expensive system of education caused the report's authors to be predictably alarmed. Ernest L. Boyer, in the report's introduction, suggested that this corporate enterprise raises "vital public policy" questions.[5] Indeed, it does, but that question's meaning for professional educators may be what to do about the existence of a major enterprise outside the direct reach of educational authorities. Its existence is both an affront and reproach.

To deal with the affront, Mr. Boyer was quick to suggest the creation of a new "semi-public Strategic Council for Educational Development" to recommend how to coordinate educational activities. To be sure, the "coordination" might be designed to eliminate the "threat" of an alternative to traditional colleges and universities. Barely but visibly evident in the report is the veiled allegation that corporations have violated the "public trust" (or, the SEC may yet inquire about the corporate effort to bust the monopoly of existing educators).

The reproach to the quality of existing education could not be clearer. While the report observes that the burgeoning corporate programs entail large costs that ultimately may be borne by the public through tax writeoffs and presumed increased costs of goods and services, it ignores the direct need of corporations to create their own educational system *in lieu of* inadequate schools. And it utterly ignores the benefits to be gained, not only by these students/employees, but also by the public from increased profits. For the last century business leaders have staunchly supported higher education. As Peter Dobkin Hall tells us:

It was, after all, business that underwrote the reform of higher education which began in the late 1860s, an educational reconstruction which, through the elective system on the undergraduate level and the reform of the graduate school and professional schools, emphasized both professional specialization and the ethos of national service.[6]

In gratitude for this beneficence the report's author, Dr. Nell P. Eurich, states that "It would be ironic if significant new insights about how we learn would come, not from the academy, but from industry and business." It may also be true and necessary.[7]

Something has to be done about the declining capacities of American education. Money cannot be causing the problems of the schools (except perhaps in too easy abundance). Excluding the $60 billion now being spent on corporate and industry educational programs, the total bill for operating our educational system, public and private at all levels, reached $215 billion in 1983. In constant (1983) dollars these costs have increased 20 percent over 1970— and there are 3 percent fewer students. Expenditures per pupil (adjusted for inflation) increased almost 5 percent per year between 1965–1978, *twice* the rate of growth in GNP, and faster than real expenditures per pupil for the preceding fifteen years, 1950–1965.

Further, intimacy in the relationship between teacher and student might seem to have grown. The number of students per teacher dropped in national averages from twenty-nine to twenty-one overall. These ratios in public schools improved markedly over the last decade, where in secondary schools there was one teacher for every seventeen students, down from twenty in 1970. Yet this increased familiarity seems to have bred contempt between teacher and student.

Dissatisfaction with discipline in the schools is the single, greatest, and continuous cause of the public's concern with education. As difficult as it is to contemplate the blighted adult lives with which too many American youths will be saddled due to inadequate education (to say nothing about our nation's future growth and tranquility), it is horrifying to consider the pathologies loosed upon the young by the failure adequately to develop their characters, an external substitute for which is imposed discipline.

Two anecdotal examples suffice. In 1984, after a near-fatal assault on a student, a Brooklyn high school installed metal detectors, together with body searches, at the school's doors in a desperate attempt to stop the flow of guns, knives, and other lethal weapons into the building. After a near riot and angry boycott of the school by the students, the authorities relented and removed the detectors. Later, according to the *New York Times,* the carrying of weapons into the school declined about 30 percent, but it continues because students fear for their lives. In California, alienated suburban youth in Milpitas knew of the murder of a fourteen-year-old girl by her boyfriend. According to public accounts, for several days her half-nude body was viewed, mutilated, and desecrated by other students. In spite of rumors flying around the high school, no student reported the incident to authorities for days. "You don't narc (inform) on people," said one friend of the victim.

Consider the vast meaning about the changes in character and the resultant problems for schools revealed in the comparison reported in Table 1.

Alarming symptoms of the decline in the character of our youth have been evident for some time, certainly pervasively known to

Table 1
Blackboard Jungle: The top seven discipline problems in public schools in 1940 and the top seventeen in 1982

1940	1982
1. Talking	1. Rape
2. Chewing gum	2. Robbery
3. Making noise	3. Assault
4. Running in the halls	4. Burglary
5. Getting out of turn in line	5. Arson
6. Wearing improper clothing	6. Bombings
7. Not putting paper in wastebaskets	7. Murder
	8. Suicide
	9. Absenteeism
	10. Vandalism
	11. Extortion
	12. Drug abuse
	13. Alcohol abuse
	14. Gang warfare
	15. Pregnancy
	16. Abortion
	17. Venereal disease

Source: Reprinted from *Harper's* Magazine, March 1985, and the *Presidential Biblical Scoreboard* with permission from the Biblical News Service, Costa Mesa, California.

educators in manifold forms as the 1960s blossomed, long before these pathologies reached present proportions. Character is more than discipline, for character refers to the beliefs, values, and habit of good behavior that shape one's life, rather than to compliance with eternal laws and regulations. Edward A. Wynne has compiled data that reveal a consistent, disturbing, and sharp upward swing in the incidence of rates of suicide, homicide, and out-of-wedlock births. And he has determined that these rates for youth increase far more quickly than for similar adult measures. It is not just the reappearance of "The Blackboard Jungle" that we witness, though delinquency and social pathologies are widespread, but the realization that what Thomas Hobbes called "the state of nature" is real and alive—and still "nasty, brutish, and short."

And it will not do, at all, for educators to excuse themselves from knowledge and action by saying that after all, these problems walk in the school's doors, that students are mirrors of society, and that "values and sex education" is an answer. Attempting to do so abdicates educational responsibilites, and denies substance to the act of education. Here, we get close to the heart of the issues raised by the public's demand for excellence and for a return to basic education. And this is the question that divides education itself: Is education for the mind alone, or for the whole man, heart and head?

At issue in the public's determination to get serious about schooling is a fundamental division between them and educators, by whom they do not mean teachers or principals but rather those pedagogues in higher education (at the pinnacle of which reside schools of education), foundations, public officials, and other upper-level reaches of the intellectual new class. The principle causing that division has been confounded, unwittingly and maliciously, by a wide mixture of issues entangling the debate over educational reform. The "good news" rebuttal is but the first professional response. What distracts attention and adds confusion to the central question in today's educational debate are the myriad diversions offered by issues such as educational budgets (more, but from whom?), merit pay for teachers (which some educators argued all teachers were due—at a 50 percent increase in starting salary), competency testing for certified teachers, and nationwide competency tests for high school seniors.

All these issues are real, and some are practicable means for marginal improvements in education—but they are all instrumental questions of policy *not* to be confused with the principle under debate. Even more bewildering, the moral purposes in the service of which the schools might be enlisted create another layer of confusion. Whatever the merits or faults of issues such as school prayer, review of library holdings, secular humanism, or eliminating sex education, entwining the "social issue" with educational purpose has only compounded the argument.

What still shines through this welter of debate about policies and practices in our schools is the public's insistence that excellence include academic performance, decent character, and civil behavior. Against these standards the Apollo-like commanders of the institutional high ground reply that equity (or access) is *the* measure by which to judge schools. In this clash of principles,

what one side sees as failure, the other sees as success. What one
urges as reform, the other resists as retrograde. What one insists
upon as right and fitting, the other insists is wrong and immoral.
A Nation at Risk was the summation of the public's complaints
about schools. The determined answer to that complaint, beyond
silence, has yet to be heard.

Joseph Adelson, in an article "Why the Schools May Not Improve," fairly summarizes the fundamental principles of our present educational enterprise.[8] In his analysis of the conflict, realities
of the classroom will be interpreted by the ideas pervasive in intellectual life. And the reflexive answer will be that there is no such
thing as excellence, only self-expressions.

Sharp exception to that prevailing opinion has been voiced by
William J. Bennett, Secretary of Education, and Richard Ekman,
the director of NEH's Division of Education Programs, under
whose brilliant leadership NEH has demonstrated that educational excellence can be nurtured and expanded. Yet the continuing reactions to Bennett's efforts can be seen from the response to
his asking teachers what books should high school seniors have
been expected to read. That reaction betrays the real grounds for
the current arguments about the purposes of education.

Out of the 500 questionnaires returned to Bennett in answer to
this question, most of which came from high school teachers in
humanities (just inspired by having participated in an NEH Summer Seminar for Teachers), there appeared substantial agreement on ten classic authors. Of these ten, four wrote in classical
antiquity and six in modern times. Only one wrote in the twentieth century. The list was as follows:

1. Shakespeare

2. Selected American
   historical documents

3. Twain, *The Adventures of
   Huckleberry Finn*

4. The Bible

5. Homer, *Odyssey, Iliad*

6. Dickens, *Great
   Expectations, A Tale of Two
   Cities*

7. Plato, *Republic*

8. Steinbeck, *Grapes of Wrath*

9. Hawthorne, *The Scarlet Letter*

10. Sophocles, *Oedipus Rex*

The expectable criticisms of the exercise came not from class-room teachers but mostly from "professional educators," officials of educational associations and government lobbyists. The critics variously argued that students could not understand these works; that the list lacked appropriate sexual and ethnic balance; that the list slighted the accomplishments of minorities; that the list promoted patriotism; and, that the list discriminated against all other works.

While the remarkable level of agreement among teachers about these ten great books is impressive, what infuriated Bennett's critics was the idea that *any* books could be identified as more important than others. As Adelson foresaw, the heart of the problem is the lingering relativism that continues to grip education to the point of nearly extinguishing its collective capacity to choose among purposes.

To Reclaim a Legacy, NEH's report on the humanities on college campuses, is yet another measure of the movement away from any basic curriculum, the continuation of which was Auden's concern. In the last forty years colleges have permitted the erosion of curricular requirements so that bachelor's degrees can be obtained from 86 percent of colleges without having studied the classical civilizations of Greece and Rome; from 75 percent, without having studied European history; and from 72 percent, without American literature or history. The significant change is the foreign language requirement, which 90 percent of colleges had waived by 1966, but that nearly 50 percent now require.

Finding Our Way

What is quietly remarkable in NEH's work, and by extension in the other reports on excellence in education, are the underlying presumptions supporting that agreement. First, there is a consensus that schools at all levels must concentrate on nurturing the love of academic learning and assuring for all students a comprehension of the philosophic foundations for their nation and civilization. Second, they remind us that true education is for every student a fundamental act of justice, overcoming the hardships of birth or upbringing, and enabling each to select, and then more fairly to achieve their own dreams.

Reaffirming these truths a decade ago would have gained its champions' abuse for their tyrannical, repressive, deformative, or even less civil descriptions of their wish to restrain young minds.

All these victories also affirm an inherently moral dimension of education and the moral effects of being educated. We are no longer forced publicly to choose between a technocratic education that destroys human spirit and the granting to students of a voluptuous license to do whatever they please. We are, again, in sight of the lofty goals resting upon requisite mental discipline, which was the sole virtue of the traditional "3 Rs" to instill.

It is not yet known whether the public means to follow the bandwagon of excellence when the road gets rough, as it surely will when the full intellectual magic of "equality" or "equity" is invoked against resurgent traditionalism in the classroom. Excellence means recognition and rewards on merit. The excellence of a society is measurable by the qualities called forth in its citizens, and the success of our society especially depends upon the intellectual and moral qualities of citizens. The "rising tide of mediocrity" will, after all, overcome only *us*. And if a majority, even of today's youth, were to become oppressive, narrow- or empty-minded, there would be no preserving of society.

If schools are to remain the engine of opportunity by which America has produced its remarkable equality and mobility, then every student, at every level, must be able to draw upon his full abilities. Even when the results vary, the purposes for which all strive must be commonly understood as the common good. And from the list of purposes to which schools and pedagogues bend their efforts we must strike several categories that have been given high place since the 1930s. Among the purposes of education we can no longer afford the expensive delusions of the past, such as the hostility toward academic subject matter and the related determination to focus on the student's "adjustment" to society. Despite all the care lavished on a youth due to his "cultural deprivation," that very preoccupation has served to cast such students into an iron cloak of race, class, ethnicity, or sex as determinative of their lives. Education considered as an adjustment process reconciling one to society's ills may well have been the external constraint on life that could never be overcome, and the thing that may have prevented self-liberation.[9]

A confusion, if not a cowering paralysis, over the purposes of education has plagued educators for too long. For too long the power of progressive education has blinded educationists to the disastrous consequences of its actual practices. Since Robert M. Hutchins and Arthur Bestor created in the 1950s the lingering crises whose end we are witnessing, it has been painfully evident that ill-considered ideas distort practices long after their intellectual foundations have been exposed and destroyed.

Leadership, in education as in all endeavors, is both rare and irreplacable. But it need not be punished, as David Reisman has described current procedures for selecting university and college presidents. Even if we had a Robert M. Hutchins today, could he become a college or university president? The answer is, probably not, and not just because of the ruffled feathers of faculty peacocks or the determined alumni football fans demanding a winning team. Those problems have always been with us, but we have not always made them legitimate concerns. By doing so now we make them into structural problems in governing institutions, turning what are human weaknesses into almost constitutional problems. It is we who have decided to live, however unhappily, with the unwanted legacies of the 1960s by tolerating the democraticization of the presidential search procedures in higher education, procedures designed with exquisite regard for the presumed sensibilities of any and all "constituencies" of the school, but with a brutal disregard for the results of those procedures upon the institution or the enterprise. Like the reforms of the Democratic Party in national politics, higher education prevents itself from identifying its best leaders because it forgot why and for what purpose it was selecting them. And like another leadership group crippled by short-term perspectives, corporate chief executive officers, college presidents now have an average tenure of about seven years (CEOs last about six).

We impatiently await the full debate from which education may sort out a purposeful course for making our schools what most teachers and parents wish, an enterprise responsible for much of the nation's continuing well-being. And while we await agreement among educational leaders, we might usefully consider some small practical steps to remove our self-created obstacles.

3

FRANCIS KEPPEL

Standards — By What Criteria?

As the title implies, there is no single standard for education in the United States; there are many. This raises questions about priorities. Which purposes are most important? How do educational institutions at all levels influence the priorities of different groups—students, parents, rich versus poor, the local community, the state, business and labor, intellectuals, scientists, and the nation? How do priorities change over time?

Even a cursory look at the history of education in the United States in this century shows that the priorities set for schools and colleges have included varied topics such as teaching the key subjects to all youth; providing equal access without regard to race, sex, national origin, or economic condition; imparting democratic values; teaching responsible social behavior; culling high talent; and preparing for the world of work outside the schools. Different decades seem to have put higher emphasis on one or another of these goals, but at no time have any of the goals been eliminated entirely. This suggests that *all* of them have to be considered in setting standards and deciding criteria, and that relevant data have to be collected *regularly* so that judgments can always be made on the progress toward, or retreat from, the goals.

There are two essential problems here. First is the incredibly complicated job of identifying, collecting, and analyzing data measuring results in relation to each of these very different areas. Such measurement obviously puts a heavy burden on the social sciences—cognitive and social psychology, psychometrics, political science, sociology, and anthropology, among others. Given limitations in the state of these arts or sciences, one should be cautious about relying on putatively "scientific results." Moreover, it is clear that no single measure, by itself, can provide a basis for judging performance for any standard. We are forced, therefore, to deal with complex variables and complex interpretations of data, as well as to decide on where to put emphases.

The second problem, of course, lies in judging *which* standards are considered priorities at any moment in time. The recent educational reform movement, which is the subject of this book, addresses the decline in performance on the quality of student learning of "basic" subjects. This chapter will therefore focus on this standard among the many others set forth above.

The list of basic subjects varies somewhat over time, but reading and writing, mathematics, the several sciences, and the social studies are on every list, often with the addition of the arts and foreign languages. That pleasantly vague skill of "learning how to think" may also be included. These standards of accomplishment are relevant for the individual and for every group in society.

The 1970s and early 1980s brought more attention to the need for higher "academic" standards in the schools. It seems reasonable to assume both that this focus will continue in the 1980s and 1990s and that it will extend from the schools to higher education. Furthermore, criteria and measures developed to set standards in this area of education often turn out to be the basis for assessing progress toward the goals of equal access, democratic values, the identification of talent, and preparation for work. This author takes the position, therefore, that in any strategy for reform, attention must first be given to how well the schools and colleges teach these basic subjects and how well the students learn them.

What Data Are Needed?

Who wants data that are used to set standards and how will the data be used? At the national level, do the Executive Branch and the Congress need something comparable to the Annual Economic Report, which provides data on a host of variables and projects future developments? Is the same kind of report needed by states? Are these kinds of data needed by individual schools and colleges or accrediting commissions, or is something more comparable to a thermometer reading and a blood test more appropriate? Is it adequate to infer some standards, as we do today, by using other kinds of data, such as faculty qualifications, institutional resources or financial strength? Are those concerned with such reports interested primarily in the present situation, or is it more important for the reports to show trends over time? Does the choice of those who apply the standards affect the standards themselves? To put it another way, can the medium become the message?

The American people, who ultimately pay for whatever educational standards they get, have varied in their views both among themselves and over time, on what criteria are the more important. For a decade a sample of the public has said that the "biggest problem—the very serious problem" of the public schools is "lack of discipline" (35 percent) and "use of drugs" (18 percent).[1] Thirty-one percent of the teachers, who themselves make up a not inconsiderable fraction of the people, think that "parents' lack of interest/support" is the biggest problem, while only 5 percent of the public agreed. A number of state legislatures in the early 1980s, on the basis of their own studies and encouraged by a cluster of national reports, have decided to raise college entrance requirements; yet the 1984 Gallup Poll quoted above reports 59 percent of the public does *not* feel that colleges should do so. What do the words "standards" and "criteria" mean, for whom, applied to whom, and when? And do the words change meaning depending on who is in charge?

For centuries success or failure on examinations from a fixed curriculum set the educational standard of the day. The individual learner's performance was the unit of measure, and his relative performance on academic measures was the multiplier factor by which the total standard was measured. It is only recently that the philosophy of education, political ideology, and sociological theory have shaken faith in this single standard. Social class, poverty in youth, family influence, racial isolation, the "climate" of the school, pedagogical theory and practice have all been reported as important factors for the learner's "cognitive" measure of performance. These developments have led to the proposition that there should *not* be a single standard for education: the standards have to be relative to be fair; the measure should assess progress toward a goal not the meeting of a single standard; and the overall measure of educational success or failure of the educational system has to include factors other than individual performance. The very idea of "standard" has come to include measures of the learner's home setting, how well the school is organized, the dropout rate in schools, or the retention rate in colleges.

These changes in what criteria are important to measure, of course, have accompanied the democratization of access to high school and college in the twentieth century. The single measure of cognitive achievement for the few became inadequate for the many. The pendulum began to swing toward social rather than individual measures, and by the third quarter of the century the focus was put more on access than on the performance of the individual student. As we face the closing years of the century, we see signs that the pendulum is swinging back again. Have the changes in schools and colleges during these years made it necessary to change standards and criteria for student learning?

We first have to remind ourselves of the educational setting in the United States. There has never been a single standard for any subject or any age of student, nor has there been any effective effort by either national or state government to impose a standard. Available data make it clear that there are large variations in student cognitive performances within a given school, between schools in a community, and between parts of the country. It is probable that the best student performance in a particular subject in one college is below the weakest performance in another college. At all levels of education, though perhaps particularly in higher education, the lack of comparative data on what students learn has led to an informal rating system of the quality of institutions, based partly on fact, partly on social class consideration, partly on publicity, and partly on gossip about how the children of friends fared in different colleges.

The important point is that the data now used at all levels of education, on which judgments by parents, students, economic or political leaders are made on academic standards, are a mixture of information about individual students, particular institutions, and particular social settings. Often there is no dependable way to make comparisons or calculate probable developments. Consider, for example, the information about how an individual student is performing. What most parents with children in schools hear concerns grades in particular courses, some comparative information on tests widely used across the country, and if the student is going to college, some data on SAT or ACT tests at the end of high school. Once in college, the data about a student's performance are comparable only within that college. In the last year of college a minority of students take aptitude tests for graduate study or for entry into the professions. Then "scores" designed to inform admissions officers about probable success at the next stage of education are available but are usually not intended as measures of how well the student learned a particular subject—though the public and leaders in private and public life often assume that they are. The result is that the standards of an institution are often judged by criteria devised for another purpose. In the 1980s the conclusions reached about the quality of high schools based on GRE score are a frightening reminder that "correct" data may actually lead to incorrect conclusions unless put in proper perspective.[2]

It seems clear that data now collected on student learning are not necessarily useful, or even comprehensible, for those concerned with setting standards.

The Uses of Data

For what reasons are data needed? For teaching or advising a particular student at a particular age? For accrediting a school or college? For assessing the national situation in knowledge of science or the comparative quality of research and development? It is clear from such questions that different kinds of data serve different purposes. When it comes to the individual student, fine-grained information, studied in relation to his age, his family, his social setting, may be needed by teacher and parent alike. How he compares to his age group may be interesting data for use in motivating him to study harder or behave better, but such comparative data at a particular point in his malleable youth should not be used (but are) to fix him forever in relation to a particular standard of performance in a particular subject. Teacher and parent need to see development over time—a moving picture, not just a photograph in a frame.

Is this kind of detailed information on *all* students needed for accreditation of a school or college? Will a sample taken every few years serve the purpose? The history of accreditation in the United States (see Chapter 16) suggests that assessment of student performance has in fact been only a part, and even a minor part, of the overall judgment of institutional performance.[3] The 1980 Carnegie Council final report on the next twenty years for higher education, titled *Three Thousand Futures,* makes no mention of comparative data on student performance as a part of accrediting institutions, and in general takes the position that judgments of educational quality and standards should be left to the educators.[4]

Yet the years since 1980 force a reconsideration of the Carnegie position. Initiated by governors and other political leaders in many states, and usually not by educators, tests designed to measure student performance are being required to justify the award of a high school diploma. Increasingly, statewide tests of the "basic" subjects are being required at earlier grades. Public institutions are being forced by government to set standards for admission, usually in the form of requiring minimum years of study of subjects deemed essential for college level work. There are even examples of states requiring that students in the first year of college study pass tests of this sort to stay in college. Apparently the traditional reliance on accreditation reports is weakening, giving place to direct supervision by the state, despite the Carnegie statement that:

... the associations with responsibility in these matters need to starting using ... more meaningful standards in academic areas ... Better performance by the accrediting association is the best defense against establishment of more direct government controls.... The federal government and the states should continue to rely on private accreditation.[4]

In planning for standards and criteria, therefore, it would appear that the question of "what for?" will have to expand to "for whom?" In the case of the schools, it seems possible that standards and criteria are already being used to set minimal levels of student performance satisfactory to employers of youth and to political leaders. These standards increasingly have to be based on data which are understandable and useful to the layman, not the educator. As Nathan Glazer wrote in 1984:

> This new wave of educational reform comes not from the educators, not from the students, not even I would hazard from the parents—who seem more disturbed by lack of discipline and presence of drugs than by the quality of the education their children are receiving—but from opinion-makers distant from education, and specifically businessmen who are dismayed by the quality of the education young Americans have received. These spurs to action one can assume will be with us for a while. They are not going away. One cannot expect that feet of clay will be revealed underneath the new Japanese, German, and French superiority in a variety of fields. Russia's achievements in space were backed by no triumphs in civilian technology. In that sense, catching up with Sputnik was easy compared with catching up with Japan and Germany in automobiles and video products, or France in mass transportation, where advantage is not based on a supreme effort in one field but on a solid underlying base of competence that should properly make us uneasy[5].

What Glazer writes about the schools may soon apply to the colleges. There are some parallels that leap to mind. In the 1970s, the schools had fewer students, cost more, and yet showed lower academic performance at the high school level, according to the reports of the National Assessment of Educational Progress (NAEP). Higher education by the early 1980s enrolled fewer of the "traditional" age group, i.e., recent graduates of high schools, and filled up their rosters with older, and usually part-time, students. Costs have been rising more rapidly than inflation, both to the state governments that pay the basic costs of institutions for almost 80 percent of those enrolled, and to students and parents in the form of tuition. And there are indications that academic standards are declining, if data on grade inflation, "gut" courses, and academic discipline are correct. These are the same factors that affected the actions of state governments in the 1970s and early 1980s designed to jack up the standards in the schools. However, no evidence is available for higher education comparable to the

NAEP for the schools, which would make it possible to show trends over the decade and to compare results in different groups of the population and different parts of the nation.

Higher education's time for external review may have arrived, therefore, without adequate agreement on what data are needed, how collected, for what purpose, and designed for whose use. It may be significant that the Chief State School Officers in the fall of 1984 decided, in an unprecedented action, to work toward annual reports on their schools, on a variety of issues, including data on what students are learning at different ages. The minority voted against such reports, at least partly on the ground that a demonstration of lower student performance in some states would bring down unfair and unwarranted criticism on the schools of those states, whose difficulties were caused by economic or other factors outside of their control. But the majority prevailed, basically on the ground that the public and their political representatives, demand both the data on their own state and comparative data from other states. The NAEP idea, which was designed to obtain sample data adequate to show comparisons between major sectors of the nation at ages nine, thirteen, and seventeen, in the familiar school subjects, may now be spreading to the state governments. And it is not impossible that state leaders will ask for similar data about what college students are learning in "core" courses, similar to the "basics" in the schools. Higher costs for fewer students are likely, sooner or later, to be resisted by the taxpayer's representative unless there is evidence of better results, i.e., of progress in a desirable direction.

Conclusion

Different participants in the educational system, as in most areas of life, need different kinds of information. Economic and political decision makers need general kinds of data for action on budgets, on minimal standards for diplomas and degrees, and on programs implemented for the state or national welfare. Such general information is the sort that goes into the President's Annual Report on the Economy, and it is very different than the information sought by parents or teachers who deal with an individual student, or even by a school principal or college dean who seeks to improve the quality of the performance of the students and teachers, and to assure adequate standards of learning. For these purposes the individual, with all his strengths and weaknesses, with all his idiosyncrasies, must be the focus of attention.

But such detail on the individual is not needed by decision makers in the great majority of issues of policy or budget allocation. Sophisticated samples and trend lines over time are usually sufficient. This means that in setting state or national standards—though not in selecting talent or making awards—it is not necessary to engage in massive "testing" programs, with all the risks that such testing involves in rigidifying the curriculum and encouraging teachers to teach for the test rather than for student learning. One of the first tasks in deciding on standards and criteria therefore may be to make sure that all concerned are sensitive to the issue of when data on individuals are needed and when data on samples of individuals (and often small samples at that) will serve the purpose. A second task is to assure that data are collected on a regular and comparable basis. This will probably turn out to be far easier to write than to accomplish, for it may require a substantial increase in the responsibilities and the costs of the National Center for Educational Statistics and the National Institute of Education—especially if data on student learning in higher education are required—and if state comparisons are demanded.

This analysis leads to the conclusion that standards change both over time and depending on those who make the decisions. For the next few decades American education might wisely plan to put top priority on standards for student learning, and develop both more sophisticated and more economic methods and criteria to measure how well our schools and colleges are doing. But it would be unwise to give up the setting of standards and the search for criteria in the other areas for which society holds education at least partly responsible: equal access, responsible social behavior, citizenship, preparation for work, identification of talent. On many of these topics the annual report of the Department of Education's *The Condition of Education* has done an increasingly impressive job in recent years, and has earned the right for more support. One may hope that the efforts of the Chief State School Officers will result in comparable reports at the state level in the years to come for the schools, and in the fullness of time for higher education. Without such a solid basis of fact and analysis of trends, the setting of standards and choice of criteria may continue to be episodic and subject to the risk of judgments flawed by poor data and misunderstanding of their meaning.

4

RUTH B. LOVE

Educational Standards: A Public Educator's View

The discussion of educational excellence is not new in the United States: in effect, it has become an important recurring theme in American life. Much of what is said today about standards seems familiar to one who passed through the period of the late 1950s. Then, the appearance of Russian technological superiority, as demonstrated by the launching of the Sputnik satellite, forced educators in our country to reexamine curricula and attempt to reformulate them with a new emphasis on science, mathematics, and foreign languages.

Most of us appear to see education as a cyclical process. Like Edgar Allan Poe's pendulum, our commitment to education swings back and forth. As a nation, we are either filled with fervor and dedicated to excellence in education or we are content to let our schools run on sheer momentum.

The quality of schooling is in a steady decline, say the cynics among us. To listen to them one would believe that the trend in the

1980s toward excellence is an aberration. After all of the dire warnings contained in many noteworthy reports on education, we must see to it that the pendulum will never swing back. After thirty years in the profession, I believe that it is time for Americans to commit permanently to a system of public education that works effectively.

This commitment then must lead to new educational frontiers. Today the prospects are favorable for a nationwide infusion of confidence in and support for public education. Lest we allow the negative trends, which have played a role in misshaping educational standards, to repeat themselves, we can make the kinds of positive changes that will help our schools meet the needs of the twenty-first century.

A Brief History of American Public Education

Ask Americans what they believe are the three important elements needed to guarantee an effective education, and "a strong curriculum" will most likely be among those named. Then, ask them to define the elements they would include in "a strong curriculum" and be prepared to get a variety of answers. Mandating curricula has never stumped state and local school boards, but establishing curricula with definitive standards has baffled them for decades.

Unlike some other societies around the world, which have centrally designed and imposed national education programs for their schools, in the U.S. state and local district levels decide what and how much is taught. Some schools, for example, may allocate a larger percentage of their teaching force to the fields of mathematics and science; some to the field of English; and some to the field of vocational education. The same pattern is seen in the amount of time that is devoted to the various subjects. Some schools assign more time to the teaching of science or mathematics. Others spend more time on teaching social studies or the language arts.

Such a varied educational program does a disservice to both students and teachers, whose concerns and preferences are largely ignored when curricula and time-on-task are mandated. It also does a disservice to society at large, which has a right to expect every graduate to have learned specific skills and to have become proficient in utilizing those skills. As a nation, we too often have lacked a common vision for our schools, perhaps because we too often have lacked a common vision for other institutions as well. Our schools, since their inception, have reflected society as a whole, and they have been bent and swayed by the winds of prevailing political influences. Much of the time, the effect has been progress in education, but it has been progress in fitful starts and stops, characterized by major disagreements between the schools and the public on what is required for education to be effective.

Over 300 years ago, the concept of education centered on the religious and legal aspects of living in our society. Today, the schools are called upon to provide parenting, socialization and assimilation, manners and morals, immunization, and sex education. Education has suffered with each new demand, because it is impossible to be effective when the educator's efforts are spread too thinly.

The problem is aggravated when taxpayers begin to fume that they are not getting a dollar's worth of education for their tax dollar, when parents consider removing their children from public schools because they sense a decline in quality, and when employers complain that too many graduates lack the basic skills and attitudes to do a good job.

A brief history of educational trends over the decades tells much about how we arrived at the present state and gives us strong clues as to where we should be headed.

Recent Trends in Public Education

It is interesting to note that in the latter part of the nineteenth century, Americans were revising curriculum and instruction to address a system of education that they deemed inferior to that of Europe's.

By the decade of the 1930s, the nation's schools—particularly those in urban areas—had improved substantially. But as the "urban crisis" in housing, employment, recreation, and health evolved, and the move to the suburbs started, urban education began to decline. Massive reforms of the public schools were called for by the leaders of that time.

The post—World War II years saw the continued decline of urban education as a result of the accelerating movement of middle-class residents from the cities to the suburbs. While surrounding communities expanded, urban areas began to suffer from the erosion of their tax bases. Accordingly, financing for the inner city schools plummetted, and so did educational standards.

Most of us view the latter part of the 1950s as the start of a get-tough policy in education. But even the early part of that decade saw a strong back-to-basics movement to combat the widely held belief that students were not reading up to standards. What we most remember, however, is the National Defense Education Act (NDEA) of 1958, enacted by the Eisenhower Administration.

Coming after Sputnik, which shocked the nation into an immediate reordering of its priorities and pushed the schools into the limelight, the NDEA put the federal government's muscle and funds behind the teaching of science, mathematics, and foreign languages. Teachers were trained and retrained. New programs in chemistry, biology, and physics were funded, and prominent educators were provided subsidies to write new textbooks. The teaching profession was invigorated with a new crop of professionals whose pledges to teach for at least five years in public schools had saved them up to half of their college tuition. The NDEA provided grants, matched by state and local school districts, that allowed schools to purchase equipment and materials for science laboratories and to rehabilitate them. Of the first appropriation of $57.4 million, $56 million went to the local schools.

Title III, under the NDEA, paid for additional instructional materials for schools. Helpful roles were played by the Atomic Energy Commission and by other federal agencies. Because of Title III, schools made the transition from traditional but obsolete curricula to new science and mathematics courses being developed under private and public sponsorship.

Two years after Sputnik, the National Science Foundation supported programs that included special secondary institutes, funded by some $30 million. For about a decade the programs' budget remained that high or higher. By the end of the 1960s, about half of the nation's high school teachers of mathematics and science had received institute training.

Attention to education, dramatized by the NDEA, did not falter with the coming of a new decade. Buoyed by the progress being made, the federal government was encouraged to increase its support dramatically. By the middle of the decade, the Johnson administration had expanded the scope of federal involvement in education: Project Head Start included youngsters who had entered school, and the Elementary and Secondary Education Act (ESEA) dealt with students from disadvantaged backgrounds who attended elementary and secondary schools.

Yet, at the same time, something ominous was happening. Mirroring the general trend toward permissiveness that began to spread throughout society, schools placed less and less emphasis on competition and achievement. Following the lead of corporate management and the work force, rules, regulations, policies, and practices were relaxed, changed, or often done away with altogether.

Many academic requirements were dropped, and curricula were expanded to include something for everybody. Classroom behavior was less strictly monitored, and more so-called freedoms were given to staff and students alike. Parents and the community abdicated their responsibilities to the learning process, and in many instances, educators were happy to be left alone.

When teacher unions became so powerful that schools were threatened with work stoppages, demands were quickly met without giving much thought to the ultimate effects of such settlements. Permissiveness caused our schools to lower standards and expectations and to demean our children by not holding them accountable.

It has become somewhat fashionable to place the blame for declining standards and expectations squarely on the shoulders of "Great Society" programs such as Project Head Start and ESEA. But history has vindicated those programs. If not for the massive outpouring of resources to help upgrade the academic skills of poor and disadvantaged children, their prospects would be far worse than they are today.

Because of those federal initiatives, millions of children were turned toward success, not only academically but socially. Recent studies have documented substantial gains in the achievements of children served by Project Head Start and ESEA. I predict that future studies will continue to confirm a closing of the gap in their academic achievements when compared with those of other students.

The decline in city school enrollment, which began in the late 1940s, continued in the 1970s to the dismay of educators who encountered thousands of white and black dropouts. That decade also generated a public outcry. For the first time in history, it was a response aimed at the system of public education itself. Faced by rebellious taxpayers and unable to garner the funding they had once enjoyed, many school systems teetered on the brink of bankruptcy. Most had to slash their budgets and to cut personnel and services for students. The public and political climate of that period was one of general disinterest in maintaining and improving the schools. Urban schools suffered most of all, because federal orders to desegregate pupils and personnel brought disruption and violence over busing and accelerated the white flight from urban schools. Many schools became increasingly populated by poorer and socially disadvantaged students who needed remedial help. In such cases maintenance of adequate standards of performance and achievement became extremely difficult.

Some would characterize the decade of the 1970s as the nadir of public school quality. But others would prefer to remember the period in a different light. Certainly, they were years of highly inflammatory and destructive developments that threatened the survival of public education in America. Yet, they were also years that saw the first planting of the seeds for the current movement toward educational reform. Although education had lost its high place on the national agenda and in the hearts and minds of those who had fled from the public schools, it became a major issue of concern for parents and educators who were left to grapple with the critical problems. They voiced their demands for a safer school environment, more effective instruction, and more accountable leadership. Because of their tireless efforts to obtain recognizable curricular and instructional improvements, the stage was inevitably set for the pendulum to swing toward reform.

A Start Toward Reform

Reports in the early 1980s concerning the decline of educational standards refer to the very real problems, frustrations, and fears of the previous decade. It should have come as no surprise, therefore, that we took a long hard look at all of the schools—urban and suburban—and discovered low standards and expectations. Today, fewer than half of the nation's public high schools require more than a year of science and mathematics. Fewer than one in ten high school students study physics. Only 16 percent take one year of high school chemistry. Many students graduate with only the equivalent of grade school levels in mathematics and science. In many elementary schools, science labs are nonexistent or inadequate, and even high school lab equipment leaves much to be desired.

When I look at schools in Chicago and throughout the state of Illinois, I find that more than half the freshmen in the system's high schools take remedial mathematics classes. In the suburbs, the number ranges from 10 to 40 percent. Only 30 percent of the high school districts in the state offer calculus, and only 8 percent of the state's high school students study calculus.

Only 28.5 percent of Illinois students take three years of high school mathematics. While national associations of mathematics and science teachers recommend that all students take at least three years each of mathematics and science, only 5 percent of high school students in Chicago take at least three years of mathematics.

Elementary school teachers in Illinois need only a year of a college science, and even junior high school teachers need not be specialists if they teach science or mathematics less than half the time. I believe that colleges should require more science of students preparing to be teachers. Some require one course or one year when they should require six hours of biological science and six hours of physical science for certification.

Today, the national climate is one of reform. We are addressing the decline in standards on federal, state, and local levels. Not only are educators preparing to revitalize education, but a growing number of parents, business and community leaders, and government officials are working together toward that objective. Where once we went along with the concept of automatic promotions, today we insist that no student moves up in grade unless he or she has mastered specified skills. Where once students were allowed to receive diplomas though they had never taken one basic, solid course, today we demand that every prospective graduate fulfill minimum course requirements. Where once the community avoided meaningful involvement in our schools, today such participation is on the rise.

We have reordered our priorities. Indeed, there is reason to believe that the 1980s will be the decade in which public education will flourish as never before. As this book demonstrates, positive results are emerging from our renewed commitment to quality education.

During the three-year period 1982–84, 53 percent of the 16,000 school districts nationwide as a condition for graduation have increased the number of credits they require in such core subjects as English, mathematics, and science, and by 1985 another 38 percent will have similarly upgraded their standards. Since 1980, 69 percent of all school systems have launched efforts to increase daily attendance, and no fewer than twenty states have passed tougher certification laws, with the goal of making sure that a teacher has mastered certain basic skills before ever entering a classroom.

In a political climate where federal support is shrinking, educators are looking to others for leadership and support, e.g., our state chief executives, many of whom are rising impressively to the challenge. Arkansas, for example, approved the most comprehensive education program in the state's history. It will mean stricter standards, curriculum improvement, and more importantly, the requisite funding. The governor also pushed—against heavy political opposition—a system of merit pay that he defended persuasively on national television. In California, far-reaching educational reforms such as stronger high school graduation requirements, higher salaries for beginning teachers, loans for teacher training, and funding for master teacher programs were backed up by $800 million in added state support. Mississippi's State Department of Education is developing a five-year plan for educational improvements, which will be the basis for bigger budgets and for legislative initiatives. And in Florida, the legislature has enacted sweeping reforms and improvements including strengthened high school graduation requirements, incentives for students who take college level courses, and stress on mathematics, science, and computer instruction.

Altogether, there are some forty-five states where serious school reform is either being proposed or carried out in the areas of curriculum, standards, teaching, parental and community involvement. Students are being challenged not only to learn to read, write, and compute, but also to think, to analyze, to respect differences among their peers, to appreciate diversity, and to develop positive self-concepts.

By setting formidable standards in the schools, we are saying that we believe students can achieve. That belief has paid off, even in the nation's most populous urban school districts, where expectations and standards have long been extremely low. The Council of the Great City Schools, a coalition of thirty of the nation's largest urban school systems, has noted that during 1980–84, twenty-seven of the council's districts, composed mainly of minority students, raised their test scores for elementary school reading and mathematics.

In this era of increasing technical and global political complexities, we must make the schools centers of excellence, cement lasting partnerships between schools and the country they serve, and return public education to its historical place of honor and influence in our society.

If we are to succeed in revitalizing education to meet contemporary needs, leaders in business, government, and the community will have to agree on a policy of constantly reviewing and upgrading educational objectives and procedures. Then they must act and not simply take a position. That is a concept that too often gets lost in the meeting rooms where policies are created and decisions made that affect the quality of the schools. There are still those who are more concerned with politically safe positions rather than with the difficult issues of matching education with rapidly changing needs.

Elements of Quality

Before we can achieve quality education on a continuing basis, we must decide:

1. What should students know when they graduate from elementary school? And from high school?

2. Are we effectively and realistically linking the education product at all levels to the world in which our students will live and
   work?
3. Have we taken into account the partial shift of our economic
   base from manufacturing to service?
4. Have we taken into account the increasing number of young
   people who will likely be making their living through interaction with overseas markets?
5. Are we merely teaching students how to use computers, or are
   we also teaching them how to apply computer knowledge to
   their lives?
6. Are we merely teaching English usage, or are we also teaching
   students how to apply these skills in an era where communication is dominant?

In other words, are our education expectations squaring with
reality?

We also need to decide how time in school should be allocated to
ensure effective instruction and meet society's needs. Many
educators now believe that more time in school must be spent on
teaching and on tasks. There must be less administrative paper
shuffling and less interruption of the learning process. There
must be more consolidation of various kinds of programs to increase efficiency and effectiveness. Improved classroom instruction is also needed. This means either a longer school day and/or
year. A policy to extend the school day and/or year will call for
adequate financial support. In the meantime, the business community needs to join more actively with the school systems to increase both the quantity and quality of the educational product.
Some businesses are already paying teachers for additional learning programs after the end of the school day. Others are donating
time, personnel, and equipment to enhance the learning process.

One of the most significant reforms we must push focuses on
recruiting, educating, rewarding, and retaining good teachers and
administrators. We must elevate the status of education as a profession and thus attract the best minds in the nation to public
education. Once we compensate them adequately, we must hold
them accountable for the results they produce. We need to consider the pattern by which teachers in the post-secondary schools

advance educators not only financially but also in status: teaching assistant, instructor, assistant professor, associate professor, and full professor. In many school districts, the starting salary for teachers is too low to attract the brightest people. Teachers with ten to fifteen years of seniority may be earning less than the maintenance personnel in their schools. Clearly, starting salaries for teachers must be raised, and the compensation packages restructured. I have no problem with concepts such as merit pay. No one can deny that extra compensation is laudatory for those who excel. However, we will never be able to recognize all of those who are outstanding in school systems that average 24,000 teachers. If we utilize merit pay, we must couple it with an upgrading of the entire teacher salary structure and demand correspondingly better teachers. Concurrently, teachers will have to want to do a good job. Their working conditions should be adequate because they serve as an added incentive for creativity and excellence. It is important that good teachers find teaching important and sufficiently gratifying to remain in the classroom. They should not look to administrative positions or any other career in order to earn more or to be held in higher esteem. In other words, public education must be funded at realistic levels, and the source of that funding must be predictable, so that school systems can depend on it and plan with it.

Education is costly, and good education costs even more. There are no shortcuts. Yet, education is much cheaper and cost effective than the alternatives. Welfare programs and unemployment compensation to offset illiteracy cost taxpayers over $6 billion annually. Some $6.6 billion is spent annually to keep 750,000 largely illiterate prisoners in jail. American business spends additional billions of dollars annually to teach their employees functional skills in reading, writing, and computation, even though they should have acquired them in school. The federal government can and should stimulate local and state support for the schools. Educators alone can do little to keep pace with the rapid scientific and technological advances as we approach the twenty-first century. Specifically, politicians should persuade more business and community leaders to do their share. The private sector employs 60 percent of all scientists and engineers, nearly 1.9 million people. If even one-tenth of this resource became active in precollege education, every school in the country would have access to two or three scientists or engineers. In addition, the federal government cannot safely further reduce its share of financing for elementary and secondary education. That share has dropped from 8.7 percent in fiscal 1981 to 6.4 percent in fiscal 1984, the lowest level in two decades.

Having achieved a reasonable consensus as to the ingredients of educational excellence, we must fund education realistically. Elected officials must have the wisdom and courage to contribute solutions that are right, not just expedient.

Shakespeare wrote: "For courage mounteth with occasion." The occasion in our generation calls for curricula to meet the realities of a rapidly changing society and world. We can produce literate and thinking young people if graduation requirements become more stringent at the elementary and high school levels. That means offering no credit for remedial courses, and allowing no student to spend more time on physical education than on mathematics and science. School systems must see to it that time-on-task increases, that only the best teachers are in our classrooms, and that principals provide the requisite leadership and backing. Those are only some of the things that will have to be tackled in the quest for educational opportunities and advancement for all young people. I emphasize both because we cannot have one without the other. Students need to know that they are receiving a fair shot at personal achievement, that if they work hard for thirteen years they will have acquired valuable knowledge and skills, and that they will have a chance to use them to advantage in later life. Equal access to a solid education will greatly improve job openings in the business sector for minority groups, as well as women. In turn, that sector must also develop a close, sustained partnership with education. Our public schools need regular guidance and help if they are to keep up with on-site technological and social changes and to deliver useful and timely education to match them. Furthermore, vocational education must be converted into technical education. Students who have not gone the academic route have traditionally taken obsolete or obsolescent vocational training and, too often, have ended up with skills for which demand has sharply declined. Somewhere along the way, the notion developed that academic pursuits are more worthy than technical pursuits.

This must change as we prepare students for the twenty-first century. I am reminded of what John Gardner said: "Those who value philosophy because philosophy is an exalted profession, but denigrate plumbing as a lower occupation, will have neither good philosophy nor good plumbing, and neither their theories nor pipes will hold water."

Schools may also be helped through more shared time programs, which have as their primary feature the teaching of multiple and transferable skills that will enable students to learn and adapt to change. It would be disastrous for us to create a society in which large numbers of young people cannot expect to work and live a life of purpose and promise.

I have faith in the nation's leadership. It knows what is right for America and, based on such knowledge, must make tough decisions and formulate realistic policies for implementation. Either we are for significant educational reforms to meet the challenges ahead, or we are not. Either we support and believe in quality education for all, based on our public schools, or we do not. Willingness to accept full responsibility for the education of its youth— with everything this implies—is probably the ultimate measure of a nation.

II

Standards for Various Grade Levels

5

MADELINE HUNTER

Building Effective Elementary Schools

Our educational system is a critically important institution because it influences whether or not America has informed, responsible citizens. That system is the only institution that we as educational professionals control; and since elementary schools form the initial experience in the system, they are probably the most important level in achieving those educational goals.

The responsibility for educators is evident. And awareness of the schools's power is obvious from the rash of reports on schooling that have swept the nation. We experienced a similar "jolt" when Russia launched Sputnik. Then, however, people felt the curriculum was to blame, not the teaching. New math and science courses were delivered to schools. It was assumed this was all that was necessary to correct our deficiency. At that time no one was challenging our professional skills—the concern was academic knowledge.

It was just as well. A quarter of century ago we had identified few cause-effect relationships that teachers could use daily to promote learning. Now we are well armed with professional knowledge, not all we need, but enough to take steps that could result in dramatic acceleration of students' learning.

The answer to the current challenge, however, is multifaceted and lies not only in professional skills but in curricular decisions, materials, technology, and the financial and attitudinal support essential to a successful educational enterprise.

The National Association of Elementary Schools Principals convened some of the best minds in the country to define the question of what standards we should use to evaluate our schools. The result was the 1984 publication *Standards for Quality Elementary Schools, Kindergarten through Eighth Grade.* Rather than review the twenty-one standards and their quality indicators or focus on an assessment of a school to determine discrepencies, this chapter will identify some of the most important ways schools can be moved from where they are to where educators and the public would like them to be.

For brevity, those standards have been grouped into the categories of leadership, training and development, instruction, curriculum, evaluation and assessment, and school climate. While this is not the order of presentation in the original document, this chapter will argue that this order will most effectively close the gap between what a school is and what it has the potential to become.

Leadership

Recent research has corroborated what all of us knew intuitively: that the principal must lead in setting the goals, climate, and achievement in a school. The principal needs, first of all, to be an instructional leader. *Instruction is the business of the school.* All other functions exist to support instruction. In addition, the principal must have human relations, organizational, and political skills.

In the past, organizational skills were considered to be the major criterion in selection of a principal. Now, instructional leadership skills have emerged as more important. Clearly when students are successful in their learning, human relations and politics become lesser problems.

This is not to minimize the importance of organizational skills; they are essential if a school is to run smoothly. Principals, in most cases, once were effective teachers in terms of organization. They face only the problem of transferring those skills to a larger scale operation. Very few schools are ineffective because supplies, materials, or buses are not where they should be.

Political and human relations talents also are essential. Both of these skills, however, require "know how" in dealing with people so they feel comfortable and self-fulfilled as they advance in productive ways. In this process, leadership and teaching are identical: the use of one's skills to move people more reliably in a desired direction.

The principal who has internalized successful instruction uses those same skills to increase staff, parent, central office, and community motivation, as well as students' motivation; the rate and degree of their learning; and retention and transfer of that learning to other appropriate situations. Remember that feelings, attitudes, and appreciations also are learned. What is learned can be taught, and teaching is our business.

Unfortunately, these powerful, psychological cause-effect relationships still are not being taught in most administrative preparation courses. Experience suggests that a minimum of sixty to eighty hours of instruction and practicum is needed to equip principals with the skills necessary to know and use principles of human learning. Then principals can design and implement a successful staff meeting, discipline with dignity, observe and analyze an episode of teaching, follow it with a growth evoking conference, evaluate teachers, and work productively with individual parents and parent groups.

Following initial instruction and practicum, most principals need about two years of practice in using these principles, with systematic coaching, in order to internalize skills so they become artistically performed and, eventually, become abiding characteristics of that principal.

An effective principal uses these skills to observe teachers, diagnoses their strengths and weaknesses, holds a conference to increase strengths and remediate weaknesses, then does follow up observations to validate the success or failure of the supervisory process.

Many attempts have been made to short-cut this process with check lists, recipes, and other quick fixes. Such things simply will not work. There is no short cut to acquiring competence in supervision for there are no absolutes in this area. Every generalization in learning needs to be considered along with the conditions under which its use is effective or, if ineffective, *not* to be used. Supervisory focus needs to be on quality not quantity.

Closing the gap between current knowledge and the principals' performance is probably the single most important element in the creation of successful schools. If the principal knows, articulates, and models appropriate cause-effect relationships between leadership (teaching) and performance (learning) it is highly likely that teachers will acquire these skills. Accordingly, most research shows that the principal is the single most important element in a successful school.

Training and Development

A second critical need to ensure effective schools is to maintain an ongoing development program for administrators, teachers, support staff, paraprofessionals, and parents. For teachers this means, through initial teacher education, transmission of the knowledge we now possess. Then, to stay abreast of new developments that emerge from research, teachers in the field need continuing inservice so that knowledge can be translated into daily practice. This is a constant need throughout a professional's life. Although it is a costly part of the educational budget, money spent on continuing teacher education represents probably the single most valuable investment of the tax dollar; and educators must educate their school boards about this important dividend to avoid pressures to short-change it.

Continuing teacher education cannot be a "patchwork" of the yearly changing vogues but must become a long range professional tapestry to which illuminating detail is constantly added. In the past, a purveyor of inservice has been like Ponce de Leon, seeking the fountain of eternal literacy. *We are convinced it does not exist.* Educators, like all professionals, must be decision-makers. No one can tell a teacher or principal what to do. The job of inservice is to equip that professional with the knowledge that will support whatever decision is made, and the practice, with coaching, that changes initial efforts into artistic performance.

Instruction

Many people including teachers, paraprofessionals, specialists, aides, central office personnel, and parent volunteers may contribute to a planned, unified instructional program. Without good management, and if their efforts are not consonant with the principles that promote learning, their various contributions to education can be disjointed, wasted, or even actually subversive of good education.

Teachers. Highly trained teachers can 1) diagnose what each student now knows, and what is next ready to be learned, 2) develop successful learning strategies for individual children as well as techniques for judging whether they have actually learned, 3) use research-based procedures to increase students' motivation to learn, the rate and degree of learning, retention of that learning, and its transfer to new situations that require creativity, problem solving, and decision making, and, 4) discipline with dignity.

Most people who are willing to put in the necessary time and effort for learning, practice, and internalization can achieve these skills. Granting differences in natural ability, outstanding teachers aren't born, they're made in the same way that doctors, attorneys, and engineers are made—by acquiring knowledge plus practice with coaching.

A model school builds in that essential practice with coaching through frequent observations, followed by growth-evoking feedback. In addition, continuing inservice renews skills and adds new techniques as they are developed by research, which is field tested for practicality.

Paraprofessionals. It matters less whether the school has paid aides or volunteer parents than whether or not these adults have systematic initial and ongoing training, then demonstrate their ability to work productively with students. Wanting to be helpful, they can inadvertently foster dependence when the school is encouraging independence, rote memorization when the school is emphasizing higher-level thinking, and convergent responses when divergent ones are indicated. Untrained personnel can be as dangerous in teaching as they are in surgery. Consequently, careful training about how to deal sensitively and productively with students is essential—even for personnel who work only in the office or library.

Parents. Parents are an incredibly rich resource for support and assistance. But again, without training, they can become partners in accomplishing our mission or they can become adversaries. To work collaboratively with us, they should be able to help in establishing goals and should have opportunities to learn ways that contribute to their accomplishment.

Parent advisory groups and parent education classes are the most economical means to achieve an informed and proficient parent body. Also, reporting individual students' progress through parent conferences throughout the year will encourage a more collaborative partnership. Satisfying parent conferences also depend on systematic inservice and practice, with coaching for both teacher and parent.

Specialists. The need for specialists obviously depends on student needs. A school nurse, for instance, should be available as a consultant for health education and to detect any problem requiring early intervention, but not as a first-aid helper.

A school psychologist and social worker should be available for teacher consultation and/or parent referral. The best therapy for most students, however, is success in the classroom. Therefore, rather than "pull out," remedial classes, in most cases special teachers in academic subjects should be "put into" the classroom to team with the regular teacher. Not only does this avoid the waste of time of students changing rooms but it eliminates the stigma of leaving for special help. An additional dividend is that special and regular teachers have opportunities to observe and learn from each other.

Student-teacher ratio. The "right" number of students per teacher has been debated for decades. One reason a research-defensible answer has never been found is that the question is based on the faulty premise that one student equals another student. Yet, we know there are light years of difference between a healthy, bright, eager learner who is supported by an enabling family and an undernourished, tired, slower student who has no support at home. How can we say that one equals the other? The latter student is going to require considerably more teacher time and skill than the former, yet we talk about the "right" number of students as if the *kind* of student made no difference.

To compound the problem we assume that one teacher equals another teacher: that the professional virtuoso is equal to the beginning teacher and that they should have the same number of students "to be fair." What could be more unfair to both student and teacher?

Whatever the student-teacher ratio (and we, too, hope it would be low), students and teachers should be assigned on the basis of needs and competencies. As a result, the numbers in each class *may not* be the same. The beginning teacher may have fewer or more students than the virtuoso, but they will not require the extra time and skill of those in the more competent teacher's class. We are aware that this is a revolutionary idea in a profession that divides teachers and students as if each were identical. Productive schools, however, for years have been intuitively making such assignments successfully but usually have not articulated the reasons that support their criteria for assignment.

Curriculum

The reason for listing curriculum (what to teach) after leadership, inservice, and instruction (how to teach) is not because the former is less important. To teach exquisitely that which is not worth the effort is an educational sin parallel to teaching ineffectively to the most loftly goals. Because "how to teach" is a newer science, the lag between knowledge and performance is greater. If schools actually accomplished what is in most curriculum guides, we would be considerably ahead of where we are now in education.

It is essential that school staff and parents agree upon and articulate their curricular goals, assign responsibility for achieving them, and have a document that will make these decisions clear to any inquirer.

Curriculum content should be selected for its transfer potential. This does not necessarily mean only "practical use" but rather that the concepts and skills learned will be conducive to new learning and problem solving, creativity, and the making of responsible decisions throughout life. In short, knowing how to think and to learn.

Clearly, the ability to read with understanding, to write and speak clearly and artistically, and to solve quantitative problems are skills that are useful throughout life. Rather than teaching students to memorize facts, the social sciences should teach key concepts that help the student understand that differences in cultures and people are not deficiencies and that most events and feelings are predictable results from identifiable causes rather than chaotic happenstances.

In our contemporary technological world, it is more important than ever that students are able to use the scientific method and understand the difference between correlational and causal relationships. We now have computers to tell us the consequences of making a particular decision before we actually make it, and thereby can greatly expand our ability to accomplish the goals we all seek. Computers, like other tools and machines, are extensions of the human mind and body and can provide powerful assistance in creating a better world. A successful curriculum must communicate skill in using these tools and eliminate the myth that technology is unhumanistic.

Certain things are conspicuously absent from plans arising from the current "back to the basics" frenzy. The most important of these is "knowledge of self as a physical, social, emotional, and intellectual being" so one's own human functions can be brought into either predictability or control. A beginning has been made in the physiological, emotional, and social areas; still, much more needs to be done. The area of intellectual functioning, "learning how to think and to learn," has in the past been conspicuously neglected except for entrepreneuring "how to" courses for popular consumption. Recently, meta cognition and dialectical thinking, and noetic science have brought "thinking about thinking" to the education profession but little has been done to alert the public to this critical area of the curriculum. Also, we are in danger of adding twenty minutes of "thinking" to the school day with the remainder being "business as usual."

A curriculum that provides knowledge of physical self should stress the constants in structure and function of all humans as well as idiosyncratic features that can make an individual proactive rather than merely reactive to his physiological self. For example, the principles of nutrition as they relate to an individual's daily intake of food should result not only in knowledge but in the selection of a diet balanced in the variety and amount appropriate and satisfying to *that particular individual.* Need for exercise should be translated into the kind and amount of exercise that is helpful and enjoyable for *that learner.* The anatomical and physiological strengths and weaknesses of the learner's own body, the optimal amount of sleep necessary for him or her, sensitivity to one's body's inner regulators and warning signals systems, the personal source, kind, and duration of energy; such are the topics that distinguish contemporary education from the stockpiles of anatomical and physiological data, "no-relevance-for-me" health education of the past.

Recently, knowledge of humans as emotional beings has burgeoned. Fact and fad, self-improvement programs have permeated education. The pendulum has swung from a denial of all emotion to a bacchanal of feelings that is tantamount to not being psychologically housebroken.

A critical area of curriculum study is the commonality and interpretation of a human's subjective experience. Out of this should emerge the ability to discriminate between those conditions under which release of emotion is authentic, healthy, and therapeutic, and conditions under which such release is potentially destructive and control is indicated.

A curriculum that includes such items then teaches young people to act more maturely—to gain some measure of self-awareness. This includes helping them address problems associated with the inevitable waxing and waning of feelings; anticipation of and preparation for feelings triggered by certain circumstances; awareness of one's "hot buttons," which when touched set off predictable overreaction, and the development of compensatory or regulatory activities to ameliorate the effect; and an awareness of the philosophical and empirical base of one's values and their consonance with behavior. All of this knowledge has the power to change an individual from a bewildered, depressed, or angry person who can only *react* to his or her environment to one who can *act* upon the environment and live an emotionally rich, productive life.

Along with this emotional sophistication should emerge an individual with a healthy self-concept based on feelings of worth and competence in those areas deemed appropriate by each individual. These areas may vary from traditional school subjects to aesthetics or athletics or crime depending on the human environment, but there always exists some field of action and body of content that a student must master to respect himself. Neither feelings of worth generated from the respect of significant others nor competence is enough in itself—both must be experienced to produce a positive self concept.

Current educational trends clearly indicate the need for more understanding of and competence in *social interaction.* Teaching students how to work productively with others—how to understand and respect their responses, as well as how to influence the effect one desires to create in others—is an extremely important aspect of the curriculum's social dimension, and programs dealing with these issues are expanding very rapidly.

Skills that act as social lubricants can be taught and predictably acquired with integrity and sincerity by most individuals. In a world where human contact escalates with an exponential ratio to human density, such social skills are a survival dimension of the future.

Just coming into focus is a curriculum that deals with the intellectual power of the individual. Based on genetic assumptions, individuals often have adopted a fatalistic stance about the ability to learn. Binet promulgated this deterministic assumption by estimating the intelligence quotient of the individual. Terman added to the predictive value of such numerical "brands" to the point where numbers became cherished hallmarks of intellectual quality. Questions have recently arisen, however, about whether these studies have been measuring genetic endowment or environmental influences. Apart from genetic variables that could limit individual achievement, research has identified psychological principles that have a profound effect on learning. In fact, teaching earns its status as a profession by using these principles to accelerate learning. Unfortunately, teachers are still emerging from teacher education programs without the knowledge, much less supervised practice, of such principles.

We cannot, however, be content with this rich lore of psychological truth becoming the private domain of only the professional educator. Those principles must be transmitted into the conscious knowledge and resultant practice of each parent and student in the same way that knowledge and practice of the principles of nutrition are transmitted for the well-being of every individual. Use of these learning principles will enable most students who choose to learn, to do so efficiently and effectively.

Learning how to think and how to learn, knowing the factors that exert an influence on the function of the world's most complex and unique instrument, the human mind, may well become the essence of education. Of equal importance is a sensivity to those same factors that, used by others, (such as television, advertising, political speeches, etc.) can have a powerful influence on the learner's behavior. An individual's response should be the result of intent not the result of default or manipulation by others. Only by understanding the potential effects of principles of learning such as modeling, reinforcement, redundancy, and transfer, can one be free to be master of one's own learning rather than be a mere reactor to the stimuli and experiences encountered.

The curriculum, if it is to meet learning needs in a world where knowledge is exploding, must equip learners to deal efficiently and effectively with the learning tasks that confront them. This implies that psychological principles affecting human learning will be systematically taught using those same principles to promote positive transfer of that learning to future learning tasks. Each individual can discover through experience and experimentation the variables that increase his motivation to learn as well as the factors that accelerate the rate and degree of his learning. A student should be able to determine the amount and duration of practice optimal for *him*, decide whether overt or covert participation is more productive, assess, and, if necessary, adjust *his* level of aspiration, determine what generates meaning for him and which are his most powerful reinforcers. Along with these idiosyncratic factors, a student should be sensitive to properties inherent in the content to be learned, such as position in sequence, potential interference, and relationships that can impede or accelerate achievement. With sophistication about variables that accelerate initial learning, a student should learn to make use of factors that promote retention of what has been learned plus the most powerful accelerants of all, those factors that promote transfer of learning so the student can realize all the gains of positive transfer of that learning to new situations that require it for problem solving and creativity. All of this knowledge of "how to learn" is essential in the curriculum. Teacher and administrator preparation should equip educational professionals with knowledge and facility in use of the principles of how to learn.

A deplorable curriculum casualty in the "back to the basics" blizzard is the fulfillment of humans' aesthetic needs. As technology removes concerns about physical survival, people will experience increasing amounts of leisure. Since this means reduced accountability, it is not surprising that past civilizations, relieved of pressures to worry about survival, revealed contrasting potentials for either deadly sedation or creative renewal. This explains why the concern about leisure is so widespread—why so many books have been written about it.

Concern about leisure highlights the importance of the arts—music, drama, dance, and the visual arts. The curriculum should provide opportunities for students to act as both consumer and producer of the arts, since nonverbal, artistic expressions (including those using the physical body) serve as a valuable counterweight to the strong traditional curricular emphasis on verbal expressions.

Evaluation and Assessment

Teachers should be mindful of the need to do ongoing assessment, using both formal tests and "dip sticking," throughout a lesson to determine whether, at this moment, they should move on, go back and reteach, or generate more than one "catch hold point" in the lesson. It is possible for the content to remain the same, but those who have achieved the learning can be stretched while those who need more teaching will receive it.

A paper-pencil test usually is not necessary for "dip sticking." Signaled responses, telling a neighbor (with the teacher sampling the responses), choral responses, or *brief* written phrases alert the teacher to students' current state of learning. Waiting until the end of the lesson or the end of the unit to assess learning is no longer defensible. Reteaching or remediation should be provided as soon as "dip sticking" indicates it is needed.

School Climate

School climate has been placed last, not because it is unimportant, but because it is not something you *do:* it is the result of *what* you do.

If the principal provides skilled and inspiring leadership, if ongoing inservice enables teachers, paraprofessionals, and volunteers to generate the best instructional practice each day, if learning is monitored so success is attainable and predictable, a warm, responsive, stimulating school climate is assured.

Summary

Whatever emerges in the future, clearly our students will be the issue resolvers and decision makers. Preparation for resolving those thorny issues and making those tough decisions is the main imperative. Producing individuals who have basic skills, who know and accept themselves, who can work productively with others, who know how to think and how to learn—this is the contribution of an elementary school toward making citizens of the future.

6

PAUL M. POSSEMATO

Secondary Education

Agreement on the need for high academic standards is not universal. Predictions continue that raising standards of academic achievement will increase student absenteeism and dropouts by producing anxiety and frustration. Detractors point to poor socioeconomic conditions that thwart the most positive efforts to achieve established standards. They question whether it is possible to set uniformly high academic standards for all students considering the economic and cultural heterogeneity of American society.

Both within and beyond the school environment, many forces can influence the reform movement. If these forces are not dealt with, they can be harmful. Properly understood and directed, they can help encourage constructive educational innovations. In considering the problems of our schools, we must begin as background by understanding certain social constraints impinging on education—some of them operating positively and others negatively.

The most fundamental of these constraints are the broad social expectations we have of education. Americans, in fact, have certain fundamental beliefs about education. They expect the schools will teach fundamental skills and basic cultural values. These include proper use of the English language; the ability to reason systematically when solving problems; an understanding of the basic principles of democracy, civic responsibility, and fair play; the duties associated with the work ethic; an appreciation of the need for a sense of community among members of the society; the values of personal and mental health; and an appreciation of the fine arts, music, and the love for life-long learning.

A second constraint is the urban environment. The inner city problem begins with a burgeoning of non-English speaking immigrants, who have had no previous formal education. More than eighty languages are spoken in the homes of the Los Angeles Unified School District (LAUSD) students, and a growing number of students live in homes where English is not spoken at all. In the LAUSD, that number now exceeds 40 percent—in absolute terms it grew from 5,663 in 1970 to 28,903 in 1983. The situation is further exacerbated by a cycle of poverty, which may work counter to the value system of both school and society. Students from extremely low income families rely almost exclusively on schools for the intellectual stimuli that are necessary to language competence.

Another constraint comes from the media: motion pictures, television, videotapes, and radio, which often present anti-intellectual images in a fantasy world that actively distracts students from work. Automobiles, cruising, and partying also belong in this category, but they are so well known to prior generations of students that one need hardly dwell on them here.

Schools themselves can sometimes inhibit learning. Especially in the inner city, school environments themselves often militate against positive academic achievement.

To focus attention on the importance of learning in the inner cities, Los Angeles, as one of several other urban school districts, encourages large numbers of students to take the Preliminary Scholastic Achievement Test (PSAT) and the Scholastic Achievement Test (SAT), even though their school records suggest that they might not do very well on the tests. The reasoning is that putting urban students in a highly competitive situation helps them to understand the kinds of academic preparation needed to compete in later life, and thereby contributes to their overall growth.

As a result of this program, many upwardly mobile foreign-born students take this test after having had significantly fewer than twelve years of English instruction. The effects are evident from the statistics on those taking the test in Los Angeles versus the state of California as a whole. Thirty-four percent of all LAUSD seniors took the latest SAT examination—although L.A. represents only 13 percent of the total student population in the state. This effort to encourage broad participation is also reflected in the comparative data on the numbers of seniors who took the SAT and were also enrolled in honors courses in the subjects tested. The number in Los Angeles is significantly lower than in the state and nation (approximately 14 percent in the district; 29 percent in the state; and 25 percent in the nation).

In the spirit of broad community expectations of the schools, other constraints that influence education include the expectations of parents, teachers, and students themselves. At recent LAUSD meetings of parents and school personnel, parents voiced expectations that schools will teach—as one would expect—educational skills, but took responsibility themselves for things such as student vandalism, lost (or stolen) textbooks and equipment, and overall student attitudes toward classroom conduct and education.

Teacher surveys, letters to the editor, and magazine articles reveal a disturbing consistency in teacher attitudes and aspirations. Teachers are confused and disheartened by negative press and educational decisions they do not understand. They feel helpless in effecting change; they are overwhelmed by nonteaching responsibilities and are demoralized by low pay and lack of respect from those they teach. What they want follows entirely from this. Besides increased compensation, they want smaller classes, more recognition for their contribution to society, and a differentiated workload. They also want a general increase in administrator visibility on campus and in the classroom, administrative support to maintain a good learning environment, and higher standards for student behavior and responsibility.

Despite enormous distractions that students face in our youth-oriented consumer society, certain recent polls indicate that today's students are markedly more goal oriented than preceding generations. For a large majority of students, education is the vehicle to attain personal goals and economic advancement; and this datum—perhaps more than anything else—augurs well for the movement to increase academic standards.

In a sense each sector of the educational community imposes standards on the others; we might even say that the entire educational process rests on the maintenance of interrelated standards. There is no part of the system where this structural necessity is more pronounced than in secondary education, the bridge between childhood and adulthood for all who pass through schools. It is in our secondary schools that the crisis over standards is most acute, and it is not unreasonable to believe that it is there that success will have to be measured. A student who fails at some early step in primary school and, at the other end, in the college setting, is provided with many more chances to take corrective steps. But a lapse of study habits, or conduct, or on the other side, a failure to gain access to the right resources, at the secondary level, may be magnified and prove uncorrectable. It is, then, at the secondary level that the fight for higher and better standards must be most seriously waged.

Some Proposals

The most fundamental reform to be undertaken is improvement of the educational environment. This is most fundamental because in an important sense everything else depends on it. Individual reforms will accomplish very little without a broad commitment to reform, a commitment that reaches into individual homes, politicians' offices, and the centers of business, as well as the classroom.

Reforms have their best chance when commitment to them comes from the superintendent, who can then recruit school board members' approval and enthusiasm for a general plan of action. Such a plan should include a statement of direction and purpose, an organized and structured curriculum, a common core of classes, and a list of special interest courses which strengthen prevocational, vocational, or academic offerings. The course descriptions should identify goals and objectives, and suggest strategies for reaching them. And finally, the expanded curriculum should include student, teacher, and parent responsibilities related to conduct, attitude, and expectations.

Beyond the school itself, successful reform depends on reaching out to other individuals and institutions that can help in various ways. Political support is the most obvious of these, but strong relationships with the higher education and business communities can also be extremely valuable.

Active cooperation between university and public school educators is important because a major burden of secondary school teachers is to transmit the current state of learning as it is refined and intensified in higher education. For this purpose, encouraging scholars in higher education to hold seminars, discussions, and other training sessions for secondary school officials and teachers can be extremely helpful in communicating new intellectual developments.

The general process of reform can also be encouraged when school districts establish partnerships with business and industry. These partnerships often bring business and industry spokesmen to schools to provide special assistance for advanced skill training of teachers, management skill training for administrators, and seminars to outline the quality and types of skills needed by graduates.

The problem of hiring and retaining first-rate teachers must be a central part of any serious effort to improve academic performance. A major issue in this regard, which others in this book have addressed, is the problem of compensation, which is far below earning opportunities in competing occupations. Besides realistic compensation and adequate recruitment, several administrative reforms can make a substantial difference in trying to keep good teachers. Teacher involvement in decision-making is one. Another is assurance of consistent and fair administrative and operational procedures. Both will empower teachers and encourage them to participate more fully in the total school program.

It is important that school boards allow department chairpersons to decide about the curriculum and supervise instruction, but with a formal process that allows individual teacher input into the decision-making process. A strong structure of authority will permit focus on department goals, especially for the purpose of establishing standards regarding vertical progression of skills, homework policies, standardized test scores, acceptable student achievement, progress reports, enriched courses, and communication with counselors and parents.

Improving the quality of teachers depends in part on the strength of university programs to prepare them for their profession and on school district leaders working with university officials to that end. Intern programs for both teachers and administrators can be helpful. All training programs should ultimately ensure that teachers are, above all, good planners. This means seeing instruction as a precise experience, beginning with course objectives and concluding with a summation that permits evaluation of actual learning. In the end, of course, the experience will be successful if the teacher has managed to develop a learning environment that is precise, planned, and motivating.

Mastery of language is the single greatest determinant of success, and it is therefore important to emphasize the language of individual disciplines. Teachers should require students to master the discipline vocabulary and apply it both within and metaphorically outside the subject area. Class discussion can be an important part of this process, as it forces students to listen and discuss in order to gain insights into concepts in a broader context than they may appear in a textbook. In this process the acquisition of standard English is paramount because it is the prevailing language of learning and because of its importance in the job market. In this context, bilingual instruction should reflect commitment to an accelerated transition from instructional use of the native language to saturation use of standard English.

The importance of the learning environment is also greatly influenced by school administrators who must insist that students attend school regularly, report to class on time, pay attention in class, respond to the teacher's authority, and in general make a serious effort to achieve class objectives. Administrators' willingness to support teachers' attempts to maintain order will help them to hold students accountable for their deportment, effort, and achievement.

All school employees—including even secretaries and custodians—have a responsibility to motivate students and help to reduce the number of dropouts. This latter problem may be addressed in various ways—by part-time job offers, individualized learning, and by a generally caring environment. Other programs that can be helpful include vocation/high tech centers tied closely to an industry that provides training and part-time employment; counseling that concentrates on potential and actual dropouts, and on their parents; reduce graduation costs; and ultimate assistance in job placement of graduating students. Finally, a student data bank that allows the school district to identify and assist potential dropouts will help schools intervene early and keep students in school.

In the instructional leadership role is the principal, who has the responsibility both for the educational quality of all school programs and for the climate of high expectations and positive attitudes that makes the educational experience meaningful. The principal is the focal point of the planning process—working with all other actors in the educational system, including parents and students.

Most important in the effective, comprehensive high school is an instructional program that implements the district's broad educational objectives with courses producing measurable and observable results, as developed by individual departments.

Entry level assessments will evaluate student needs and strengths. An effective comprehensive high school has an individual profile defined by standardized test scores, providing the means to measure student growth. In such a setting, teachers and administrators recognize their roles to promote instruction and student learning and accept the concept of "student advocacy." In turn the student population then senses that it has a caring, yet directive staff. At an appropriate level of expertise and responsibility, students can be involved in the operation of the school. When such a team works together toward shared goals, student growth improves—as measured by standardized tests. Follow-up studies have demonstrated improvement in performance at the college level and in first jobs.

As an indicator of the recent response to demands for higher academic standards, a study of curriculum and enrollment trends reveals an increase in the number of students who take and pass three years of mathematics, three years of science, and four years of a foreign language. The study also shows, in contrast with past tendencies, an increase in assignment of appropriate homework.

In the Los Angeles School District, school administrators supervise instruction through visits to the classroom, and the district supports a standard program of teacher evaluation that incorporates sound lesson plans, learning theory, methodology, and collegial assistance.

Standards for the Larger Community

Public education does not exist in a vacuum. This social organism functions in the larger arena of parents, community members, legislators, government agencies, and business and industry, all of whom affect or are affected by public education. If each group has slightly different needs, all have a fundamental interest in producing thinking citizens. When one group abrogates its responsibility to public education, the institution is poorer for it and other groups must carry the burden. Standards can be defined for these groups.

Parents. The role of parents is well known. Nevertheless, the lack of parental involvement in education remains a major problem. Parental interest in all dimensions of learning obviously reinforces values learned at school, and when students are deprived of that reinforcement, it is hardly surprising that the school's task becomes enormously more difficult. In the broadest sense, the most important point here is the teaching of good behavior and self-discipline, which help children learn to work in groups, to study, and to adjust to the classroom environment.

Business. Business leaders can demonstrate their commitment to education directly by supporting the Adopt-A-School programs and, indirectly, by working with other citizen groups that favor high educational standards both at the local school board and the state legislative levels. To encourage closer relations between business and schools, administrators and teachers might make open-house presentations to local business groups and organizations— in exchange for which business could train school administrators in new management skills that could be effectively applied to education. During teacher sabbaticals or summer vacations, businesses might provide job-training opportunities for teachers in fields related to their teaching—which would permit teachers to bring new and practical knowledge into their classrooms. Business leaders can also inspire students directly by participating in school programs and by visits to their workplaces, or they could provide off-campus instructional sites in practical work settings. Businesses could also establish any number of work, tutoring, and counseling programs for students during their vacation periods.

The state legislature. Local school boards have lost much of their power to make educational decisions in recent years, and the power of state legislatures has grown enormously. As a result, legislatures have become active partners in the education of citizens, and individual legislators have had to become knowledgeable about education. This increased role for state legislatures makes it necessary that they, too, be held accountable for high academic standards and educational reform.

As has been discussed elsewhere, funding is obviously a central concern here. Legislatures must also make an active effort—which is often very difficult—to resist political pressure from fringe groups, which want to use public schools to promote a particular point of view or ideology. In the same way, they must also resist the temptation to try to make schools become all things to all people. The primary purpose of the schools is education, not the treatment of all of society's ills.

The urban environment. Many parents have taken flight to the suburbs as a means of avoiding the negative aspects of an urban environment. Many families cannot flee, and in recent years some young adults have been returning to the cities to partake of the cultural and creative aspects of urban life.

For some, urban life is transitory, as one immigrant replaces another. And within each ethnic or economic stratum considerable movement occurs into and out of the community. Cities create temptations and challenges for children as they grow up, causing anxiety for parents, school officials, and other public figures. The nature of urban life is such that a major cooperative effort is necessary by local governments, public and private agencies, and school officials to mitigate negative influences on school-age children. Among the most important such efforts are programs aimed at actively resisting the distribution of drugs, and curbing street violence and other behavior hostile to established authority. These programs may include a neighborhood watch, liaison between community and police, and active contact between legislature and community.

In the inner cities, some students can only take advantage of educational opportunities if they can earn a supplemental income while they are in school. Economic assistance can often help at the margin in creating school/vocational programs that will allow these students to remain in school. Moreover, such a school could serve those young people best if it switched to a twelve-month year and a weekday operation from 8 AM to 9:30 PM. This would allow students from the lower income families to (a) seek part-time work that may be available only during specific time periods, and (b) still take all the subjects needed for graduation. Properly scheduled, intensive use of some existing facilities need not call for greatly increased staffing and operating costs. Whatever modest increases might be involved will be far less than the costs added to society by the school dropouts. A small number of these "flex-time" arrangements within inner city areas would ultimately be cost effective and benefit all of us. In any event, all job-training programs organized through the schools, business, and industry should emphasize the value of the work ethic as an intrinsic part of student responsibility.

The economic health of such communities would improve if parents and students were more aware of the economic value of completing high school. Their educational development would also advance with counseling about vocational opportunities and about the possibility of enrolling in a college. The media, especially television, can also help in this regard—changing public attitudes toward education through ongoing reports of school activities, including reports on how education is related to employment opportunities.

The student. Last but not least are the standards that must be set for students—inducing them to become citizens capable of making a positive contribution to the larger community. In considering the minimum expectations that are appropriate at graduation from secondary school, students should have acquired specific knowledge and skills. Among these, the most basic is obviously a command of the English language—learning to speak, read, and write clearly and grammatically. After that comes the ability to analyze and solve problems—knowing how to employ a scientific method in gathering and organizing data and drawing conclusions.

To be a responsible and productive citizen, it is important to acquire a broad range of substantive knowledge. Such knowledge should include an ability to trace the origins of the American democratic system and its institutions; to evaluate the benefits of American society and its economic system; to analyze the historical processes of civil rights, social justice, legal justice, and government functions; and then to apply such understanding to individual rights and responsibilities.

A similar area of personal responsibility, in which the student must be expected to have acquired some fundamental understanding, involves the value of a positive personal work ethic and attitude. The moral aspect implicit in the development of any career choice encompasses a recognition of the value of cooperation between people, while comprehending the value of the individual's contribution. In addition, meeting obligations in a timely and efficient manner is a necessary ingredient of a good work attitude that must be encouraged.

Students can be guided toward a real, active respect for an interest in education, extending from secondary education through college and beyond. Apart from narrow educational norms and emphases, other personal characteristics are important for the growth of such a positive outlook. These include a real feeling of self-discipline, understanding of and respect for art and other intellectual achievements of human society, an interest in physical and mental health, and in sound relationships with others, and a sensible perspective on the value and use of leisure.

Conclusion

The student is a product of all the years of formal education. His achievement belongs as much to the kindergarten teacher as it does to the third, seventh, or twelfth grade teacher. In the end, however, it is difficult to talk about "educational reform" as if it were something separate and apart from the rest of society.

Schools are not separate and apart. And for this reason reforming the schools really must be considered in relation to reforms of the larger society. Our national leaders have increasingly become aware of this connection, and educators thus have an opportunity to work for progress in a more supportive environment.

At the secondary level, the responsibilities of students and teachers change when compared with primary education. Secondary schools tend to represent a special case in the standards debate. Students in secondary schools are faced with more sophisticated, more demanding, and more challenging subject matters. Psychologically, the student is then at a period of his or her life when long-term decisions are or should be made. Faced with this potentially volatile mixture, the secondary teacher must make a special effort to guide students, to help them in career or vocational choices, and all through that period to foster good classroom and schoolwide relationships.

7

HOBERT W. BURNS

A View of Standards in Post-Secondary Education

The thesis of this essay is that, due in large but not complete part to the "student revolt" of the 1960s and the emergence of a "new egalitarianism" in the 1970s, higher education has misplaced its central purpose and, in consequence, its academic standards have suffered to the point in the 1980s where, as the National Commission on Excellence in Education has said, "Our nation is at risk."

The Loss of Direction

"Cheshire Puss," [Alice] began, rather timidly . . . "Would you tell me, please, which way I ought to go from here?"
"That depends a good deal on where you want to get to," said the Cat.
"I don't much care where," said Alice.
"Then it doesn't matter which way you go," said the Cat.[1]

Any view of academic standards is clear only when illuminated by the light of the purposes of education, for standards in education are the criteria by which we assess how well students, faculty, and schools are realizing the purposes of educational institutions.

It is not at all too abstract or "too philosophical" to say that the most persistent, contaminating problem in higher education today is that the earlier consensus about its central purpose has collapsed, and confusion about purpose has entailed disintegration of academic standards in the admission, curriculum, instruction, evaluation, retention, and graduation of students.

This is a serious problem because there is an inescapable relationship between the kind and quality of education and the kind and quality of society we shall have. There is an organic and causal relationship between standards of achievement in education and the preservation of a free society in a highly complex, technological, interdependent, and nuclear world. The disintegration of purpose and, in turn, of academic standards is no mere "academic" problem: a failure to reestablish appropriate purposes and standards means not only the failure of education but social, political, and economic failures of such magnitude as to endanger the existence of a free society.

Such reasons led David Gardner, President of the University of California, and his colleagues on the National Commission on Excellence in Education, to warn us that:

> Our Nation is at risk . . . [because] the educational foundations of our society are presently being eroded by a rising tide of mediocrity that threatens our very future as a Nation and a people. . . .
>
> If an unfriendly foreign power had attempted to impose on America the medicore educational performance that exists today, we might well have viewed it as an act of war. . . .
>
> Our society and its educational institutions seem to have lost sight of the basic purposes of schooling, and of the high expectations and disciplined effort needed to achieve them.[2]

Collapse of any primary social structure, political, economic, or educational, cannot accurately be attributed to any single cause or reason; and the definitive analysis of the loss of central purpose in higher education is yet to be made. Even so, it is possible to identify some of the principal conditions and events that contributed to the present confusion and debilitated condition of higher education.

The "knowledge explosion" of the post–World War II decades

continues to be a significant factor as it creates legitimate demands for continual changes in curricular content, often requiring new academic priorities and so complicating the stability of consensus about central purpose.

The unprecedented, almost unimaginable growth of post-secondary enrollment in the quarter-century following World War II (over 500 percent from 1940 to 1975) led not only to the expansion of existing colleges and universities but to the creation of new ones, particularly at the state college and community college level. The expansion of old institutions and the emergence of new ones involved not only huge increases in the size of faculties,[3] but also often resulted in faculty compositions in which the majority did not participate in and were therefore less committed to the earlier, long-standing consensus about the central purpose of higher learning. Indeed, many faculty members rejected the carefully, narrowly focused ends of education and the high standards required as means to those ends, not only for their students but for themselves. As George Will, no doubt too uncharitably, put it,

> Many faculty members were on campus because the education boom [of the 1960s] made the academic job market undemanding.... they were bored by scholarship, and their self-esteem and comfort were threatened by traditional academic standards. So they had powerful incentives to demote those standards.[4]

Those standards for faculty members, principally involving the requirement for scholarly activity and research ("publish or perish") were not so much denigrated in themselves as subjected to benign neglect on the ground that, in non-elite institutions at least, teaching was the first, most important, and perhaps only priority. There is great truth in the importance of teaching, but it is also true that teaching is less easily evaluated than scholarship and there is no convincing evidence that neglect of scholarship improves teaching or that attention to scholarship harms teaching.

Such demographic and epistemic conditions as these helped lead, as David Truman has said, to ". . . changed commitments by and demands upon faculties [as well as] a decline in the confidence necessary to discharging the responsibilities of establishing priorities. . . .[5]

Additionally, the growth in demand by students for post-second-

ary education—involving the enrollment of hundreds of thousands of those who might well have not gone to college under the
socioeconomic conditions that existed prior to World War II—
forced many states to divide the task of providing higher education among universities, state colleges, and community colleges.
This tripartite arrangement, while necessary and more beneficial
than not, did result in different (and often differing) missions
among the different segments and, as a result, differing values
and commitments that made consensus on a common central purpose and appropriate academic standards more difficult than ever.

Such great growth signalled, as Theodore Lockwood put it, the
erosion of ". . . a shared set of beliefs about the fundamental goals
of undergraduate education"[6] and left higher education open to
the further erosion of academic standards.

But no single event conduced to the disintegration of purpose,
and thus of standards, in higher education so much as the "student revolt" from the late-1960s through the early 1970s. As Martin Trow described it:

> The constant attacks on universities for their "irrelevance," their
> neglect of students, their "institutional racism," their implication in the
> war in Vietnam and in the "military-industrial complex" have deeply
> shaken the belief of many academic men in their own moral and intellec-
> tual authority. Many . . . no longer really believe they have a right to
> define a curriculum for their students or to set standards of performance,
> much less to prescribe [as a central purpose of higher education] the
> modes of thought and feeling appropriate to "an educated man."[7]

The cry for "relevance," following the erosion in consensus of
purpose, rather rapidly resulted in the reduction or abandonment
of normal standards for student admission, evaluation, and retention. It also led to the reduction or dismemberment of curricular
requirements, not only in general and liberal education but in
academic majors (with exceptions, of course, generally in the sciences and science-based professions) at both the undergraduate
and graduate levels, as well as to the proliferation of new and,
shall we say, unique, courses. The nature and magnitude of this
was encapsulated by Gary Knight and Peter Schotten in these
words:

> In the 1960s liberal education was declared irrelevant because its cli-
> entele, the students, felt it did not prepare them for a vigorous, socially

relevant life. Faculty and administrations alike responded by eliminating en masse requirements of all kinds. . . .[8]

In most but not all colleges and universities much of the curricular structure was built up over many decades. The structure consisted of certain course requirements, specifications, and prerequisites designed to yield scope and sequence and focus upon a set of curricular priorities based on a consensus about the central purpose of higher education. Such a structure was in greater or lesser degree dismantled by the faculty, with the consent of the administration, in favor of curricula that had courses or other "delivery systems" characterized as new, innovative, responsive, pertinent, and relevant.

It was a fundamental change, based principally on the elective principle in which students had all but unlimited opportunity to choose the courses, and the kinds of courses, they wanted to serve their own purposes from an increased number of course, instructional, and curricular options. Samuel Hux says,

> The older universal requirements were dropped. In their stead: either no requirements save a course in composition, or [the cafeteria curriculum]. Since it is practically impossible . . . to accumulate 120 credits over four years without sampling the cuisine in some scattered fashion, the [cafeteria curriculum] is, for all intents and purposes, *no* requirements.
> This was called "cultural pluralism." It was not, however, anything so well thought out as that term suggests; it was an unmanly throwing up of the hands. . . .[9]

The elective principle, extended so far, convinced many that it necessarily undermines the interrelationships of knowledge, the epistemic wholeness that should characterize the higher learning.

The assignment of cause-and-effect relationships is extremely difficult, and probably impossible, in the evaluation of education if one wishes to view curricular content and structure as "cause" to the "effect" of student academic achievement. Still in all there is a growing agreement that recent college and university graduates are less prepared than students of an earlier generation who graduated from a more structured curriculum with more rigorous standards.

While it may not be defensible to say that the replacement of structured, prescriptive curricula by a relatively unstructured, piecemeal, elective curriculum produced the decline in student knowledge and skills, there is no doubt that there have been consistent and dramatic deficiencies in student academic achievement.

These deficiencies are said to be in large part the result of lowered academic standards, as most dramatically illustrated by "open admissions" and "grade inflation," which are largely the creatures of a new egalitarianism in higher education.

The New Egalitarianism

"What *is* a Caucus-race?" said Alice ...

"Why," said the Dodo, "the best way to explain it is to do it.". . . . First [the Dodo] marked out a race-course, in a sort of circle ("the exact shape doesn't matter," it said), and then all the party was placed along the course, here and there. There was no "One, two, three, and away," but they began running when they liked, and left off when they liked, so that it was not easy to know when the race was over. However, when they had been running half an hour or so ... the Dodo suddenly called out "The race is over!" and they all crowded round it, panting, and asking "But who has won?"

This question the Dodo could not answer without a great deal of thought, and it sat for a long time with one finger pressed upon its forehead ... while the rest waited in silence. At last the Dodo said, "*Everyone* has won, and all must have prizes."[10]

As Thomas Sowell has said:

"Equality" is one of the great undefined terms underlying much current controversy and antagonism. That one confused word might even become the rock on which our civilization is wrecked. It should be defined.[11]

But there is no meaning of "equality" to which all would subscribe. Certainly the meaning of "equality" is not at all as clear and simple as the new egalitarians would have us believe, as they seem to assume that "equality" means "identicality." On this definition equal rights means identical rights; equal treatment means identical treatment; and equal opportunity means identical opportunity.

It is on such a definition, and considerations more of ideological than lexical nature, that the new egalitarians conclude that no one should be judged better than anyone else; that no one should be treated differently than anyone else; that if conditions of status or result or achievement are not identical they are not equal, and therefore intolerable in a society of equals. The new egalitarian morality thus requires society to make uniform, to level, those differences by placing artificial restraints on some and providing special treatment for others.

It takes no logician to note the contradiction in such an egalitarian thesis: in the name of equality inequalities are justified.

Equality as identicality can only refer to the civil and political rights we assign ourselves, individually and collectively, in a social compact. It cannot possibly refer to individual skills, abilities, interests, potentials, efforts, or achievements for none is equal in those respects if by "equal" we mean "identical."

John Gardner, himself a passionate defender of equality who fears the dangers of the new egalitarianism, is well aware that an egalitarianism

... which ignores differences in native capacity and achievement, has not served democracy well. Carried far enough, it means the lopping off of any heads which come above dead level. It means ... the individual smothered by the group. And it means the end of that striving for excellence which has produced mankind's greatest achievements.[12]

Egalitarianism in practice results in a sameness that can only be called mediocrity, a mediocrity that breeds more of the same. The eventual result of a well-motivated but mean-spirited egalitarianism must be, as that Gloomy Dane, Soren Kierkegaard, predicted, a mediocrity that is ". . . unrelieved by even the smallest eminence."[13]

In a free society, in the liberal society, the full expression of equality comes in equality of opportunity. "Equality" means the liberty to pursue one's goals on the basis of a freedom whose own meaning is explained, but not exhausted, in terms of the existence of alternatives, the right and ability to evaluate and choose among existing alternatives or to create new ones, and the opportunity — uninhibited by the accidents of race, color, creed, sex, national origin, or other artificial considerations — to try and implement the life choices that one makes.[14]

The new egalitarians pervert the meaning of equality of opportunity by a circuitous rationalization that if equal opportunity does not yield equal results then those results prove the opportunities were not equal. As Richard Lyman, the former President of Stanford University, has put it,

... a tendency is rapidly developing which, as Daniel Bell and others have pointed out, alters quite drastically the *meaning* of the search for equality. According to this new tendency, equality of opportunity is not enough; what must be guaranteed is equality of result.[15]

The only justification for that would be if all individuals were in fact equal, that is, identical, in their natural gifts or abilities; equal, that is, identical, in their interests and efforts; and equal, that is, identical, in their purposes. Yet thousands of years of human experience have failed to sustain such a rationale, and a theory of equality that runs so contrary to the course of human experience ought not be invested with a great deal of confidence. Thomas Sowell puts paid to the egalitarian argument by saying that:

A good umpire calls balls and strikes by the same rules for everyone, but one batter may get twice as many hits as another.

In recent years we have increasingly heard it argued that if outcomes are unequal, then the rules have been applied unequally. It would destroy my last illusion to discover that Willie Mays didn't really play baseball any better than anyone else, but that the umpires and sportswriters just conspired to make it look that way.[16]

The undeniable fact of unequal abilities and differential efforts will result in unequal outcomes in the context of equal, or even identical, opportunities. So it is clear the achievement of equal outcomes must necessarily be artificial.

Do we in fact *want* equal outcomes? Who could justify equal results in which the indolent student gets as high a grade as the hard-working student, "the careless fool as much as a careful and intelligent craftsman," or the boorish teacher as much as the inspiring teacher?[17]

It is foolish to assert that equal treatment of unequals is unjust. Yet in the name of justice that is what egalitarians commend, and where that commendation is rejected they attempt to enforce—by law and policy—a theory of "equality" whose practical implementation mandates the forced imposition of inequalities.

It was just such an egalitarian thrust, stimulated by a real failure to offer equal educational opportunity to many who were qualified (remember Governor Ross Barnett barring James Meredith from the door to the University of Mississippi?) that led to open enrollment with normal qualifications ignored.

From Mass to Universal Higher Education?

> "There's no sort of use in knocking," said the Footman. . . .
> "Please, then," said Alice, "how am I to get in?"
> "There might be some sense in your knocking," the Footman went on without attending to her. . . .
> "How am I to get in?" she repeated, aloud.
> "I shall sit here," the Footman remarked, "till tomorrow . . . or the next day, maybe". . . .
> "How am I to get in?" asked Alice again, in a louder tone.
> "*Are* you to get in at all?" said the Footman. "That's the first question, you know.". . .
> "Oh, there's no use in talking to him," said Alice desperately: "he's perfectly idiotic!" And she opened the door and went in.[18]

The first and most dramatic of our national documents declares "We hold these truths to be self-evident, that all men are created equal, that they are endowed by their Creator with certain unalienable Rights." Our failure to honor that commitment for all Americans, regardless of the accidents of race or color or national origin, was instrumental in the justifiable demand and drive for equal civil and political rights that was vigorously renewed in the 1960s.

For many, belief in that kind of equality—that each and all individuals have innate moral worth and equal civil rights—grew into the new egalitarianism. Coupled with that is a Jeffersonian-like belief that a free society requires, as means to that end, universal public education.[19] That belief is strengthened by the undeniable truth that historically, first, universal elementary education and, then, universal secondary education have been of inestimable value in the growth, development, and prosperity of the United States and its citizens.

From such a set of values and facts two things followed in the minds of the new egalitarians. First, if universal elementary and secondary education are right, necessary, and good, then universal higher education is right, necessary, and good. Second, just as some Americans—again, due primarily to those accidents of race, color, and national origin—have been denied their right to elementary and secondary education so, too, have they been denied their right to higher education.

Paul Kurtz describes the new egalitarians' position succinctly when he says they believe ". . . that the democratic ideal implies universal higher education. . . . [and] The open admissions policy [in higher education] is an effort to fulfill this ideal."[20]

That ideal was implemented, not for the first time in American higher education but certainly in the most dramatic way, at the City University of New York. CUNY was known as the institution that for decades had selected students from the immigration melting-pot that New York City has always been and, by offering an excellent education with high standards, helped the underprivileged but talented enter and achieve in mainstream America.

Although not in office when CUNY implemented its open admissions policy in 1970, its long-time President, Buell Gallagher, explained his rationale for it, based on his experience in 1962 when he served as the first Chancellor of the then newly-founded California State University and College system:

> [The need for open admissions is] best illustrated in the three-track system of public higher education in California [where] admission to each of the three segments . . . is determined by rank in high school class and standing on SAT tests: to be admitted to [The University of California, a student] must be in the upper 12.5 percent; in the top third for admission to [The California State University and Colleges]; and the junior colleges admit all the others. This automatically guaranteed that black enrollments in the university would be less than 1 percent; less than 3 percent in the state colleges; and at the 7 percent level in the junior colleges.
>
> The same error was repeated by [CUNY before open admissions]. . . . [and] The manifest unfairness of an admissions policy that penalized black and Puerto Rican students because the lower schools had not adequately prepared them for academic success . . . was defended in the name of "standards" and "equal opportunity on the basis of achievement."[21]

Open admissions to CUNY began in 1970, after it had been forced to close for three successive spring semesters due to racial rioting, and the doors to the university were thrown open.

Four years later, after only 110 students graduated out of 3,687 who would not have been admitted except for the open admissions policy,[22] it became clear that universal higher education as implemented through the policy of open admissions at CUNY had failed: the lowering of standards had not contributed to the educational benefit of those for whom it was designed nor to the institution. "Open admissions solved the political issues on which it began," said the Chairman of the Board of Higher Education in New York City, "but it has not fully solved the educational issues."[23]

To say open admissions did not solve the educational issues was an understatement, for in 1976 CUNY ended the policy. But not without serious academic consequence, for, as John Silber observed:

> [CUNY] did not . . . return to its earlier admissions standards, but instead established as the minimum qualification for admission the competence expected of an eighth-grade education. . . . [W] hile prospective students at CUNY must now have reached an eighth-grade level, they must also be high-school graduates—so, in theory, they must also have attained a twelfth-grade education. Implicit in the admissions standards of CUNY is a one-third devaluation of the New York high-school diploma.[24]

Despite the debacle at CUNY it should be pointed out that a policy of open admissions per se was not at fault. For many years many state universities had been required to admit all state residents who applied and met the admissions criteria—there was no "cap" on enrollment for qualified applicants. Even today almost one-fourth of all four-year public colleges and universities must, by state requirement, admit every high school graduate. The debacle at CUNY was due not so much to the throwing open of the doors but to the throwing out of admissions standards based on academic achievement. The crucial distinction is between the admission of all and the admission of all who are qualified, and the crux of that distinction lies in the definition of appropriate standards for admission and retention.

The creation of such appropriate standards is complicated by the declining academic preparation of high school graduates. For example, The California State University (CSU) system for more than twenty years has committed itself to the admission of all who meet its requirements (based on a formula drawn from high school Grade Point Average and SAT or ACT scores), and four percent who don't.

In 1975–1976, under the leadership of its former Chancellor, Glenn S. Dumke, The CSU, concerned about the student ability in English, decided that all its new students, whether from high schools or community colleges, would be required to take an English Placement Test. A few years later, under the leadership of its new Chancellor, W. Ann Reynolds, The CSU also decided that

its newly admitted students would be required to take an Entry
Level Mathematics Examination.

"Since the English Placement Test was first administered," reports William E. Vandament, "increasing percentages of entering
students have been unable to demonstrate competence." He goes
on to say that:

In 1977–78 approximately 43 percent of test-takers failed to achieve
the desired minimum score which has been determined to demonstrate
minimal entry-level skills in reading and composition. This translates
into an estimated figure of 14,440 students requiring remediation in
writing.

By 1983–84 the rate at which students failed to demonstrate competence [in reading and writing] had increased to 60 percent, or an estimated 18,012 students. . . .

Of all the students required to take the [Entry Level Mathematics
Examination] in 1983–84, about 53 percent failed to demonstrate competence in arithmetic, elementary algebra, and geometry. . . .

He further offers the discouraging observation that:

A sizeable proportion of these students failing to demonstrate competence [in reading, writing, and mathematics] were first-time freshmen
from among the upper one-third of California's high school graduates.
It is estimated that three-fourths of those students not passing the
EPT and ELM examinations were students meeting regular criteria for
admission. [25]

Such an observation makes one wonder about the quality of curriculum, instruction, and standards of student achievement in
high schools when so many in the top third of their graduating
classes fail tests of basic skills. One wonders as well about standards of admission that require such tests after rather than before
enrollment is granted.

The presence in colleges and universities, including community
colleges, of so many students lacking the fundamental skills
needed to benefit from higher education has inevitably led to an
increasing amount of remedial instruction in our institutions of
higher learning. Contradictory as that concept is, paradoxical as it
may seem, the solution of the problem is neither easy nor within
grasp in the immediate future.

That is because educational policy is not, and cannot be, set
independently of larger social policies. If the new egalitarians' pro-

posed social policy of universal higher education has been shown to be infeasible, neither is it feasible in the short run to restrict our commitment to mass higher education only to those who are qualified on sound academic standards. The sudden reimposition of truly defensible standards of secondary achievement as prerequisite to admission to colleges and universities would eliminate large numbers of ambitious and natively able students, including many from minority populations, and social policies will not now tolerate that even in the name of academic quality.

So remediation in higher education of student defects from elementary and secondary education, though highly controversial, is likely to be a feature of collegiate curriculum and instruction for another decade—and longer, if the lower schools are not reformed.

The argument for remediation is powerful: if institutions of higher education admit, for reasons of social policy or not, students who are deficient in the knowledge and skills required to benefit from and complete college then those institutions have an obligation to provide the curriculum and instruction needed to help those students "come up to speed." Many of these students, members of minority groups or not, are graduates of schools that place less emphasis on preparation for higher education than on other curricula, so students are disadvantaged even though they may well have the native capacity and personal desire for a college education. And, truth be known, any historian of American education can show that collegiate level remediation of defects for admission is about as old as American higher education itself.

But the arguments against remediation are equally powerful: the very rationale for higher education, the pursuit of higher learning as based on adequate secondary school preparation, is wounded, perhaps mortally, if the failed tasks of elementary and secondary schools are passed along, with their deficient students, to colleges and universities. Remedial instruction thus perverts the very mission of the university; it forces the faculty to offer instruction at a level at which they are not necessarily competent, and certainly far below that at which they were employed to teach; it corrupts the curriculum for non-remedial students, as intellectual and other resources devoted to remediation are drawn from the normal courses of instruction, debilitating the scope and

quality of education throughout the entire institution, contribut-
ing to the further loss of central purpose and the further decline of
academic standards. Moreover, it is inordinately expensive to do in
college what should have been done in the lower schools.

The egalitarian pressures for open admissions, remedial instruction, and retention of students who under traditional standards would be "flunked out" have combined with those other conditions noted earlier (e.g., the substitution of the elective principle
in place of a more structured curriculum and the desire by some
institutions to protect resources—particularly jobs—by maintaining enrollment) to contribute to the phenomenon known as
"grade inflation."

Grade Inflation − Achievement = Academic Deflation

"We had the best of educations" [said the Mock Turtle]—" in fact, we
went to school every day—"

"*I've* been to a day-school, too," said Alice; "you needn't be so proud as
all that".…

"I went to the Classical master," [said the Gryphon]. "He was an old
crab, *he* was."

"I never went to him," the Mock Turtle said with a sigh: "he taught
Laughing and Grief, they used to say."

"And how many hours a day did you do lessons?" said Alice.…

"Ten hours the first day," said the Mock Turtle, "nine the next, and so
on."

"What a curious plan!" exclaimed Alice.

"That's the reason they're called lessons," the Gryphon remarked:
"because they lessen from day to day."[26]

A few years ago a journalism student wrote that:

Inflation has become a household word. It seems everything is going
down in value, and up in price.

Education is no different. A student is rewarded for performing his job,
not with money, but grades. Due to grade inflation, a student's reim-
bursement is clearly worth less.[27]

Implicit in that student's generalization is the presupposition
that grades have risen without a correlative rise in student
achievement, that grade inflation reflects the deflation of
academic standards. The case that student grades and GPAs have
risen while student achievement has not requires some empirical

demonstration. Consider the following data, drawn from a large state university system.[28]

In the spring of 1974 33.8 percent of all undergraduates got A's, and 91.6 percent were average students or better, getting C's or higher; 95.9 percent received passing grades, so that only 4.1 percent failed their courses. At the graduate level 61.2 percent got A's, 33.2 percent B's, and 4.2 percent C's, so that 98.6 percent were average or above; only 1.1 percent failed, so 98.9 percent passed their courses.

A decade later, in the spring of 1984, there was not much difference—29.6 percent of undergraduates got A's, and 88 percent were average or better getting C's or higher; 93.6 percent received passing grades, so that only 6.4 percent failed. At the graduate level 62.7 percent got A's, 32 percent B's, and 3.4 percent C's, so that 98.1 percent were average or above; only 1.6 percent failed, so 98.4 percent passed their courses.

One could easily conclude from those data that the average achievement of undergraduates is above average, and the average achievement of graduate students is clearly above average. But that seems a logically odd thing to suggest, so alternative interpretations are in order. As no act of evaluative will can justify the conclusion that "the average is above the average," one is left with the explanation that average student achievement has proved to be higher than average achievement expected—that students are better than ever, requiring a new definition of "average," perhaps because, as some elementary school teachers have put it, many students are "overachievers."

George Will, however, dissents:

Everyone is "supremely gifted?" Well, then, grade inflation makes sense: it merely says that almost everyone is above average. And never mind that academic life may come to resemble the "Caucus-race" as explained by the Dodo to Alice in Wonderland.[29]

It might be said that high selectivity in the admissions process has generated only superior students or students superior to those upon which the old norms and expectations were premised; or that students have not so much changed as instruction has improved; or both; and in those ways explain a skewed distribution of grades to the high end. It might also be said that, human nature being what it is, neither student achievement nor faculty instruction has improved all that much, so the jump in grades and GPAs could be the result of generous, even forgiving, academic standards.

Is that latter conclusion unfair? If the standard of quality is to be judged by performance on normed tests of academic achievement—such as the Scholastic Aptitude Test, the American College Testing Program, or the Graduate Record Examination—the answer is "no." We have seen a steady twenty-year decline in SAT averages on both verbal and mathematical scores,[30] confirming assessments based on other data as well as more subjective judgments that students have been increasingly less prepared for normal collegiate level achievement.

We are left with some intriguing conclusions: student achievement in pre-collegiate academics is generally down as measured by normed tests, but generally up as judged by secondary school GPAs. Similarly, students enter college less prepared than in years past but receive grades higher than in years past. How can such discrepancies be explained?

For a long time the declining levels of achievement on SAT and ACT scores were said to be the result of increasing numbers of students taking those tests, implying that more students in the lower percentiles of high school classes were taking them, thus dropping the average. Despite the tinge of controversy in such an explanation (as more minority students were taking the tests), that seemed a plausible explanation until some few years ago when the number of test-takers leveled off, making it more difficult to attribute the consistent decline in scores on a consistent increase of poorer students taking the tests.

Indeed, analyses showed fewer and fewer students were scoring in the higher ranges of the tests, leaving the conclusion that even the most prepared students in recent years were less prepared than their counterparts in years past. Even so, they receive higher grades and GPAs.

There is no single or simple explanation for the inflation of grades and the concomitant deflation of academic standards. The causes are multiple, interrelated, and often confused and confusing. There is more than a grain of truth in Martin Trow's judgment, quoted earlier (see note 7), that many faculty members no longer have confidence in their right or ability to set rigorous standards of achievement; and it is true that, for many reasons at all levels of education, faculty members are demoralized; too many have grown cynical, and too many are too burned-out to care very much.

There are of course other reasons as well; some of the more important can be described briefly:

1. The increase of such evaluative techniques as pass/fail or even pass/no grade; of courses and programs of non-academic activity (e.g., athletic cheerleading, election to student government) that receive academic credit and grades tends to subvert the value of academic effort, academic achievement, and academic transcripts.

2. The ideological commitments of some faculty members (e.g., during the Vietnam War that no male student be "flunked out" lest he be drafted) and of some institutions (e.g., that the admission of normally unqualified students entails the obligation to provide them with special instruction and consideration until they "catch up") has contributed to grade inflation.

3. The recent decreases in enrollment, which by most resource allocation policies result in decreases of faculty positions and funds, have led to fears that rigorous standards of achievement and grading would drive students away to "easier" departments or even other institutions, and this has contributed to the continuation of grade inflation. As the National Commission on Excellence in Education says, "In some colleges maintaining enrollments is of greater day-to-day concern than maintaining rigorous academic standards."[31]

4. The "spiral down effect" is at work, too: many faculty members, who regret and resent grade inflation, feel that maintenance of their own higher standards will work to the disadvantage of their students—that their students will be penalized when compared with other students getting "easier" grades— so they tend to ease up in an attempt to be fair to their students and find some equal level. But an equal level in higher education always proves to be a lower level, and this contributes to grade inflation.

5. There are some faculty members, one hopes very few, who are

not as competent as they might be either in their own subject
specialty or in their teaching, and are unable to distinguish
among levels of achievement and so grade all with generosity.
As Charles J. Brauner and I said twenty years ago, there are
too many who:

> ... teach and grade after the manner of bull-session rhetoric without
> realizing there is a level of scholarship quite beyond [their] own ac-
> quaintance, hence totally beyond [their] students' reach . . .[32]

These reasons are near the mark, and they did not come upon
higher education "full-grow'd," like Topsy, but as already noted
had their antecedents in the academic self-introspection of the
1960s and 1970s, which, in turn, contributed to the loss of central
purpose.

Although those events have been over for many years they have
left a festering sore in higher education through the wounding of
academic standards. Peter Burger says, of those days, that:

> The less visible—but much more consequential—change has been a
> pervasive softening of academic standards. The abolition of required
> courses, the statistically demonstrable inflation of 'A' and 'B' grades, the
> spreading notion that scholarly capacity is, at best, one of very many
> qualities needed in a college teacher . . . these and similar developments
> on the level of curriculum and faculty policy, including personnel policy,
> are where the long-range effects of [those days] must be sought. . . .

Is it too late to rebuild into higher education, he wonders,

> . . . objective standards and criteria of evaluation instead of the currently
> fashionable chaos of subjectivity; respect for hard intellectual labor in-
> stead of the cult of self-expression and "creativity" . . . ?[33]

If it is too late, if grade inflation—which is no more than the
reluctance of faculty members and their institutions to make
meaningful discriminations among individual students on the
basis of their academic achievements—is to be with us permanently, what does it mean?

At least this: the refusal of colleges and universities to continue
to serve as the socially sanctioned sorting or selecting or certifying
agencies for society. Perhaps that is too far-fetched, but it is certainly reasonable to conclude that letter grades and the GPAs
derived from those grades are the principal means to serve the
socially commissioned role of selection, and if that role continues

to be contaminated by grade inflation, then all—students, faculty, higher education, and society—suffer. Edward White puts it directly:

> The problem is not merely the familiar 'decrease in standards' or 'inflation of the grading system'. . . . The problem is that a major function of higher education is openly based on fraud: Important decisions about people's lives are made all the time on the basis of an accreditation system that cannot be trusted. . . .
>
> [N]o one from the outside, looking at a student's grades, can have any real idea of what they mean. . . .
>
> [But] of course, those involved in the corruption of the grading system . . . hope . . . that all grading cease. . . .[34]

Roben Fleming has said:

> There is a body of opinion . . . which takes the view that the educational world would be improved if we never made any comparisons between individuals, and if our records reflected nothing more than a kind of equality among students. This seems to me a total delusion. I have spent too many years in the classroom, and had too many students, to allow myself to believe that their academic aptitudes are all the same. . . .
>
> When we act as though all students are equal we deceive only ourselves [and] we are not even acting consistently with our own practices outside the academic arena. . . .
>
> Why, then, should we be so reluctant about rating students? And why should we apologize for insisting they perform at a high level of quality? . . . . [because] an academic experience in which one can never fail is contrary to every other life experience which the student will have. . . .
>
> There is considerable evidence that there is already an increasing public acceptance of the fact that the university is not for everyone . . . [and] I would hope that we would have the courage to say so, and not be deterred by a misplaced sense of egalitarianism.[35]

What is the price to be paid if higher education neglects or spoils the sorting and selecting task? John Silber says "[T]here lies behind the egalitarian cliche a profound conflict of interest and it must be relentlessly exposed."[36]

That conflict of interest has to do with concepts of authority, responsibility, and accountability, and the new egalitarian thrust is aimed, if not deliberately nonetheless effectively, at academic authority, responsibility, and accountability. It has led to diminution, sometimes voluntary, sometimes not, of professorial authority. John Gardner believes that:

> Those who derive their authority from the institutions of a free soci-

ety—professors, for instance—have seen their position seriously undermined in recent years. In a time when authority ... is scorned, the
teacher-student and master-apprentice relationships are weakened at
the core ...

But when we reject apprenticeship, when we scorn the learner's role,
we demolish the path that leads on to craftsmanship and mastery. And
then we discover that the most intransigent tyrant of all is hard reality.
You can't vote yourself into the company of great heart surgeons or con-
cert pianists ...

Professors should strive to understand the needs of students, but they
need not forsake their own role nor for one moment doubt its validity.
With respect to [a subject matter] at hand there is an inequality that can
only be altered through the hard process of learning.[37]

And, it might be added, the correlative responsibility to evaluate
achievement—to grade. The purposes of grading should be well
known, but it is never inappropriate to restate the two principal
ones.

First, grades tell a student about the quality of his achievements, or lack thereof, and the relationship of his work to that of
other students; they let a student know in honest terms where he
stands. Surely not to do so, or to mislead students by declining to
make such discriminations or to disguise them harms students
most of all.

Second, those judgments, recorded on a transcript, indicate
something of value to others, within or outside the university, who
must themselves make decisions or judgments about an individual's qualifications—the sorting and selecting process so essential
to progress within both higher education and society itself.

Those purposes are denigrated by the inflation of grades, says
David Kenny, because:

[Inflation] diminishes the student's ability to profit from his undergraduate education by coming to a better sense of himself and his particular
intellectual qualities. It further undermines the utility of the grade-
record to others, and thus ironically tends to negate the benefits that
many naively assume to flow automatically from a "good transcript."[38]

It is possible to reach an important conclusion: there can be no
academic standards for students if there is no grading or if grading is relative to effort alone or to egalitarian social policy rather
than individual achievement. Academic institutions that cannot
or will not make such distinctions must, in the long run, suffer

because there is a functional connection between academic standards and the health of higher education—health in higher education is in large part dependent upon the academic standards that guide the activities, the life, the very being of colleges and universities.

If that is so then the decline of academic standards, as most clearly illustrated by inflated grades based on policies or practices that fail to discriminate among levels of student achievement, signals a fundamental corruption of higher education and a betrayal of its duty to society. That is exactly why, as John Gardner has put it,

Those who are most deeply devoted to a democratic society must be precisely the ones who insist upon excellence, who insist that free men are capable of the highest standards of performance. . . . The idea for which this nation stands will not survive if the highest goal free men can set themselves is an amiable mediocrity.[39]

Most people are certainly not willing to settle for "an amiable mediocrity" in and from their schools. Nor do most subscribe to the belief that schools, especially colleges, should try and be all things to all men and teach whatever and however students or faculty want. To this point Daniel Patrick Moynihan, scholar and United States Senator, has said that:

If egalitarianism lies deep in the American character, so does competitiveness. . . . There is precious little evidence that any significant portion of American opinion, much less the public at large, desires that high standards—based on competition—be reduced. . . .

There exists no populist groundswell in favor of abolishing standards of academic excellence.[40]

Indeed not, and as recent public opinion polls have shown there is increasing public support for the reform of education, from preschool through graduate school, the better to turn again onto the path toward sound academic purposes and defensible academic standards. In response to, or in tune with, this public desire for renewed competence in education state legislatures, boards of regents and trustees, academic senates, school boards, and parent-teacher organizations have taken the first steps—if only through recognition and discussion of the problem—necessary to repair the damage.

Postscript

"I can't believe *that!*" said Alice.

"Can't you?" the Queen said in a pitying tone. "Try again; draw a long breath, and shut your eyes."

Alice laughed. "There's no use trying," she said: "one *can't* believe impossible things."

"I daresay you haven't much practice," said the Queen . . . "Why, sometimes I've believed as many as six impossible things before breakfast."[41]

Is it reasonable to believe these six things: that (1) the public and academics will develop the will to improve higher education; (2) admissions standards will be tightened and made more specific; (3) curricula will be made leaner, cleaner, and sounder; (4) remedial instruction will be contained, reduced, and eventually minimized; (5) retention standards will be reinforced and grade inflation taper off; and (6) graduates will more frequently exhibit the qualities of mind and possess the knowledge and skills that higher learning is supposed to help generate?

Put cautiously, those who believe all that may not be believing six impossible things. But those things cannot be achieved in higher education alone, for if we want to improve higher education we must first, or at least concurrently, improve lower education. Secondary and post-secondary schools must work together and help each other if they are to help themselves, and some things need to be done first:

1. High schools must clean up their curricula and raise standards for the diploma that they say qualifies students for admission to higher education. Michael W. Kirst, a former President of the California State Board of Education, observes that:

   [When schools] have been pressured into [offering] courses in drug abuse, sex education, moral education, energy, career education, ethnic studies, parenting, environment, and so on [rarely is it asked] what is to be excluded . . .[42]

   and, advising schools to clean up their curricula, he says ". . . the secondary schools should surrender most of their programs in health, the worthy use of leisure, driver's training, and vocational skills . . ."[43] to other institutions.

2. Colleges and universities can assist in that, and contribute to their own need for more qualified students at admission, by

requiring higher levels of knowledge and skills—especially in the basic subjects of reading, writing, and mathematics. They must also be more specific and prescriptive about the acceptable courses and content of secondary education. There are even now some signs of this for, as Ernest L. Boyer, the distinguished former United States Commissioner of Education, has reported:

> By the early 1980s, efforts were underway to tighten standards and let high school students know what would be expected of them. Admissions requirements were being changed or reviewed for public systems of higher education in twenty-seven states.[44]

In California, for instance, a joint effort by the academic senates of the University of California, The California State University, and the California Community Colleges resulted in a set of recommendations specifying what secondary school graduates should know if they are to succeed in college. The California State University, to illustrate one result, increased its admission requirements in 1984 to include four years of college preparatory English and two of mathematics; a third year of required mathematics is planned, along with other specific subject requirements.

3. Most importantly, perhaps, if higher education is to help itself it must reinvigorate and improve—dramatically—the teacher training curricula. This must be done in close collaboration with state agencies and public school districts, and involve an *all*-university approach to and responsibility for teacher education, because schools of liberal arts and sciences actually provide teachers in training with more instruction than do schools or departments of education. The standards for admission to teacher education curricula need to be raised significantly. Martin Trow notes that:

> The problem has many dimensions, but perhaps the most critical is the quality and morale of the teaching profession itself. From 1972 to 1980, SAT verbal scores for college-bound high school seniors planning to major in education dropped from 418 to 339, a loss of 79 points, while the SAT math scores in that population dropped 31 points, from 449 to 418. This is a much steeper decline than the national average for the SAT over the same period . . .[45]

None of these things can or will become possible except as one other thing happens: the investment of by far, far greater amounts of monetary and human capital in our schools. We are seeing some signs of this, small as they are, and one might take them as omens of more to come. As John Bunzel has observed:

Although there is no solid agreement as to whether more money should be spent on education, most of the polls show that the American people are willing to pay higher taxes if they believe they will get better-quality education in return.[46]

It is not too much to hope that within the next decade—it will take that long—higher education will have refound its central purpose, that its academic standards will have been revitalized, and that it will serve well the nation and those who live and work in the twenty-first century.

8

SALLY B. KILGORE

Educational Standards in Private and Public Schools

Observers frequently distinguish private from public secondary schools by their use of entrance standards. Indeed, data support the focus on this distinction. The High School and Beyond (HSB) 1982 survey of high school administrators[1] suggests that about 3 percent of the public high schools have entrance requirements— including successful completion of eighth or ninth grade course-work.[2] In contrast, approximately 60 percent of the Catholic sector schools and 52 percent of the non-Catholic private schools report some type of entrance requirement.

In setting entrance standards, private-sector schools are limited only by federal tax laws that prohibit racial discrimination for those educational institutions claiming a nonprofit, tax exempt status. Most public schools are perceived as either victims or beneficiaries of administratively defined areas that either include or eliminate a large number of educationally disadvantaged students. However, to conclude that the quality of students acquired by private sector schools through the control of admissions is the most significant consequence of the use of such standards is to miss a more subtle, but perhaps more important, function of entrance standards at the secondary school level, namely, facilitating institutional support.

The use of admission criteria is only one of several ways in which public and private sector schools differ in the application of standards. Observers also emphasize differences in conduct and performance standards. In this chapter I review each of these distinctions. My objective is to illuminate the role of standards more generally, emphasizing that portion of the private sector that enrolls most of the students who attend private secondary schools, the Catholic sector.

Entrance Standards

Entrance standards for educational institutions are of two types: objectified and personalized. I classify some as objectified not because of their relative validity or accuracy, but because of their greater degree of quantification and comparability across students. Such standards include: (1) some level of attainment on an aptitude or achievement test, (2) some level of performance in previous educational settings, and (3) the content of previous schooling. The second type of standard, personalized measures, includes those evaluation mechanisms that permit relatively idiosyncratic qualities of students to emerge as relevant to the admission decision. Such standards include: (1) satisfactory performance in an interview with school personnel, (2) written recommendations from educators regarding the potential of the applicant, and (3) written recommendations from civic or religious leaders attesting to the moral character of the applicant.

Private sector schools differ in their use of these standards in at least four ways: (1) in their decision to employ or not to employ entrance requirements, (2) in their selection of which types of standards to use, (3) in their selection of an acceptable performance level for a given standard, and (4) in the relative weight attached to each criterion employed.

Much of the variation among private sector schools in admission standards is likely attributable to differences in mission and in applicant pools. Obviously, the obligations of a religiously affiliated school may require that they give attention to the religious affiliation of applicants. Conversely, the financial obligations of a struggling secular school may preclude entrance requirements completely. The following discussion is restricted to institutions that give at least equal weight to some factor other than the moral character or religious affiliation of the applicant. The objective of this section is to explore why private sector schools institute entrance standards, not the actual content of those standards. In subsequent sections I shall address the actual substance of the standards.

Educational institutions purportedly design and weight various entrance standards to insure that a student will be successfully educated at a given institution. However, it is no secret that at all levels these standards vary over time at an institution with no prior change in curriculum or expectations. The change in standards more than likely reflects a change in the attributes of the applicant pool. Where demand for entrance is great—as in the more prestigious medical and law schools—educational institutions may introduce objectified standards to reduce the pool of applicants requiring extensive serious consideration. It is these functions—insuring successful students and managing applicant reviews—that are commonly known and thereby constitute the manifest functions of entrance standards.

Several latent functions of entrance requirements also exist. At the college level, entrance standards partially define the status of an institution and the value of its degree. As a consequence, private educational institutions have incentives to elevate entrance standards as much as possible. The hypothesis I would like to entertain, however, is that entrance requirements are more important to most private secondary schools for the commitment and respect they instill in their students than for the capacity of these requirements to differentiate good students from bad students or to create an added value to their certification. The evidence I provide in support of this hypothesis is, I think, persuasive if not conclusive.

Consider first the applicant pool to which private schools apply entrance standards: What is the demand for private sector secondary schooling? Data from the HSB administrators survey indicate that only 38 percent of the Catholic sector schools and approximately half of the non-Catholic private sector schools have a waiting list—a list of students who wish to gain admittance but cannot due to space limitations. Another, perhaps more informative, survey of Catholic secondary school administrators suggests that, on average, Catholic sector secondary schools are operating at 85 percent capacity.[3] Thus, evidence suggests that a number of private secondary schools fail to have a demand for their services that exceeds the supply they are prepared to offer.

A second condition of private sector schooling is perhaps more informative and critical. It is the constraint of finances. For both Catholic and non-Catholic private secondary schools, data from the HSB survey indicate that half use tuition fees to meet 80 percent or more of their operating costs. Nearly all of these schools (more than 80 percent) use tuition fees to meet at least half of their operating costs.[4] To the degree that schools are dependent on tuition for a large portion of their operating expenses, student enrollment must attain a certain level to insure survival. The addition or subtraction of four students can, for some private secondary schools, constitute the addition or subtraction of, say, one part-time French teacher.

Together, the variable of demand for services and the dependence on tuition fees constrain the application of high entrance standards and/or strict application of modest entrance standards to a subset of private sector schools—at best, probably half of the schools in the private sector. (Some preliminary evidence suggests that Catholic schools may be more likely to report such standards when the demand for their service appears weak than other, non-Catholic private schools.)

To the extent to which parents and children are aware of a school's heavy dependence upon their tuition fees, the day-to-day operation of the school is vulnerable to a myriad of intrusions. Such a dilemma is peculiar to private sector schooling and to alter such a balance of power school officials must somehow communicate the substitutability of one family's tuition money for another. Under these conditions of financial dependence, schools may employ entrance procedures (perceived as standards by the applicant and his or her family) as a mechanism to encourage certain positive beliefs about the applicant, his or her potential peers, and about the school itself. In creating an aura of selectivity the school officials have communicated a student's substitutability. In these instances admission procedures are ritualistic events, not screening devices. They encourage students to acquire a positive disposition toward the school and perhaps only secondarily help the educational institution to identify those students who have satisfactory academic and conduct records.

Public sector schools may also encourage positive orientations. School traditions, legends, and ceremonies that accompany admission are not the exclusive domain of private sector schools. Public sector schools can create traditions of excellence and rituals of entrance that foster dispositions toward the school that are similar to those that result from private sector entrance admission standards. Unfortunately, courts as well as educators have often ignored the role of institutional heritage in the educational process.[5]

As public sector secondary schools were transformed from selective institutions to schools providing universal education, school entrance standards disappeared, and program and track admission standards emerged. Most public secondary schools now have a pre-college or academic track, a general track, a vocational program, and an honors program. Similar to private sector school entrance standards, I argue that the degree to which the standards for admission to such tracks or programs is articulated and enforced is a function of the demand for the credentials provided by each program. Where a low demand for the program or track exists, entrance standards will be lower than in places where there is a high demand. The source of this variation, however, is slightly different than in the private sector.

The pragmatics of running a comprehensive public high school require at least some students to enroll in each program. For vocational programs, the heavy capital outlay requires continued justification. Teacher interest and status are often embedded within the academic and honors programs and constitute a demand for such services.[6] Thus, student demand for programs or tracks interacts with institutional requirements to create measurable variation in the level of performance required for entry into a given program or track. If student demand for the academic curriculum is low and the potential pool of enrollees is of average achievement, then the standards for admission to the program

will be lower than the standards applied at, say, a suburban high
school where the demand for a pre-college curriculum is high and
the achievement of students is above average. Generally, such
variation is similar to that of the private sector but, as I hope to
show in the subsequent section, the sectors differ in the weight attached to specific standards when faced with similar conditions.

Defining and Weighting Entrance Standards

In the previous section I classified entrance standards (such as
standardized tests and coursework completed) and personalized
standards (such as personal interviews and recommendations).
Both sectors employ each type of standard but differ in the point
at which the standards are applied and in the relative weight
assigned to them. In particular, private and public sector schools
with similar demands—for entrance into their school or into a
pre-college curriculum—differ in the relative weight they assign
to objectified and personalized standards.

Table 1 shows the types of school admission criteria mentioned
by private sector schools. As seen in the first and second rows of
the table, a majority of these schools use some type of standardized test in the admission process but very few list student
transcripts as their first or second criteria. My own exploratory

Table 1

Types of Admission Criteria Used in Private Secondary Schools
(Percentage of Schools reporting listing item as first or second criteria)

Measures	Catholic	Other Private	Elite Private[a]
Standardized Test Scores[b]	56	51	72
Attendance Records	8	17	31
Interviews	5	10	33
Recommendations	8	3	29
	N=84	N=27	N=11

[a]Private schools with the greatest number of National Merit Finalists in 1979.
[b]Included in standardized tests are achievement tests, placement or aptitude
tests, and entrance exams.

Source: High School and Beyond Administrators' Survey, 1982.

research of public sector schools[7] suggests that admission criteria for academic programs are weighted equally between student transcripts and achievement tests.

Differences appear more substantial, however, when comparing schools with similar demands for services. In the same exploratory research, I found that public school districts serving a population with a high demand for a pre-college curriculum tend to objectify the admissions criteria by establishing minimum grade point averages and standardized test scores for college track or honors programs. Teacher recommendations are used, but only to sort exceptional cases within the pool of students who have met the objective standards. The role of counselors is negligible. In contrast, in those school districts where there is a low demand for the pre-college curriculum, the evaluations of counselors and teachers may be used to "override" the objectified information. A general description then, would be that a public sector school with a high demand for academic and honors programs tends to objectify its standards, whereas a public sector school with low demand for such programs gives more weight to personalized criteria.

In contrast, it appears that secondary schools in the private sector with similarly high demands for services—elite private schools—introduce more personalized criteria (personal interviews, teacher and principal recommendations) than do the less prestigious private schools that assign more weight to objectified criteria.[8] Table 1 shows that both types of private schools consider objectified measures important, but that elite private schools are more likely to include personalized criteria.

These differences across and within sectors reflect the larger context within which each type of school operates. In public sector schools, public accountability is always present. For track placement, this accountability is activated only in schools where a high demand for the curriculum exists. The school must naturally buffer itself against charges of unfairness or discrimination. Consequently, with a good applicant pool, public sector educational institutions are pressed to objectify their entrance standards.[9]

In contrast, private sector secondary schools operating in an environment with a good applicant pool do not experience a concomitant increase in public accountability at the point of admission. Rather, accountability to alumni and donors increases and personalized standards can permit some latitude in meeting these private interests. To the degree that these same elite institutions gain some financial independence from these private interests, it would appear that the weight of objectified standards might again increase simply—as in the public sector—to buffer the institution from the private interest pressures.

We tend to think of objectification of entrance standards as a master trend at all levels of education. Moreover, we tend to think of personalized criteria as some aristocratic residue of class-based education, when in fact it likely operates at all levels and sectors. I suggest that it is most common at the secondary level in public sector schools dominated by low SES students and in the prestigious private sector schools. It is beyond the scope of this chapter to evaluate the substance of entrance standards, except to say that the experience of our professional schools should suggest that complete objectification of entrance standards is not desirable and that different opportunity structures exist even within our public sector schools because of these variations.

Conduct Standards

Common perceptions regarding public and private school differences begin with the entrance standards discussed in the first section of this chapter and move quickly to incorporate what is perceived as the natural consequence of those entrance standards: well-behaved students in the private sector. According to a 1983 report by Williams, Small, and Huter, discipline is second only to academic quality as the most frequent reason parents give for transferring their children from public to private sector schools.[10] Again, a cursory examination of the facts supports that common perception. Student misbehavior appears to occur much more frequently in the public sector than in the private sector. In the Catholic sector, even the scope of rules appears extensive, and perhaps exhaustive, compared with the public sector schools.[11]

However, it is curious that the incidence of disciplinary action is approximately equal in the Catholic and public sectors.[12] One of two differences exist: either students in the Catholic sector are more likely than public sector students to be caught and disciplined when they break rules, or they are disciplined more frequently for minor infractions.

The first explanation—higher probability of disciplinary action for any misbehavior—may be reasonable. Catholic schools, on average, have a smaller student enrollment. School size can affect the effective enforcement of rules.[13] The problem is illustrated with a simple, hypothetical example.

Suppose the upper limit of any teacher's knowledge of student names is 200 and that the probability of a teacher knowing a given student is independent of the probability that another teacher will know that student. Suppose, further, that on any given hall there are four teachers observing the movement of students from one class to another. In a school with 800 students enrolled, there is a high probability (.68) that most of the students passing through the hall will be known to at least one of the four teachers. For a school of 4,000, in that same hallway, the chances of name recognition is much smaller—following the same assumptions, about one chance in five (.19).[14] Thus, if some incident does occur in the larger school, the likelihood of successful enforcement of rules is hampered by the inability to communicate personally with a misbehaving student, much less convincingly report it to higher authorities. Whether or not this is the specific mechanism by which Catholic and public sector schools achieve equal rates of disciplinary action remains unverified. It does suggest how school size may explain the rates of discipline.

The second explanation of the equal rates of disciplinary action—the variation of actual enforcement standards—is more intuitively consistent with the data. Given that students report higher rates of misbehavior in the public sector than in the Catholic sector and that the disciplinary rates are relatively equal (12 percent in the Catholic sector and 13 percent in the public sector), one may argue that Catholic school administrators must react more strongly to less glaring types of misbehavior than public sector administrators. However, this assumes that more serious forms of misbehavior result in disciplinary action at an equal rate in both sectors. If such a difference in enforcement exists, then the interesting question is whether or not the use of disciplinary action for less serious offenses actually affects the rate of serious misbehavior. Both explanations, size and enforcement, are consonant with the evidence explored to date; to answer the question satisfactorily, further exploration of variation within the public sector should be pursued.

Some observers attribute the difference in student conduct between the two sectors to the initial screening; that is, the opportunity in the private sector to reject students with a history of disciplinary problems. The differences, however, are not as striking as one might presume. In the 1982 HSB administrators' survey, 11 percent of the public school officials reported that their schools could refuse admission to a student with a history of disciplinary problems. Eighteen percent of the Catholic school officials and 39 percent of the non-Catholic private schools that have no academic entrance standards reported similarly.

Such data suggest that in creating an orderly environment Catholic schools may rely primarily on strict enforcement of rules whereas non-Catholic private schools rely more heavily on screening students. Public sector schools utilize some screening but may be limited in the successful application of strict enforcement if school size proves to be a critical component of such a strategy.[15]

Performance Standards for Certification

Efforts to insure the quality of academic training include the establishment of performance standards as requisites to obtaining some type of certification—in this case, a high school diploma. Four mechanisms are available at the secondary school level to impose performance standards: (1) course requirements, (2) minimum grade point averages required for graduation and/or for participation in other school activities, (3) general competency exams, and (4) entrance standards at post-secondary institutions. Given the intricate relations among these standards, I will not attempt to discuss them separately, but rather I will try to illuminate the nature of their interdependence.

It is not news that coursework standards in public secondary education have changed considerably in the past twenty years. The *Nation at Risk* report gave considerable attention to the substantial reduction in coursework required of all graduates of high schools. All of the major reports on education recommend increasing the number of required courses for all high school students in all subjects.[16] A recent survey of state education agencies suggests that state legislatures are responding to these proposals. As of 1983, 80 percent of the state legislatures were considering reforms that would increase the academic coursework required for high school graduation. Most of the recommendations and reform efforts focus on minimal course requirements for all students.[17]

Less attention has been given to the required coursework for students enrolled in a pre-college curriculum as well as the minimal requirements for entry into four-year colleges and universities. Given this inattention and its significance in comparing public and private secondary schools, I begin this section by focusing on these two interrelated problems: course requirements for pre-college track students and curriculum requirements for entry into four year colleges and universities.

Table 2 shows the distribution of course requirements by sector for students enrolled in the pre-college track. In general, private sector schools require that students in the college preparatory track complete more semesters of mathematics, science, foreign language, and English than do public sector schools.

The most substantial difference appears to be in the area of language arts. Seventy-six percent of the public sector schools report that they require no foreign language courses and only 13 percent require three or more semesters. In contrast, almost half of the private sector high schools require three or more semesters of a foreign language. In English, the difference is also quite apparent: sixty-five percent of the Catholic sector schools require seven to eight semesters of English; 60 percent of the non-Catholic sector schools and 43 percent of the public sector schools have a similar requirement.

Regardless of sector, very few schools require more than four semesters of science. Over half of the public sector schools require only one to two semesters. For mathematics, students in a pre-college curriculum in the public sector are required to complete substantially less than those in the private sector: ten percent of the public sector schools require these students to complete more than four semesters as compared to 32 percent of the schools in the Catholic sector and 43 percent in the non-Catholic private sector.

It is reasonable to ask what the outcomes of increasing requirements may be. The obvious answer—more is always better—may not be consistently true. Preliminary analysis suggests that student achievement in science is not enhanced by additional requirements.[18] For mathematics, the added increments to growth

Table 2
Public and Private High Schools
with Various Levels of Course Requirements
for College Preparatory Students
(Percent[1])

Subject	Public	Private Catholic	Private Non-Catholic
Mathematics			
None	3	1	0
1-2 Semesters	49	19	30
3-4 Semesters	38	47	27
5-6 Semesters	7	28	43
7-8 Semesters	3	4	0
Science			
None	4	1	0
1-2 Semesters	58	30	33
3-4 Semesters	32	50	48
5-6 Semesters	5	15	19
7-8 Semesters	2	4	0
Foreign Language			
None	76	32	25
1-2 Semesters	11	22	30
3-4 Semesters	11	37	19
5-6 Semesters	2	8	18
7-8 Semesters	0	0	8
English			
None	2	1	0
1-2 Semesters	1	0	0
3-4 Semesters	36	34	40
5-6 Semesters	17	0	1
7-8 Semesters	43	65	60
	N=893	N=84	N=27

[1]Figures may not total 100 due to rounding.

Source: High School and Beyond Administrators' Survey, 1982.

are apparent only where three or four years are required.[19] If further evidence supports these preliminary findings, one must ask if there are other reasons to support the increase in course requirements. I answer a tentative and qualified "yes," for two reasons: first, for the general effect on school climate and second, for the effects it may have on disadvantaged students. The qualification of the support I give to additional course requirements is simply that they should be school- or district-specific, not mandated by state law. I elaborate on this position in the conclusion of this chapter.

Course requirements and school climate. In the first instance, the effect on general school climate, the ratio of required to elective courses may have consequences well beyond the relative proportion of students who complete advanced courses in, say, mathematics and science. Under certain conditions, the distribution of requirements may compromise the quality of education. Where a great number of courses are required of all students, some dilution of the content may occur to accommodate the less able students. At the other extreme, where few if any courses are required, dilution may occur to attract the minimum number of students needed to justify the existence of the course. Many of the proposed reforms in performance standards may move schools from one albatross to another—from dilution prompted by low demand to dilution prompted by student interest and capabilities.

In the past ten years public sector teachers have had to place many of their courses into a marketplace, that is, they compete for student interest to secure an acceptable enrollment level in their courses. (Honors courses, coveted by certain segments of the student population, may constitute the only exception to this general pattern.) Teachers in a market environment must promote some attractive course attributes to sustain a reasonable, acceptable enrollment. For any pool of individuals, charisma is the gift of the few, and teachers are no exception. As a consequence, we should expect that a variety of other attributes such as entertaining films, little homework, no research papers, or simply easy grades will be introduced to attract a sufficient number of students.

The problems of a market curriculum are exacerbated when post-secondary schools have few requisites and/or when secondary schools, by design or by happenstance, come to emphasize one aspect of the secondary school experience to the exclusion of others.

Public secondary schools unquestionably operate in an environment where their students anticipate few curricular requirements for entry into college. If colleges fail to require some courses, why should students bother with the additional effort in high school? Reform efforts notwithstanding, such a situation will be very difficult to change while colleges face a declining pool of applicants.

Despite the disincentives to raise college standards, some evidence supporting that need should be offered. Both *A Nation at Risk* and the study of Kilgore and Lewin-Epstein suggest that students and secondary school personnel are responsive to the standards set by post-secondary school environments.[20] If, for instance, colleges do not require completion of two years of a foreign language, secondary schools may not require it of students in a pre-college curriculum. The rational response of students, however, is even more informative. Kilgore and Lewin-Epstein compared students who dropped out of a pre-college curriculum between their sophomore and senior years in public high schools with those who remained in that curriculum.[21] The study found that regional variation was quite important. In those regions where the favored colleges and universities had high admission standards, the students dropping out of the pre-college curriculum were decidedly different from those in regions where the most attractive colleges and universities had minimal standards. Specifically, in less competitive regions, students who dropped out of a pre-college curriculum were not any less confident of their abilities to complete college than those who remained, when achievement level, family background, school performance, and conduct were held constant. In contrast, we found that students in competitive regions (where colleges have high entrance standards) who dropped out of a pre-college curriculum were significantly less confident of their ability to complete college than those who remained in the pre-college program. Such data suggest that students in less competitive regions are less likely to view enrollment in a pre-college track as a prerequisite to successful completion of college. Thus, the satisfactory introduction of a rigorous pre-college curriculum is contingent upon a rather unlikely circumstance: increasing the prerequisites for entrance to our major colleges and universities.

The potential for changing the disproportionate emphasis of one aspect of the high school experience over another is more encouraging. Magnet schools—with some explicit focus on a subject, skill, or art—reflect an understanding of this problem. However, in schools where a singular emphasis evolves slowly and without explicit commitment, few recognize the inevitable consequences. Large and time-consuming athletic programs are the most obvious examples. Here, where students' social esteem becomes intricately linked to athletics, students will seek an academic experience that enhances their athletic performance, including minimum grade point eligibility requirements. In such instances, the ratio of required to elective courses must be high to constrain the search for easy courses. If not, the natural consequence of a market curriculum interacting with students' priorities will continue to dilute academic performance.

Course requirements and disadvantaged students. Students may be academically disadvantaged in one or two ways—they may not have obtained the requisite skills and knowledge for satisfactory performance at their current grade level and/or they may not have access to information regarding what information or skills they need for successful performance in future academic endeavors, such as a pre-med or pre-law program.

Public and private school comparisons regarding course requirements are especially valuable when evaluating both types of disadvantaged students. For those schools with a high proportion of low-achieving students, Catholic sector schools appear to increase the course requirements. For instance, in the HSB survey of 1982, a greater proportion of administrators of predominately black Catholic schools (80 percent) report requiring eight semesters of English than do other Catholic school administrators (63 percent). A recent study of mathematics curricula in Catholic secondary schools suggests that remedial students receive an additional year of elementary arithmetic but also complete a year of algebra and geometry.[22] In surveying teachers in Catholic schools that study found that "while only a third of them consider a college curriculum best for everyone, over three-quarters agree

all students should take and master a core academic curriculum —
regardless of students' background or educational aspirations." In
elaborating on these high standards, one teacher commented:

I require that certain standards be met. I try to be compassionate. I listen
to them and sometimes accept their excuses if they fall short (e.g. their
homework is late). . . . But I also let them know that they can and will
learn if they work at it, and I expect them to do that."[23]

Thus, low-achieving students in Catholic schools may have more
course requirements than the average student. But these requirements, along with more general expectations, are designed to enable these students to achieve at a level more comparable to other
students.

In the case of students who are disadvantaged with respect to
information, generally low-income or working class students,
minimal course requirements may have unfortunate consequences. For these students, requirements substitute for information — information regarding what coursework constitutes critical
preparation for subsequent work in college. A highly ambitious
student with college-educated parents is more likely to acquire
information regarding, say, the importance of trigonometry as a
preparation for a calculus course in a pre-med program than students from less advantaged backgrounds. A working class student
is, as it were, completely "school dependent" for information.
Course requirements may be the most judicious means of communicating these linkages.

Two studies support this argument. First, Coleman, Hoffer, and
Kilgore found lower effects of family background on achievement
in the Catholic sector than in either the public or non-Catholic private sector, particularly in language arts (reading and vocabulary).[24] Note from my earlier discussion (regarding Table 2) the
substantial difference — at least for the academic track — in the
requirements by sector. Almost two-thirds of the Catholic sector
schools require four years of English. The effects of family background may be reduced by "information" communicated through
course requirements.

Second, Bryk et al., find that social class effects on academic
achievement are significantly mediated by track and coursework.
Thus, low-income students would have achievement levels more
equal to others when they were required to take a high proportion

of academic courses.[25] Both pieces of evidence draw attention to the critical role course requirements may have for those lacking information regarding the preparation that matches their ambition.

Minimum competency exams are an increasingly common instrument designed to enhance the quality of education secured by at least one portion of students in secondary school—low-achieving students who are unlikely to pursue post-secondary education. According to the 1982 HSB survey of administrators, approximately 68 percent of the public sector schools require successful completion of such an exam. That constitutes a 25 percent increase since 1980. Only 3 percent of the private sector schools report requiring such an exam. It is beyond the scope of this chapter to address the various issues surrounding these exams; their historical context and technical issues have been presented elsewhere.[26] What is important is that such exams are part of a larger trend toward criterion-referenced testing that could, in principle, prove to be an exceptionally useful tool in enhancing the overall level of subject mastery. As presently constituted, however, minimum competency exams are oriented toward knowledge considered to be essential for minimum survival in our modern society—balancing checkbooks, completing job application forms, and so forth. To the extent that criterion-referenced tests are developed for each grade level and incorporate the knowledge required for successful mastery of material covered in subsequent grades, that type of certification standard serves a broader range of the student population.

What can we expect from the efforts to raise certification standards in the public sector? First, the introduction of rigorous standards for a limited number of students, those in the pre-college curriculum, will not likely be met with great success. Consistent with national trends, the choice of universal standards is more appropriate. The incongruity of such rigorous standards with a "buyer's market" in post-secondary education may discourage students from pursuing a pre-college program. Second, standards should be allowed to vary at least by school district, if not by school, to better approximate the time required by different types of students to master certain subjects.

Conclusion

In this chapter, I have discussed how admission, conduct, and performance standards function in the public and private secondary school sectors. Private schools, I argue, utilize admission standards to enhance the school climate—not simply through screening out undesirable students, but also through instilling respect and commitment in the admission rituals. Public schools can, I argue, achieve some of the same ends through other mechanisms that generate traditions of excellence. With respect to student conduct, some evidence suggests that the enforcement of standards may be as important as their substance.

Attempts to alter the performance standards, particularly those concerned with high school certification, constitute the major focus of educational reform today. In particular, the introduction of minimum competency exams and additional course requirements reflect a master trend in public education today: the movement to state control of secondary education. One of these, minimum competency exams, represents an output standard that is generally resisted by educators; the other, curricula requirements, is a process standard that is generally met with considerable consensus. My own position inverts the response; that is, state control should be limited to output standards, and state finances should be directed toward facilitating local school districts in meeting such output standards.

Efforts to enhance the quality of education through state mandated curriculum content and even homework are, I argue, misguided efforts that contravene the few principles of learning for which both psychologists and sociologists have empirical support. Proponents of enhanced curriculum requirements have incorporated an important principle: time on task affects learning; the more time spent, the more learned. However, the companion principle is virtually ignored: different students require different amounts of time to master the same material. The blindness to this second principle is understandable when such reforms are targeted at the state level. How can one mandate variable course requirements and homework? Rather than introducing variable standards, the state should be introducing variable funding that actually permits schools to offer different amounts of time on task.

State policy should not dictate, it seems, curricula standards, curricula content, or length of school day. Instead, these policies should vary at least by district, if not by school, according to the estimated exposure and effort required by most students to meet the state imposed output standards. Thus, for instance, urban city schools, with large concentrations of educationally disadvantaged students, may establish twelve month programs that increase the amount of school contact hours available to those children. State funding would be directed toward subsidizing the additional costs incurred by those school districts providing additional exposure to subjects and toward the administering of statewide tests that evaluate student subject mastery and grant student promotions accordingly. The development of criterion-referenced testing for each grade should proceed not on the basis of what teachers teach, but what should be mastered for subsequent schooling.

Some secondary consequences of focusing on output standards may also be positive. Removing some of the teachers' evaluative role allows them to incorporate more of a "coaching" model in their relations with students. Second, students have a greater opportunity to learn that their behavior has consequences. Annual exams and any required repetition of grades gives a student early notice of a problem. Nothing is humane about postponing such an experience.

Standards are important mechanisms for mastery in any subject or skill. State legislators have wisely chosen to raise standards universally. However, the focus on process standards, such as homework, coursework, and length of school year, may prove disappointing, especially to those who aspire to alter the outcomes of educationally disadvantaged students.

III

The California Reform Movement

9

BILL HONIG

California's Reform Program

Most people in this country believe in public education. Although they may think that many of our schools are not effectively educating our children, they are willing to support improvement. The public intuitively knows that our ability to remain globally competitive, to maintain this democracy, and to enhance individual talent depends on the success of the educational enterprise.

In 1983 the publication of several reports and books crystallized this public discontent and created a national school reform movement. Subsequent reform initiatives have stemmed primarily from two sources: first, state political and legislative leaders have passed broad structural and legislative efforts such as increased graduation requirements, longer school days and years, stronger certification for teachers, master teacher plans, and streamlined dismissal procedures. Second, over the past several years a growing number of individual teachers, faculties, and districts have raised standards, improved discipline, and upgraded instruction. These initial efforts have placed education high on state and national agendas and offered the hope of significant improvements in student performance.

For that hope to become a reality these general policy pronouncements and individual efforts must be translated into widespread specific changes in classrooms, schools, and districts. Many more teachers, administrators, and local board members must take up the banner of reform and press for higher standards, better discipline, and the creation of a powerful spirit of excellence in every school in this country. The public must understand and actively support these improvement efforts.

To reach this objective will take five to ten years and will require sustained, sophisticated support. Unless we can agree on the next steps in the reform agenda, the effort may abort because its original cast was too superficial and we may consume ourselves in squabbles about how to focus our efforts. If the drive for educational improvement is to work, we need to build a large constituency that will support specific reforms, hold a common vision of quality, and know how to keep pressure on for necessary changes and funding. Luckily, we currently enjoy broad support for reform efforts and increased revenues have given the schools resources to provide technical help.

Strategies for Reform

The following outline of reform strategies should help in determining where best to apply our efforts.

1. Effective initiatives must stem from an educational and public philosophy. In California our educational philosophy could be categorized as "essentialist" or traditional. It holds that many more of our students can profit by a traditional academic curriculum whether college bound or not. Thus, our efforts have concentrated on raising expectations, providing core curricula, increasing the amount of homework, and assuring a decent learning atmosphere.

We need to shout it from the rooftops: more children than we ever expected *can* succeed in an intensive academic curriculum, not necessarily physics and calculus, but a good strong common core—history, government, science, and literature. These courses offer the best way of developing comprehension, computing, writing, speaking, and thinking skills. Moreover, scholars such as E. D. Hirsch are maintaining that adult literacy depends as much on the knowledge base as it does on reading technique. Thus, a sustained buildup of what students know is crucial to improve literacy. Our experience in California with those schools that have successfully demanded a more rigorous academic curriculum for the vast majority of their students have corroborated this point of view.

Why is the push for stronger academics gathering such force now? There are three reasons. First, the job market is changing rapidly: if graduates are to stay competitive, our economy requires a sophisticated education for broader numbers of students. By 1995 nearly one-third of all jobs will be scientific, technical, managerial, and professional. In the other job categories, work specifications will be significantly upgraded. For example, in 1982 there were five unskilled workers for one skilled worker on a General Motors production line. By 1990 that number is going to change to one unskilled worker for every skilled one. According to Bureau of Labor Statistics, in the next decade nearly 50 to 60 percent of the new and replacement jobs are going to require the kind of education we have previously associated only with the college bound. If we are serious about giving most students the opportunity to obtain and retain attractive and lucrative jobs, we must upgrade our educational fare to include more sophisticated reading, writing, computing, speaking, and thinking. These are skills that only strong academic programs can develop.

This point of view was reinforced in a report entitled "High Schools and the Changing Workplace" released in June 1983 by the National Academy of Sciences. The study concludes that students entering the work force after high school need the same basic educational competencies as those going on to college.

Second, leaders in this country are rediscovering the idea that the continuance of this democracy demands that we do a better job of teaching civic values. We need to connect more of our students to our history, our culture, and those ideals that hold us together as a society. Schools are a key institution for transmitting the common cultural values of honesty, integrity, tolerance, fairness, magnanimity, and self-discipline that are so essential to the quality of life in this nation. The best method we have devised for engaging students in our broader historical, political, ethical, and social communities are comprehensive academic programs in literature, history, government, science, and the arts.

Finally, we surely can be more successful in opening vistas for our youth by providing more of them with a broad, liberal education. In too many instances we have betrayed the democratic dream by operating educational programs as if only the more advanced students could understand and appreciate our cultural, political, and ethical ideals. To shield the average student from the wisdom of our heritage effectively keeps students class bound and vitiates the potential power of our schools to create opportunity and broader horizons.[1]

One objection to these measures is that they are "elitist" and aimed primarily at the college bound student. This objection seriously misconstrues our purpose. We are advocating reform of existing educational programs to allow many more students to qualify for jobs, become engaged in our culture, and develop character and citizenship. Who is really the elitist—the one who thinks more children can reach these levels or the one who is willing to consign a majority to weaker educational programs because of a deep-seated doubt that most students can fulfill higher expectations?

Other objections stem from crossed communication. I am addressing the low expectations for the approximately middle 50 percent of the students who are currently enrolled in general education tracks. These students are currently receiving an incoherent curriculum and could profit from a more rigorous program.

Many educators confuse proposals aimed at the average child with their concern about the bottom 10 to 15 percent of students. These young people most certainly need special help and alternative educational strategies, but they may not benefit from a traditional academic approach. However, that is no reason to allow the middle range child to receive a diluted academic program. We can offer the right education for both groups.

2. The second strategy is to encourage commitment by educators and citizens to these ideals. Educational leaders must strive to articulate an educational vision in a variety of professional and public arenas to reinforce those who believe in this point of view, to gain adherents, and to minimize the effect of those who disagree. Getting people to believe will result in effective actions by board members, superintendents, principals, and teachers. However, there is still a large group of educators who continue to be influenced by the progressive movement, who believe—consciously or not—that a child-centered education implies hostility to academic subject matter.[2] For the most part this controversy is dated. What we teach should be arrived at by societal and professional consensus. How we teach it should be varied, flexible, and child centered.

Articulating the broad vision should be an effective method of influencing curriculum, textbooks, how and what teachers teach, how administrators lead, accountability, testing, and personnel development. It should encourage new board members to run for office and incumbents to refocus their activities. It should change the content of teacher preparation.

3. A third strategy is to galvanize the public and educational community around an educational reform package at the state level and around classroom, school, and district efforts at the local level. Winning structural reforms and increased resources fuels the reform effort and helps legitimize the local initiatives. Our experience in California will be related shortly.

4. A fourth strategy is to develop measurable goals in student performance to hold public support, further focus educational activities, and give educators enough time for their efforts to bear fruit. In California we have set statewide targets of increased enrollments in academic courses; better test scores and attendance; lower dropout rates; and greater amounts of writing, homework, and performance by the college bound.[3]

The second phase of this accountability strategy is to give each school a profile on how it is doing in these areas so that it can set its own goals in relation to the state effort. The profile is in two parts—(1) the common data we have available throughout the state, and (2) those measures that are educationally important but must be gathered at the local level. Local indicators include such items as the vitality and harmony of the school, the strength of the curriculum, the awards and recognitions received by the school, the quality of student writing, and any others the local school district deems important. The common data show how the school is doing in comparison to schools with similar student bodies and in comparison with statewide targets. Schools receive information from the state as to how they are doing both in level of performance and in growth from initial baseline levels. Some schools have already made tremendous improvements and will be recognized for the efforts they have made. Others will be recognized for making progress over time. Superintendents are building this information into principal evaluations; principals are using these reports to galvanize faculty initiatives at the site level.

 5. Finally, and most importantly, there is a whole range of strategies available to organize effective technical support to improve curriculum and instruction; the preparation, selection, support, and evaluation of teachers and principals; textbook selection; testing; the capabilities of faculties and districts; the effectiveness of parents, and the engagement of students. To organize these efforts most effectively we must start with a good conceptual map of the educational enterprise. At the center is the *student.* If we want to influence student learning, we can develop strategies to motivate students and get them to accept more responsibility for their own lives; work with parents to put pressure on their children to learn; improve the quality of the curricula in the classroom, the quality of teaching, the learning atmosphere, and the resources available (class size, availability of instructional materials); and provide special assistance where necessary.

The next level of concentration should be the *teacher.* Potential strategies to influence teachers could include teacher preparation and training, granting more autonomy within the context of professional standards, developing better faculty collaboration, salary increases, improving site and classroom conditions, improving the principal's leadership and supervision, and developing methods for evaluating teacher performance.

The third level looks at the *school.* Literature confirms that the effectiveness of the curriculum; the ethos and vision of the school; the quality of instructional leadership on the part of the principal; the development of a faculty as opposed to a collection of individuals; school policies; available resources; school climate; the existence of monitoring devices; and the gathering relevant data, both hard and impressionistic, all can enhance the effectiveness of classroom performance.

The fourth level concentrates on the *district*. What can districts do to increase the effectiveness of schools, teachers, and students? The most important strategy from a district perspective is an effective system for holding principals accountable. If principals clearly understand that they are responsible for student learning; the quality of curriculum and instruction; the learning atmosphere in the school; the supervision and evaluation of teachers; and the development of a collection of individual teachers into a problem solving, collaborative faculty, schools will improve. If, in addition, principals are given adequate resources and support, they will improve more. Districts need also to develop effective tactics for curricular definition; selection, training, and support of new principals; policies (homework, resource allocations); developing community support for improvement; utilizing standards for hiring teachers; improving staff development; and instituting school monitoring and data gathering.

Finally, there are strategies appropriate for state, university, organizational, and national levels. I have already discussed state strategies.

Universities' academic departments and schools of education need to develop proposals for educating a new generation of teachers in content, subject matter and generic methodology, and general educational philosophy. For example, all new elementary teachers should be well educated in English, math, children's literature, history, science, fine arts, and physical education, as well as how to teach writing, reading, speech, computing, and thinking. They should also receive instruction in specific pedagogy—for example, how best to teach U.S. history to fifth graders.

Universities also need to provide intellectual leadership in designing curricula for a variety of children. Universities can help answer questions such as which stories, events, and books will best teach our young. We have witnessed the absence of sustained intellectual effort in designing a curriculum that effectively engages our students in the powerful ideas of each subject.

The federal government needs to support research, expand curricular development, examine professional training, support recruitment of first rate teachers, and provide special programs for at-risk children.

The California Experience

The California experience offers some useful insights for those striving to improve educational quality in this country and examples of these strategies at work.

In 1982, a year before the major reform reports went public, the main themes of the reform movement were addressed in the California campaign for State Superintendent of Public Instruction—raising academic and behavioral expectations for all students, increasing the amount of homework, and insisting that students take more English, literature, history, math, science, and fine arts. These ideas received strong public support in the November, 1982 election.

During 1983, this electoral mandate was translated into a comprehensive reform strategy. The first component of this overall strategy was to develop a commitment from local teachers, administrators, and board members to institute a more rigorous instructional program for all students; improve student performance in reading, writing, speaking, analyzing, computing, and problem solving; increase students' understanding of their physical, social, political, and ethical worlds; and help our young people develop character and responsibility.

Key educators have also reached a consensus about the kind of instructional program which will best meet these goals. We are supporting changes that:

- Place renewed emphasis on sequenced instruction in the major disciplines.

- Increase the number of assignments requiring writing, speaking, and problem solving.

- Encourage students to read more books, write more essays, and produce more reports.

- Raise the level of homework and the amount of instructional time.

- Improve school safety and student civility.

Second, based on the commitment of the educational community to improve quality at the local level, we devised a legislative package to support the improvement efforts. This package, which was passed by the legislature in July, 1983, combined structural reforms with substantial additional funds. The bill increased graduation requirements, lengthened school days and school years, tightened discipline, improved teacher selection, inaugurated an incentive program for exemplary teachers, streamlined dismissal procedures for incompetent teachers, and provided over $800 million of new money for schools.

Several factors contributed to the passage of the reform package: (1) the educational community took the initiative in advocating reforms, (2) the reforms were combined with funding, (3) we sought a bipartisan consensus, (4) we organized support for the bill in each community in the state and obtained intensive ethnic, business, and media advocacy for the bill, and (5) we secured strong legislative and gubernatorial sponsorship.

The third leg of the strategy was a successful effort to acquire the $1.2 billion second-year funding by initiating a second major grassroots effort, together with the promulgation of an accountability program setting forth the standards by which progress will be measured. In the past two years, expenditures for students have increased nearly 20 percent or about $500 per child. As for accountability, we have established for the state for 1986, 1988, and 1990, specific numerical targets which include improvements in California assessment tests and SAT scores, increased enrollments in academic courses, decreased dropout rates, and additional amounts of writing and homework. We also have given each local school a profile to show its position in relationship to these goals and to encourage school initiatives for improvement.

Currently, we are in the fourth phase of the overall improvement plan: a long-term effort to generate the professional and technical support necessary to continue the momentum for change. We are working with key superintendents, teachers' organizations, education groups, and citizens to establish:

1. An agreed-upon curriculum; e.g., what should be a proper English sequence at the high school level or what should we be teaching in fifth-grade U.S. history? Large numbers of educators developed these criteria for each curriculum area. Under the reform legislation each district will review its instructional program against these model curricula.

2. Textbook selection procedures both at the state and local levels to reflect these standards and to make books more challenging, interesting, and consistent with good scholarship.

3. A testing program that includes more history, science, literature, writing, and problem solving and derives from our revised curricula. We now test at the third, sixth, eighth, and twelfth grades. We are revising the tenth and twelfth grade tests to incorporate these broader subjects.

4. Selection and training of principals. In California, nearly one-half of our 7,000 principals will be retiring in the next four to five years. We need on-site leaders who know what is good English, history, and science instruction. They must operate from an educational vision, have the courage of their convictions, and galvanize their staffs to work in a common direction.

5. Improved teacher preparation. A blue ribbon Commission on the Teaching Profession is developing a plan for defining what an educated teacher should be; what we want our schools to teach; and how to organize effective recruiting, training, evaluation, and support. Currently we have approximately 170,000 teachers. By 1991, we will need over 110,000 new teachers, mostly at the elementary level.

6. Widespread teacher training. If we are serious about teaching science, math, history, English, fine arts, and foreign language, we need to establish continuing education programs for current teachers. When we held a history conference at UC Berkeley in 1983, five hundred teachers attended who were hungry for intellectual stimulation. For the summer of 1985 we scheduled a large scale effort at UCLA to acquaint teachers with the recently adopted English standards.

7. A common concept of district effectiveness. What are the most

effective measures that boards and superintendents can take to improve the quality of education? We have defined accountability of principals, curriculum development, policy development, and other key leverage points and are organizing the training of boards and staffs.

Finally, there are efforts to engage in cooperative measures with the business community, to solicit the help of parents, and to encourage students' responsibility in the education process. We launched a "Parents Are Teachers, Too" campaign in 1984 which featured public service spots on every major T.V. station showing parents reading to their children, discussing events at dinner, and assuring quiet time for homework. We also printed 1,500,000 pamphlets (200,000 in Spanish), worked cooperatively with local parent training efforts and arranged with retailers to print the slogan on shopping bags and milk cartons.

I would hope that none of us will be content with only broad legislative and structural changes, but that we will also pursue the central issues of the quality of curriculum, teaching, and leadership at the local levels. Failure to do so may well halt the movement toward educational excellence before it becomes imbedded in the day-to-day operation of the schools.

English Standards

To give an example of how much work needs to be done, I will outline our approach to just one of these strategies and how the product of each effort is indispensible to the success of every other strategy.

As stated previously, a critical part of our endeavor to upgrade the instructional program and improve student performance requires tightening the definition of each curriculum area and establishing agreed-upon standards. Clearly, the consensus in California now favors a more rigorous program; yet it does little good to increase the amount of time students spend taking core courses if the curriculum lacks substance or focus. Thus, large numbers of educators in California worked together, in accordance with Senate Bill 813, to develop standards for each of the following curriculum areas: English/language arts, history/social science, mathematics, science, foreign language, and fine arts. Developing a common view has not been easy, but we have reached a good working agreement.

The following is an overview of the English/language arts curriculum standards which, along with the standards from the five other content areas, were adopted by the California State Board of Education in January, 1985. Under the law, school districts will be required to compare their programs with the model curricula every three years and report their findings to their local boards. While the standards are for grades nine through twelve, the philosophy which guides their spirit encompasses all grade levels and signifies an exciting refocusing of course content.

The reform in the English/language arts curriculum for California public schools intends to provide our students with:

- a systematic exposure to the most powerful works we possess, using them as the basis for intensive reading, writing, and discussion;

- a curriculum which transmits our beliefs, values and common goals;

- a list of high quality literary works—fiction and non-fiction, classic and contemporary—central to our culture; and

- a program where all students have access to significant examples of writing proficiency.

Goals of the curriculum standards. The goals outlined below will lend unity and direction to our curriculum and help to make all our youth better readers, writers, and thinkers.

1. *A systematic program of intensive reading of central works.* Students must read, write about, and discuss a central core of books, both classic and contemporary, fiction and non-fiction, which embody the best that has been thought and written. Taught well, these selections will intellectually and spiritually engage our students and provide the vehicle for extending comprehension, writing, thinking, and speaking skills.

2. *Direct teaching of comprehension.* Guided reading of these selected publications should develop students' comprehension

skills and extend their base of knowledge about the world—
the "cultural literacy" that scholars believe is the key to adult
reading proficiency. Through their reading, students should
expand their knowledge and understanding of the social, political, and ethical forces around them.

3. *A required individual student reading program.* We should encourage students to develop an individual reading program
   during their school careers. By the time each student graduates, he or she should have read a good percentage of a recommended list of worthy literary works that represent the
   repository of our cultural wisdom. We have developed such a
   list of 300 to 400 literary works, essays, and speeches based on
   multiple criteria: the best we have to offer, powerful use of
   language, addressing key issues, representing the diversity of
   our nation, and just plain "good reads."

4. *Integration of reading, writing, speaking, and listening.* Students must actively respond to such examples through writing, speaking, and listening activities. The emphasis on core
   works, however, is not a throwback to the old make-'em-read-
   a-book-and-do-a-book-report method of boring students.
   There must be no inert ideas that are merely received without
   being utilized or tested.

5. *Direct teaching of writing for both clarity and style.* All students
   will have to learn to write cogent, clear, concise prose. Students must learn that writing is not a one-shot attempt, but a
   process that requires time for ideas to incubate, often through
   draft after draft. The emphasis on reading will enhance writing because good literary readings provide excellent models of
   style.

6. *The study of various literary genres.* All genres should be
   taught. Students need to experience the many forms writers
   use to express fully their knowledge of the world.

7. *The study of various writings from other disciplines.* The real
   world issues raised in literature gain depth for many students
   when voices of economists, social scientists, psychologists, and
   politicians, for example, address the same concerns. Good
   writing is found in all disciplines and studying it can en-

courage young people to deeper comprehension and emulation.

8. *Strong training in speaking and listening.* We have seriously neglected instruction in rhetoric skills which are becoming so necessary in our society. Most jobs now require high levels of both written and verbal expression. By learning to listen carefully, to organize a presentation and to express thoughts clearly, students take control over their own lives.

9. *Teaching vocabulary directly and indirectly.* Students continually grow in the ability to interpret and use new words through direct classroom instruction, and through encountering new words in speech and writing.

10. *Teaching technical skills and grammar directly.* Correct grammar, punctuation, capitalization, and spelling must be taught to all students consistent with their needs. Many of the fine points of language are not learned indirectly by reading.

11. *Balancing the curriculum with other courses.* Many specialized courses based on real-world interests, such as journalism, drama, and speech/rhetoric, can also promote writing, listening, and speaking skills.

Implementation of the standards. One of the first steps in implementing this systematic program of intensive reading and writing is for districts and English departments to determine the order in which various works shall be studied.

After choosing which works will form a core of the high school English programs, and at what grade level each will be taught, the decision makers should construct two other lists—the great works students choose from individually, and the works students read mainly for enjoyment, a much larger list.

Next, the districts need to establish standards for scope. For example, after selecting some 200 works for general recommendation, the administrator and teachers might decide on some 100 works from various genres that need to be read before graduation, with the college bound students reading more complex works and more extensively.

With support as necessary from districts, departments, universities, and various professional development programs—all teachers need to decide how to teach the important works. Many excellent teachers for decades now have made literature live for all their students. Their talents and ideas are at a premium. These exemplary teachers and their programs need to be found and their impact multiplied.

Finally, teacher training institutes, both pre-service and in-service, will need to spend some time helping teachers themselves investigate the central works.

Implications. A comprehensive, systematic program of this kind has enormous meaning for what principals and faculty must do, for how staff developers and universities must operate, for textbook selection, and for district support. Furthermore, the legislature must provide funding for libraries, for classroom literary texts, and for teacher training. Statewide, district and school testing programs must reflect the rigor and substantive nature of the new content-based curriculum. And districts must revise their curricula, allocate resources, and focus professional efforts to meet the special needs of their students and follow these professional goals.

Teachers, publishers, parents, librarians, and university professors are all part of this process. What many teachers and districts have done well we now must give to all. These standards emphasize content, but they do not neglect skills.

This chapter has attempted to broaden perspectives with respect to reform efforts, and to show the relationship between philosophy, advocacy, technical support, curricula and instruction, and accountability. I hope it helps give a clearer picture of the task ahead of us for the next decade as we enter the critical stage of the reform effort. We must sustain public support while translating general improvement ideas into workable strategies for teachers, schools, and districts.

10

JAMES D. LIKENS

A Preliminary Diagnosis: The California Experience

When it comes to choosing goals for public schools[1], we Americans want everything.[2] We want our children to receive academic training, to prepare for work, to learn how to live with others in society, and to experience personal development. The news media also make it plain that we expect education to take on an even broader set of tasks; at a minimum, the schools should advance upward social mobility, achieve racial integration, socialize immigrants, prepare future scientists and engineers for national defense, provide child care for working parents, compensate for the breakup of the nuclear family, and train a labor force that can compete in the international economy.

But we Americans never have the resources to achieve simultaneously all of our educational goals; so, over time, we shift our emphasis from one priority to another, reacting one time to particular social and political forces at work in the larger society, then later reacting to new ones. Moreover, because we tend to overreact to each new concern, the excesses of our educational reform movements help bring about their successors.[3] And since education is at once public and easy to understand, policy toward education evolves in a political arena that too often creates new problems as it solves old ones.

The pattern continues with the newest reform movement, the campaign to achieve "excellence" in the public schools. As is typically the case, this movement began with apparent swiftness. Between April and September of 1983 at least eight major reports appeared that criticized education in America and presented agendas for reform. Dozens of other studies that covered state, regional, or subject matter focus surfaced at the same time. These studies received widespread attention in the press. Particularly noteworthy was the impact of *A Nation at Risk*, the report of the National Commission on Excellence. Almost immediately after its release, individual states and school boards began to enact policy changes designed to raise standards and attain excellence.

No state embraced the excellence movement with more enthusiasm and energy than California. Since 1983 it has put into place the most ambitious school reform program in the nation. Like the excellence movement in other states, California's urge to improve the public schools seemed suddenly to have begun. In fact, many of its origins can be traced to unintended consequences of past educational reforms that addressed the concerns of the civil rights movement, the war on poverty, student protest during the Vietnam war, and a recent tax-payer rebellion. And like some, though not all, previous reform movements, California's current efforts to improve its schools appear likely to produce significant long-term benefits. Yet also like those movements, this one probably suffers from enough flaws to assure that its side effects, some of which may already be discerned, will help produce a need for new reforms in the future. For all of these reasons, the California experience serves as an important case study for the entire nation.

This chapter examines the movement to achieve excellence in California's public schools. It begins with a review of the factors that produced a shift away from emphasizing equity toward stressing excellence. This is followed by an assessment of particular reforms that are not being implemented in the state. The chapter concludes with a look at the financial implications of school reform in California.

Equity to Excellence: The Emphasis Shifts

During the 1960s and 1970s, California, like the other states, focused on achieving equity and access to public education. Spurred by Supreme Court decisions, by federal law, and by court mandated busing, California made considerable progress in assuring that all its students receive an equal share of educational inputs. This vision of equity came eventually to mean that progress for the handicapped should be expanded and that poor and disadvantaged students should receive special help such as compensatory education programs and free meals.

In addition, ruling on a case that began in Superior Court in 1968, the California Supreme Court held in *Serrano vs. Priest* (1976) that the time honored system of financing school districts through the local property tax violated the equal protection clause of the state constitution because it led to unequal access to school resources. Affluent school districts could finance high expenditures per pupil with relatively low property tax rates, whereas just the opposite often occurred in poor districts. As a consequence of this decision, California struggled throughout the 1970s and early 1980s to meet the challenge of establishing expenditure parity for all school districts. In April 1983 a Superior Court judge found that sufficient parity existed and the current school finance system is constitutional. But the effort to comply with *Serrano* helped create serious side effects.

The original plan to phase out *Serrano* inequities among districts, which was contained in the 1972 Senate Bill 90, called for new state funding to be combined with revenues from the local property tax to help bring per pupil funding for poor districts up to the levels of more affluent districts. By the late 1970s, however, a weak economy had reduced the level of sales and income taxes received by state and local government and had created a climate of fiscal austerity. In addition, Proposition 13, an expenditure limitation measure approved by California voters in 1978, limited the ability of government to raise property taxes.

Since school districts had always relied on the property tax as their major source of funding, the combination of *Serrano* and Proposition 13, in practice, left the state government with little choice but to take on increased responsibility for financing education. At the local level, the problem of funding the schools was further exacerbated by underlying demographics: the postwar baby boom cohort had already moved through the public schools, and since a major portion of funding from the state is based on attendance, fewer students meant less money except in those years when the legislature could somehow be persuaded to increase the expenditure per student. To make matters worse, enrollments in private schools grew steadily, due at least in part to fears of public school integration. Thus, between 1974–75 and 1981–82, public school enrollments in K–12 fell by more than 381,000 students, while private school attendance increased by more than 116,000 pupils.

The upshot of all this was that *Serrano* did not achieve parity among all students by bringing poorer districts in line with the per pupil expenditures that had been enjoyed in the better off districts; rather, the squeezing of education budgets produced a parity more in line with historical expenditures in the poorer districts. Thus, as equity and equal access to education were being achieved as prescribed by law, they were accompanied by a decline in the level of real resources per pupil devoted to education in California and by a diminution of the ability of individual school districts to provide resources for their students beyond the state stipulated spending level.

In the process of coping with all these changes, California also moved very close to establishing a state-controlled school system. In 1970 about 70 percent of funding came from local property taxes; the state delegated to local school districts and electorates great discretion in deciding both the level of school funding and how their money would be spent. In contrast, today almost 80 percent of the general purpose revenue for public school districts comes directly from the state. Of total revenues, which include funds for capital outlay, about 64 percent come from the state. California is now exceeded only by Hawaii and perhaps by New Mexico in the extent to which the state dominates school financing. With the power to fund education shifting to the state, the governor and the legislature found themselves increasingly involved in matters of educational policy. State officials proved un-willing to take the responsibility for financing the schools and then to allow local districts full discretion for spending the money.

The shift of educational policy making from the local to the state level had several other important political consequences. For one thing, the ability of individuals in a local community effec-tively to express their educational preferences was greatly reduced. When policy is made by a local school board, an individual citizen can fairly easily direct his or her concerns to a nearby elected body which deals only with education. When decisions are made in Sacramento, however, the individual must work outside the local community and deal with legislators who consider a large set of issues and respond to a broad constituency.

On the other hand, some organized constituencies that were unhappy with the conduct or performance of local school boards found it easier to work through the state legislature to impose their views on education. Teachers' unions and the business com-munity are prominent examples.

For their part, the governor and members of the legislature also discovered they could gain political support from such organized constituencies by passing detailed education bills. These bills had to be funded, moreover, so the portion of the state budget given over to categorical funding specifically earmarked for particular programs grew rapidly as a percent of the total education budget. The federal government also directed its funding for schools to particular programs. Thus, by the mid-1980s categorical aid con-stituted more than 28 percent of state and federal funding for local assistance to California districts. The string tied to this money was that the local school district had to give up much con-trol over program planning and allocation.

The 1982 election signaled the beginning of a shift in direction for education in California. The Superintendent of Public Instruc-tion is an elected office in California. In 1982 Wilson Riles, the twelve-year incumbent, was defeated by Bill Honig. During the Riles era, a major focus of state educational policy had been equity and equal access, in accordance with *Serrano* and prevailing politi-cal sympathies during the 1970s and earlier. Bill Honig, in con-trast, who had received substantial support from the business community, was committed to achieving excellence in public education by increasing the quality and efficiency of the schools, even if this meant implicitly downplaying equity.

Honig and other advocates of educational reform called attention to the long-term decline in test scores of California students and deplored the fall-off in the ability and performance of the state's students who go on to higher education. (This appeared to be primarily a problem of the high school, though much of the fall can be explained by changes in the composition of the students taking the tests.) Also disheartening was the decline in the percent of students taking Advanced Placement tests and the reduction in the proportion of those taking them who score in the upper levels. Reformers also produced evidence that California students spent less time in school and took fewer demanding courses than their counterparts in other states.

By 1983 political momentum for educational reform in California began to accelerate. Coming together to generate change were Honig's campaign and election, the interest of the California Business Roundtable in improving education,[4] publicity given to the reports of the various national commissions, and commitments by party leaders and education committee chairs in both houses of the legislature. After several months of intense discussion and negotiation, a major piece of legislation, the Hughes-Hart Educational Reform Act of 1983, better known as Senate Bill 813, became law. In Senate Bill 813, California put in place more changes than any other state had ever undertaken at one time.

An Assessment of Educational Reform in California

Senate Bill 813 contains some eighty-three different provisions for changing schools and education in California.[5] Not all of them have been implemented, and some of them may never be implemented. What one makes of this law and the other modifications of education policy that have since been put into place in California depends much on what one chooses to emphasize.

On the positive side of the ledger, what is encouraging about these provisions is that in general they are not aimed at current fashions and trendy reforms; they go right to the core of what happens in schools. This is unusual. They address what students study, the amounts of time they study, homework, text books, student discipline, and graduation standards. These are fundamental aspects of education.

Several of the most effective changes have the additional virtue of being fairly inexpensive. For example, Bill Honig and his counterparts in Texas and Florida reached an agreement with publishers of text books that if the publishers will elevate the standards of complexity and reading in their books, Florida, Texas, and California will agree to undertake some joint purchasing. California is also encouraging teachers to give more homework. The University of California and the California State University systems are raising their entrance requirements and have developed statements of expectations of what students should learn in required high school classes.

The most expensive provision of Senate Bill 813 offers financial incentives to schools to lengthen the school year. The law establishes targets in terms of minutes per year, and school districts may qualify for special funding if they meet these targets. This program will bring class room time in California up to the U.S. average. The Legislative Analyst's office estimates that if all schools in California participate, the cost will be about $460 million over three years. Some critics of this approach believe that California would have been wiser to have pursued low cost programs to encourage schools to make better use of the time they already had available. Moreover, some school districts that will receive money under the program already meet the Senate Bill 813 target levels for instructional time, so for them this provision will add new funding without increasing the length of the school day at all. Even when schools do increase instructional time, the state will receive little extra time for its money. For example, the average high school in a sample studied by the State Department of Education could qualify for the maximum incentive award by adding only four days to its school year and six minutes per day of instructional time. Reports have also surfaced that indicate that a few schools plan to use the extra minute per day to increase the pass time between classes. Defenders of this program argue that extending the school day and year and making better use of instructional time are separate reforms. One might want to do both, and perhaps also establish after-school and weekend enrichment programs for students. Some supporters of this program also acknowledge privately that while it will create little meaningful increase in the length of the school year in most districts, it does provide additional funding for schools; for these people, new money, however obtained, is a welcome contribution to school budgets.

The California State Department of Education has also launched an impressive accountability program that ranks schools of similar socioeconomic background in up to forty-two different categories. The program sets accountability standards, establishes state targets, and initiates improvement efforts at each school and district. It establishes separate categories for elementary schools, junior high schools, and high schools. Some of the standards to be measured include: the proportion of students enrolled in the traditional academic subjects and curriculum, scores on state achievement tests, Scholastic Achievement Test scores and the proportion of students that pass the College Board's Advanced Placement tests, and grade point averages of a high school's graduates in the University of California and California State University systems. The program also includes innovative measures such as the percentage of students who are given at least one writing assignment each week, the percentage of students who complete at least one hour of homework each day, the percentage of students enrolled in extracurricular activities, the numbers and types of books students read, and the level of community support for each school. Under the program the state establishes targets for each standard over a six-year period. Each year, a "performance report" will be published for every school in the state. In an attempt to make the comparisons of schools fair, they are grouped into five different categories on the basis of the socioeconomic makeup of the students in each school. Each school district is also encouraged to develop additional assessment measurements of its own choosing; for example, some districts plan to report information about the amount and nature of extracurricular activities engaged in by their students, and others intend to report of the status of their vocational education programs.

On the other side of the ledger, serious concerns must be raised about certain aspects of the California reform movement.

Curricular Reform, Demographics, Language, and Attrition

Raising high school graduation requirements. Before passage of Senate Bill 813, to graduate from a comprehensive high school in California, students must have completed a course of study designed by their local school district and have passed proficiency tests in writing, reading, and mathematics. In 1982, California students graduated with an average of 222.4 units (a one semester course counts as five units). A survey of twenty-six high schools found that local requirements ranged from 170 to 235 units.[6] Typically, districts required three types of courses: (1) academic courses, which accounted in most instances for less than half of required courses; (2) certain specified nonacademic courses such as driver training and physical education, and (3) electives, which constituted almost half of the required curriculum. School districts also varied considerably in how units in the required curriculum should be distributed. The required number of academic units was as low as 60 units in one school and as high as 110 units in another. The number of units for required nonacademic courses ranged from 15 to 60, and 60 to 125 units for electives.

Much of this variation can be accounted for by differences in patterns of tracking across the high schools in the survey. In California it has been common for students to be placed into "upper," "college preparatory," "general," and "remedial" tracks. Students in the upper and college preparatory curricula have been required to take a larger number of academic units than their classmates in the general and remedial tracks. General students typically have taken the minimum required academic classwork and have chosen a large number of electives.

Under Senate Bill 813, however, the state now requires all students to take specific courses to graduate from high school in California. These are presented in Table 1. By upgrading the requirements for graduation, state law is forcing a realignment of what has been the typical curriculum of many high school students. Most affected, of course, are students in the general and remedial tracks. If students take five courses per semester, they graduate with a total of forty courses after four years. As can be

Table 1

High School Graduation Standards Under Senate Bill 813
(Beginning in 1983 with the 1987 graduating class)

3 years	English
3 years	Social studies, including U.S. history and geography; world history, culture, and geography; and American government, civics, and economics
2 years	Mathematics
2 years	Science, including biological and physical
2 years	Physical education, unless exempted
1 year	Fine arts or foreign language
Other course work as specified by the school district	

Source: California State Department of Education, "Hughes-Hart Educational Reform Act of 1983: Summary of SB 813 and Related Legislation."

seen from Table 1, twenty-two of them must come from the academic part of the state mandated curriculum.

Vocational education. One valuable consequence of upgrading the requirements for high school graduation is that the new curriculum will force, somewhat indirectly, changes in the importance of vocational eduction in many of the state's high schools. In the past, a substantial fraction of high school students have taken a nonacademic, vocational program that often has provided little except keeping them enrolled in school. Vocational education has long been under attack. Too often it consists merely of job training which channels young people into low paying occupations; too often it teaches out-of-date skills using obsolete equipment; too often it prepares people for trades for which little demand exists. Seldom does it prepare students for good jobs that will be demanded in the future. Worst of all, disproportionate enrollments of children from poor families, many of them from ethnic minorities, are tracked into the vocational curriculum.

A growing body of literature, moreover, argues that general academic education is the best training for work for all students, whether they attend college or not.[7] Some recent surveys of business firms also reveal that many employers believe training for specific jobs is undesirable compared with the value of general education.[8]

Though SB 813 did not speak directly to the issue of vocational education, the change it mandated in graduation requirements had the effect of reducing the number of vocational courses many students will take in the future. Alarmed by the implications of Senate Bill 813, the vocational education lobby in 1985 is engaged in a campaign to try to persuade the legislature to write vocational education back into the curriculum.

Teaching the new curriculum. Despite the obvious limitations of the curricula existing in California high schools before Senate Bill 813, it is far from a sure bet that requiring this new core academic curriculum of all students will turn out unambiguously to have been a good thing. In mandating more English, mathematics, social science, and science, California now emphasizes the courses that Goodlad tells us students like least. "Most students," he reports, "need to see, touch, and smell what they read and write about. Time spent visiting a newspaper press, examining artifacts, or observing a craftsman provides reality and stimulus for later reading, explaining, and discussing." Without these ". . . academic learning is too abstract." A problem with most academic courses is that students do not do much except fill out worksheets and listen to teachers talk.[9]

One hopeful sign that schooling can be made less abstract is the emergence of a variety of impressive business-school partnership programs. For example, the state Chamber of Commerce has instituted a Business-Education Together program, and a number of major California companies have set up adopt-a-school programs. Such programs can be designed to help disadvantaged and isolated students see, touch, and smell the world around them. Much more of this kind of activity is needed.

In the parlance of the mathematicians, a more demanding curriculum is a necessary part of attaining excellence, but imposing new requirements will not be sufficient to assure that excellence will be realized. The challenge now faced by education in California is to go beyond raising standards and increasing requirements. New ways must be sought for presenting academic classes to the large numbers of students who in the past have either taken the vocational course of study or dropped out of high school before graduation. No one knows how successful California will turn out to be in meeting this challenge.

The possibility of failing to meet this challenge looms as a particularly serious concern in California because demographic changes are increasing the proportion of the students in the state who historically have experienced the least academic success: ethnic minority students. These changes are consequences of differential birthrates within the California population and new immigration patterns.

Demographics in California schools. In California, as in the nation, the major decrease in fertility following the baby boom was almost entirely a white, middle class phenomenon. Birth rates for Asians, blacks, and Hispanics remained high. By 1990, ethnic minorities will constitute over 45 percent of the state's birth cohort.

Immigration is also producing profound changes in the school population. Though California accounts for about 10 percent of the United States population, in recent years the state has been receiving about 30 percent of the nation's legal immigrants. Approximately half of the state's population growth during the 1970s was a consequence of immigration. Whereas in the past, about 90 percent of U.S. immigration originated in Europe, today less than 30 percent comes from there. Of the legal immigrants, 80 percent now come from Asia and Latin America. Within California, almost half of them settle in five metropolitan areas. Southern California (not including San Diego county) receives 16 percent of the nation's legal immigrants. No one knows for sure the pattern of the nation's illegal immigration, but demographers believe that about half comes from Mexico and the bulk of the rest originates in Latin America and Asia. California also accounts for a large share of illegal immigration.

In the mid-1960s California each year graduated 227,000 students from its high schools; 185,000 of them were Anglo, 6,000 were Asian, 14,000 were black, and 22,000 were Hispanic. In the mid-1980s the state graduates 225,000 students per year; 130,000 are Anglo, 20,000 are Asian, 23,000 are black, and 52,000 are Hispanic.

For K—12, minority students constitute 43 percent of total enrollments, up from about 25 percent twenty years ago. Moreover, the interaction of differential birth rates and immigration means that in the future an increasing fraction of California pupils will come from ethnic minorities. The greatest change is occurring in Hispanic enrollments. Within fifteen years (by the year 2000) Hispanics will comprise the largest single segment of the school-age population in California.

Minority enrollments are already especially important in Southern California where more than 70 percent of the students in Los Angeles County schools are ethnic minorities, and where more than eighty languages are spoken. In Santa Ana Unified School District in adjacent Orange County, 84 percent of the students are drawn from a large Spanish-speaking population, a recent influx of Vietnamese, and a declining black population; at least 43 percent of these students speak little or no English.

In 1984, students with limited English accounted for 12 percent of California pupils, up from 9 percent in 1981. Though some school districts in California are responsible for educating students using more than twenty-five languages, Spanish is the language of three-fourths of California students whose English is limited. One-third of the state's Hispanic students are limited in English.

Though numerous individual exceptions can be found, the California school system has not yet developed effective mechanisms for educating and socializing the bulk of its minority students. Public education has worked best for middle class Anglo or Asian students, and it has succeeded much less well for blacks, Hispanics, and other ethnic minorities.

Consider the experience of students in California schools.[10] Of 100 Anglo first graders, 86 reach twelfth grade, 57 enter college, and 15 become eligible to enter the University of California. For Asian students, of 100 first graders, 90 reach twelfth grade, 62 start college, and 36 qualify for the University of California. But for blacks, of 100 first graders, only 68 make it to twelfth grade, only 35 enter college, and only 4 are eligible to enter the University of California. For Hispanics, only 64 out of 100 first graders become twelfth graders, 29 become college entrants, and only 4 qualify for the University of California.

Compared with Anglos and Asians, blacks and Hispanics score significantly lower on the Scholastic Achievement Test and they are more likely to need remedial work in English, mathematics, and science at the University of California. Among high school graduates who go on to college, blacks and Hispanics are over-represented in the community colleges and under-represented at the University of California. And from the above various groups of 100 first graders, the 2 blacks and 2 Hispanics who actually enter the University of California will be academically less successful than their classmates. Survey questionnaires of freshmen at the University of California reveal a remarkable similarity among Anglos, Asians, blacks, and Hispanics in their educational and professional aspirations; but black and Hispanic students are less likely to say their high school prepared them well, and less likely to graduate and reach their professional goals.

It should be emphasized that variations in socioeconomic background account for much of these differences. College Board data show that black and Hispanic students come from families with significantly lower median family incomes than their white and Asian counterparts, and their parents also have less education. Perhaps cultural factors play a part as well, such as the Asian tradition of emphasis on education, or differences in the patterns of family life. To be aware of these possibilities, however, is to make the educational challenge no less real.

In the mid-1980s, California stands closer to realizing equity, defined as providing equal access to educational resources, than at any time in its history. But now calls are being made for improving the equality of educational outcomes for students across all income and ethnic groups, and California remains far short of reaching that ideal. While past concern about equality has sometimes meant lowering academic expectations for all, under Superintendent Honig, California's strategy for moving toward this newer goal emphasizes higher standards for all students regardless of race and socioeconomic background, combined with compensatory financing for certain "impacted" districts and for bilingual education. (See Chapter 9.)

But the strategy of requiring all high school students to take a course of study that has been successful for middle class Anglos, Asians, and other middle class students will not help disadvantaged students if they do not successfully complete it and drop out instead. If the back-to-basics reform movement does produce a higher dropout rate, the reform movement that replaces it will probably concentrate less on raising standards and more on improving student retention.

Language. In California, language is politics. In the *Lau vs. Nichols* case of 1974, the California Supreme Court ruled that a student in San Francisco who spoke Chinese and knew no English had a right to attend a public school where his language deficiency would be addressed. Following that decision, California has made a substantial effort to develop, staff, and fund programs for the non-English speaking and the limited-English speaking students of the state.

Since the outset of this effort, controversy has persisted over the appropriate goals of bilingual education. The view that is probably dominant argues that bilingual education should serve as a bridge between the child's first language and developing fluency in English. A second view maintains that the child should be taught to become fluent in both his or her first language and English; a variation of this view recommends that native speakers of English be mixed in so they, too, will experience the advantages of knowing two languages. A third view, espoused most often by some Hispanic leaders, advocates that bilingual education should be part of bicultural education. Children should develop fluency in English and Spanish, and they should also be socialized into the Mexican-American subculture as well as the dominant American culture.

It is this third view that has created the most tension. Like most immigrant groups, many Mexican-Americans want to maintain their language and their cultural ties with Mexico. Bicultural education is seen by them as a way of preserving their dual heritage. Not all Mexican-Americans agree with this approach, however; some surveys suggest that many Hispanic parents want their children to focus on learning English in school, not Spanish. Hispanic leaders who support the bicultural approach continue to press the legislature to support bicultural education.

Some non-Hispanics see danger in the call for bicultural education. Their concern probably reflects a traditional value that immigrants to America should embrace its language and its culture. Some people also worry that California will become like Quebec, where differences in language and culture produce deep political divisions. Signs of concern about the growing importance of Spanish are evident. In November 1984 California voters approved a proposition to prohibit a bilingual ballot, and a bill has been introduced into the legislature to make English the official language of the state. In this kind of charged atmosphere, the role of Spanish in the schools takes on important symbolic political meaning. Views on language reflect cultural ideology.

It would be easier to resolve some of the controversy surrounding bilingual education if we knew more than we do about effective strategies for teaching English. Perhaps the sink or swim method used on past generations of immigrants works best; certainly, within a generation or two this method produced satisfactory results. But unlike previous waves of immigration, where a new ethnic group arrived over a fairly short time period and was eventually assimilated into the population, a new first generation of non-English speakers from Mexico is always present in California, and their large numbers combined with their geographic closeness to Mexico make it possible for many Hispanics to avoid becoming fluent in English. These facts may argue for a bilingual approach, at least in the case of Spanish.

One practical problem California faces is that 84 percent of the state's teachers are Anglo and only 16 percent come from ethnic groups. Moreover, the state cannot begin to find sufficient numbers of teachers for its existing bilingual programs, either in Spanish or in the many other languages presently found in California. But even if California could staff classrooms to meet its current commitments under the law, the problem of language would remain serious. Many children whose English is not limited enough to make them eligible for currently established bilingual programs nonetheless still suffer from serious deficiencies in English.

California needs to identify all of these children and offer them rigorous and sustained compensatory training. It is likely that many poor and disadvantaged children from all ethnic groups would profit from such an effort. The best time to start is when they are young. A large part of the poor academic performance and much of the attrition of poor and minority students stem from their shortcomings in English. The youngest students can survive elementary school with deficiencies in English, but by junior high school and certainly by high school, they get into academic difficulty. By then it is virtually too late to help many of them. An additional serious problem arises when older immigrant students who speak no English enter school and, because of their age, are placed in junior high school or high school. If they are assigned to English as a Second Language programs, their academic courses may be given at such a remedial level that by the time they become proficient in English they will have fallen behind other students.

California appears to be losing ground in its efforts to deal with problems associated with language, particularly Spanish. One suspects that some of the reluctance of the legislature to expand the scope of bilingual programs derives not only from the cost and the formidable practical problems presented by bilingual education, but also from the fact that language is tied up with the politics of bicultural education. The price that Hispanic activists will have to pay for an all-out attack on the language problem may include forsaking their bicultural agenda.

Governance: California's Top Down Approach

The school board in Sacramento. Unlike cities, counties, and special districts, California school districts do not have any independent sources of revenue. Each dollar they receive comes from the state either by direct allocation through Sacramento's budget process, or through controlled procedures that the legislature sets up to allocate local property taxes to school districts. A school district's revenues are determined by first going through a very complicated funding formula that determines an entitlement for a school district. From that entitlement, local property tax receipts are subtracted. The state makes up the balance of the funding.

As has been noted, since the governor and the legislature dominate funding of the schools, they are also in a position to impose controls to accompany the allocation of money to school districts.

These controls have taken a variety of forms. First, starting in the early 1960s, the state began to impose specific controls on school districts as part of its expenditure allocation. For example, state law prohibits school districts from employing more than seven to nine administrators for every 100 teachers; districts that fail to comply forfeit part of their state funding. Another state law limits average class size in a district for grades 1–3 to thirty, with no individual class having more than thirty-two. The listing of such requirements goes on and on, and these kinds of controls impinge on virtually every aspect of school administration.

Second, as school districts began to complain that state-mandated programs imposed requirements without paying for the costs of implementing them, the state in 1972 passed the first in a series of statutes that required California to reimburse school districts for certain mandated costs. For example, in 1975 a law was passed that imposed on school districts a collective bargaining process, the costs of which are reimbursed by the state.

Third, the state eventually discovered that mandating programs for school districts and then promising to pay for them could prove to be quite expensive, and that this approach could make it difficult to predict and control expenditure commitments from year to year. Thus in the late 1970s and early 1980s the state developed what are called "categorical controls" and "categorical aid." Using this approach, the state announces to school districts that it will give them a certain amount of money for mandated programs that must be spent in accordance with state law and regulations. The largest of these state categorical controls is special education for handicapped children. The state spends approximately $1.2 billion per year on that categorical program; the law specifies class size, staffing ratios, service levels, and rights of parents to help them make sure their handicapped children are receiving necessary care. Other important categorical programs include bilingual education and programs for students from economically disadvantaged areas.

The fourth and newest technique is the carrot-and-stick approach used to implement some of the provisions of Senate Bill 813. Rather than mandating programs, the state tells a local school district that if it agrees to adopt a given program, the state will give it money. An example is California's program to spend

$450 million over three years to reimburse school districts that agree to meet the state's recommended length of the school year.

In the mid-1980s the state uses all four of these approaches to control public education. Taken together, they have shifted most of the power to make educational decisions away from school districts to Sacramento. Printing the education code requires four volumes and 3,700 pages. The governor, the state legislature, and the state's department of education have become the *de facto* school board in California.

But California is so big and so diverse that attempting to run it from the capital unavoidably creates serious problems. California has 1,043 school districts. One is a Hoopa Indian Reservation School in Humboldt County with 22 students. Los Angeles Unified has 532,000 students of incredible social and ethnic diversity. San Diego's school district on the Mexican border has 125,000 students, and Crescent City on the Oregon border has 600 students. One school district in the mountains east of Fresno educates 16 students, and winter snow conditions on the roads make it inaccessible to outsiders. The ethnically diverse district in El Centro must endure great heat in the summer and cold in the winter.

It is impossible for the state to develop effective regulations, controls, processes, and procedures that meet the educational needs of a population as diverse as that of California. If the state would agree to set educational goals and standards, then provide funding for school districts and allow them to pursue their own approaches, the reform movement in California could hold out more promise for success than now seems likely.

Administrative approaches to reform. Public education is by its very nature highly decentralized. What children learn and how well they learn it depends less on the decisions of state and federal officials than on what actually happens in local schools and classrooms. Attempts to reform education will fail unless they promote appropriate changes in the behavior of teachers and principals.

Over a decade of research on the characteristics of effective schools—that is, schools that have been able to produce higher than expected levels of school achievement—has provided solid evidence about the factors that distinguish effective schools from less effective ones.[11] Four of the most important of these factors are: (1) a common school culture and agreement on instructional goals; (2) strong principal leadership; (3) a high sense of teacher efficacy, that is teachers believe they can successfully teach students to succeed regardless of their backgrounds; and (4) effective use of instructional time.

When we talk about educational reform, we are actually considering two kinds of reform initiatives. The first includes what have been called macro reforms, in most cases "big ticket" items, e.g., lengthening the school day, reducing class size, raising graduation requirements, and setting curriculum standards. The second type, micro reforms, includes a set of low-cost school improvement activities, e.g., improved staff development, and technical assistance networks.

Micro reforms assume a bottom-up approach with good ideas coming from the school site. Macro reforms assume a top-down approach with state government imposing new requirements on local districts, a strategy which of course raises serious questions about implementation. Which approach should be taken to improve education? In deciding, policymakers usually rely on some kind of implicit theory of management.

Policies and practices for education in California result from a hodgepodge of conflicting management theories. Perhaps the oldest view sees the teacher or the principal as a *professional* who is given autonomy while being guided by a set of professional standards. More recently we have seen the development of a *labor union* model, under which many significant issues are resolved in mandatory collective bargaining. That model is partly a response to still another approach, a *public administration* view under which the state and districts adopt policies, implement them, and then monitor schools and teachers to hold them accountable. In some California districts, we are even witnessing the reemergence of a *political patronage* model, under which elected school board members participate in awarding jobs and overseeing particular functions of the school district. Finally, the *modern management* view of today emphasizes the importance of team building at the local level with a key role being played by the principal as academic leader and change agent.

Except for the political patronage model, each of these models has its place in education. The key is to use each of the management approaches appropriately. But too often an approach is extended into an arena where one of the others would have worked better, and too often these competing points of view undermine one another.

For example, the public administration model makes sense when it is used to assure equity in funding schools or to set broad educational goals and expectations for education. But it is not appropriate when it is used to send top-down instructions to districts about the details of controlling classroom interruptions, allocating budgets, and managing students. More effective micro reform could be possible if only school boards, administrators, teachers, the local business community, and parents would be allowed meaningful opportunity to exercise discretion and judgment at the local level. Similarly, collective bargaining is appropriate for setting pay, hours, and working conditions, but the web of rules imposed by state law must not become so extensive that teachers and administrators cannot work together at the school site to improve learning. Though California would be wise to devise strategies that make more use of the teacher as a professional and the modern management models, the state continues to move relentlessly toward overextending the public administration model.

Some Reforms Not Being Tried in California

Smaller classes. California's average class size ranks high among the states, and periodically a call is made to reduce it. Doing so, however, would prove to be very expensive. Lowering the average class size in the state by one student would cost $1.1 billion plus an additional $900 million for school construction.

Allowing class size to rise during the past decade, of course, was a way of coping with budget restrictions. And since teacher salaries, after taking into account inflation, were falling, teachers and their unions, school boards, and the state traded larger classes for keeping salaries from eroding even more. By 1984 class size in California was the second highest in the nation.

An agenda to reduce class size in California faces formidable obstacles. Once class size becomes large, the burden of proof for lowering it falls on those who advocate change. Establishing the case with statistical evidence has not been easy. The emerging research literature on the utility of small classes is mixed at best, and so far has not been persuasive. This evidence combined with the enormous cost of lowering class size has led the California reform movement to concentrate on other approaches.[12]

Vouchers. After accepting the report of the National Commission on Excellence in Education, *A Nation At Risk,* President Ronald Reagan noted:

Your report emphasized that the federal role in education should be limited to specific areas, and any assistance should be provided with a minimum of administrative burdens on our schools, colleges, and teachers. Your call for an end to federal intrusion is consistent with our task of redefining the federal role in education. . . . So, we'll continue to work in the months ahead for passage of tuition tax credits, vouchers, educational savings accounts, voluntary school prayer, and abolishing the Department of Education. Our agenda is to restore quality to education by increasing competition and by strengthening parental choice and local control.[13]

Though the president's remarks may convey the impression that his proposals for education are consonant with those of the national commission, none of his above recommendations was included in the commission's report. In fact, the proposals of the president and the commission differ from one another both in spirit and in approach.

As advocated by the president, tuition tax credits would provide a tax deduction to parents whose children attend private schools. Tax exempt status for educational savings accounts would help families amass funds for tuition. Under voucher plan proposals, a certificate would be given to parents by the state or local school board to pay for their children's education at the public, private, or parochial school of their choice. This money would come from funds given to the states by the federal government under the Aid to Disadvantaged Children program.[14]

Supporters of the president's proposals want all schools, including public schools, to receive their revenue directly from students' parents in the form of tuition, rather than indirectly from taxes collected and allocated to schools by government. Since parents would be free to choose the schools to which their children would apply, schools would have to compete with one another for tuition. This element of choice is intended to provide strong incentives for schools to deploy resources effectively and to improve the quality of education. Government could also influence equity and access to education by the amount of money it chose to make available to particular families.

Opponents of tuition tax credits, educational savings accounts, and vouchers argue that public schools run by state governments, school districts, principals, and teachers are more likely to provide quality education than are schools driven by the profit motive, especially if parents lack the skill to evaluate educational quality. They also maintain that the public school provides a sense of community which would be missing in a tuition-supported system, and that the public schools are more likely to integrate and socialize students into a common culture than are private schools bent on competing with one another by offering educational diversity.

It is possible, of course, to increase choice for parents and their children without converting the nation's public schools into *de facto* private schools. Choice could be increased by permitting children to attend schools outside their district. Such an approach could build on successes established in a limited way in California and elsewhere such as magnet schools and special high schools for the able and talented. Lowell High School in San Francisco and the Downtown Business Magnet in Los Angeles serve as good examples. Another possibility would be to award special vouchers to children with learning problems. California State Senator Leroy Greene has proposed a bill to establish vouchers which would be administered by the courts to reward desegregation efforts and to penalize segregation.

Such ideas will not mollify the supporters of tuition tax credits, educational savings accounts, and vouchers. They want to improve education by bringing market mechanisms to education; their objective is to give parents the power to determine the kinds of schools America's children attend by the choices they make about where to send their children. Their opponents rightly recognize that at issue is the continuance of the public school as a social institution. As one of them, Gerald Holton, a member of the National commission, has argued:

When enough parents are dissatisfied with the quality of public school-ing, when [tuition tax credits, educational savings accounts, and vouchers] make an exit from public schools easy, and when the melting-pot myth has given way to a splintering along both ethnic and religious lines, the exodus from a troubled system, with its unmanaged obligations, could be catastrophic. The theory that public schools would be strengthened by a challenge to compete has to be set off against the prob-ability that they would be weakened by such flight, with the attendant loss of community support for the long-established, ecumenical mediator helping to negotiate local or individual differences.[15]

In 1985 Secretary of Education William J. Bennett takes the lead in arguing for President Reagan's proposals. In the states, the Colorado legislature is giving serious attention to vouchers, and the idea of vouchers has been endorsed by Governor Lamar Alex-ander of Tennessee.[16] The Minnesota legislature defeated Gover-nor Rudy Perpich's voucher plan. Elsewhere, including California, the efforts of the states to improve America's schools have largely ignored the advice of Ronald Reagan and have instead subscribed to the agenda outlined by the various national commissions: strengthen the present public school system.

In California, vouchers are not on the political agenda. Virtually every significant interest group involved in California's educa-tional politics opposes vouchers. Though the arguments in favor of vouchers remain as persuasive, or as unpersuasive, as they were twenty years ago, this is not a reform that will be implemented in California any time soon.

Reducing the size of schools and school districts. Many of our school districts and schools are so big that parents are at a loss in finding ways to participate in the education of their children. It is impossible in such districts and schools for principals, teachers, and parents to develop shared values and culture.

One advantage of the large school district is that its size can be used to facilitate racial integration. Integration becomes more difficult to achieve across school districts. When public education was financed chiefly through local property taxes, large districts also served the important purpose of helping equalize expenditure per student across economically divergent communities. Now that the state, in response to the *Serrano* decision, has developed a workable methodology to produce equal financial access to educational resources, large districts are no longer necessary to accomplish this goal.

In deciding how big a school should be, districts must balance the gains that come from being able to provide specialized teachers and programs against the advantages students receive from attending school in a small setting. The smaller the school, the better the chance a student has to experience a sense of belonging, to know teachers and other students and to be known by them. Accountability, rather than being mechanical and impersonal, becomes interpersonal. Students in smaller schools also have more opportunity to play significant roles in student government, athletics, and other extracurricular activities. The anonymity of the large school undoubtedly contributes to poor student performance and to dropping out.

Henry Levin observes,

"There is no educational argument for primary schools larger than about 300 students, and smaller schools can be viable down to about 150 students if they share some services with neighboring schools. Likewise, four year secondary schools can be as small as 300–400 students if they are able to cooperate through the use of some shared teachers and professionals in highly specialized areas. . . . Indeed, one of the major attractions of private schools is their relatively intimate size in which the participants are known to each other. . . . As a rule of thumb, any primary or secondary school is probably too large if the principal and teachers do not know most of the students, by name."[17]

Though Levin, Boyer,[18] and other writers have stressed the potential value of this kind of reform, California has not shown much initiative in looking for ways to break up large school districts and schools. The reasons are easy to understand. Every school district and school has administrators, teachers, parents, and students who prefer the certainty of what they already have to the less well known social benefits that might result from change. The large district helps insulate administrators from many kinds of community pressures. Moreover, though much of the state funding received by districts is calculated on a per pupil basis, the money spent on each pupil within the district need not be equal. The large district provides a way for politically skillful interest groups within the district to increase their share of the budget allocation at the expense of less skilled groups. Attempts to create smaller schools must deal with the fact that school build-

ings are already in place. In addition, California high school
teachers typically possess single subject credentials, which would
complicate the plans of districts and schools that attempt to break
into smaller units. Most important of all, no significant constituency exists to advocate breaking up districts and schools into
small units.[19]

Improving Teachers: Clouds on the Horizon

Establishing accountability programs, buying better books, and
upgrading the curriculum can help create better schools. But they
are not sufficient. Whatever reforms government may attempt,
the teacher remains the single most important ingredient in
quality education.

California is blessed with many splendid teachers. Most have
completed a fifth year of college, and a majority hold master's
degrees. Despite these strengths, a number of disturbing signs
suggests that the average quality of the state's teachers has been
slipping. For example, when one examines average SAT scores of
groups of people entering various college majors, out of fourteen
fields, only one scores lower than education. Schools of education
accept among the least able of college graduates, based on undergraduate grades, yet the grades they award their students in
education are among the highest in the graduate schools. Skepticism abounds about both the rigor and relevance of the curricula
of many of these graduate programs.

California is failing in keeping its pool of credentialed teachers
in the classroom. For every 100 beginning teachers, five years
later only about 50 are still teaching. Those who remain are on
average academically less able than those who leave.

Two factors account for most of these problems: poor pay and
low morale.[20] Compared with most other states, California pays its
teachers well. But matched against jobs requiring comparable
training, teaching is the lowest paid field in California. Education
must compete with all other employers for teachers, and in that
competition the schools have not done well in recent years.

In 1982–83, the entry-level teacher salary in California was
$13,000. New college graduates entering business earned approx-
imately $20,000. The salary differentials between teachers and

other occupations for young people with backgrounds in science and mathematics were even greater, and a serious teacher shortage has developed in these fields. The average teacher salary in the state in 1984—85 was only $26,300.

Teacher salaries also peak out at low levels compared with other fields. In the mid-1980s, a California teacher's salary reaches a maximum of about $32,000—33,000 at age thirty-five, just at a time in life when the income prospects of his or her non-teaching friends from college days are taking off. The only way for a teacher to earn more money and still remain in education is to moonlight or move into administration.

It is true that teachers work only nine months. Adjusting the 1984—85 salary of $26,300 to a twelve-month basis brings it to $35,000. But, of course, teachers are not given this twelve-month option. Faced with the choice of nine-month jobs in teaching for an average salary of $26,300 or twelve-month jobs in other fields for more pay, fewer and fewer young people are choosing teaching. One approach to the problem would be to extend the opportunity for teachers to teach a longer year. At present the state limits summer school enrollment to 5 percent of regular enrollment; if this cap were increased to 10 percent, many teachers could supplement their nine-month pay schedule with an additional 1.5 month work load.

California is also a high cost of living state, especially when it comes to housing. But in terms of purchasing power, entry level salaries for California teachers are lower than they were in 1970 and 1960.

Teaching has never been known for its high salaries. Yet through the years it was selected as a profession because it provided numerous nonpecuniary benefits. But today teachers everywhere, including California, are suffering from low morale and job dissatisfaction. Many of them work with what they perceive to be inadequate facilities and materials, and they must function without sufficient clerical support. They teach large classes and sometimes they must confront difficult disciplinary problems. On occasion, some teachers even face physical danger. Teachers become angry when they must put up with weak administrative leadership. And particularly telling, given the direction education is moving in California, they resent being treated not as professionals but as bureaucratic functionaries. Finally, compared with other professions, teaching suffers from a demoralizing low prestige.

Despite these difficulties, California has been training numbers of teachers sufficent to fill the available teaching slots, though shortages have existed for some time in specific fields. For example, in California 20 percent of the credentials are being awarded in physical education, but most of the job openings occur in other fields. A serious shortage of science and mathematics teachers has existed for several years.

Now a more general teacher shortage is beginning to develop in California as enrollment patterns begin to change. When enrollments were falling in the state, lower pay sent powerful and appropriate economic signals to young people to choose other kinds of work. In the mid-1980s, however, though the number of high school students continues to fall, growth is occurring in the early grades by enough to increase overall K–12 enrollments. If class size remains constant, a combination of attrition, retirement, and enrollment growth will require California to hire approximately 100,000 teachers between 1985 and 1990;[21] in practical terms, this means that more than half of the state's teachers will have to be replaced. Thus, California faces a serious teacher shortage in the coming years unless it finds ways to make teaching more attractive. Even maintaining the average quality of the teachers presently in the state's classrooms will be a challenge, and improving on that quality will require a substantial effort.

Some steps are already being taken. Senate Bill 813 seeks to improve teacher morale and increase the effectiveness of teaching by funding small grants of up to $2,000 to teachers under an instructional improvement program. Senate Bill 813 also allows school districts to hire "teacher trainees' for grades 7–12 if insufficient credentialed teachers are available, and it authorizes setting up a professional development plan for these trainees. This program could become especially helpful to districts in recruiting new science and mathematics teachers. In addition, Senate Bill 813 authorizes schools to establish mentor teacher programs under which up to 5 percent of a school's teachers would be paid $4,000 per year extra to guide new teachers, develop new curricula, and participate in staff development. (Some local teacher unions have opposed this approach, in large part because they perceive the mentor teacher program as a means for establishing merit pay systems.)

In the mid-1980s falling inflation and bigger education budgets will make it possible for real pay to begin increasing in California. Moreover, Senate Bill 813 permits each school district to raise the lowest salary in its compensation schedule by 10 percent a year over three years, beginning with $18,000 in 1983–84; an inflation factor is included, as well. Under this law, the state reimburses districts for these increases. However, this provision of Senate Bill 813 does not pay for salary increases for all teachers, just those of beginning teachers. (Pay increases for continuing teachers must come out of the district's general operating budget.) About two-thirds of the state's school districts have chosen not to accept this state money for entry level teacher salaries because they believe their overall budgets are not increasing enough to permit them to deal with the impact of higher entry pay on the rest of the salary schedule.

Improved salaries and working conditions will attract better qualified people into the teaching profession. Poor pay and unpleasant working conditions will lead to a continuing diminution of the quality of California's teachers. Good professionals will produce their own improvements and raise standards in hundreds of different ways throughout the state. Weak people will not, no matter what is legislated in Sacramento.

Paying for Quality: The Prospects

School districts in California spend about 85 percent of their budgets on teacher and support personnel salaries and benefits. Thus, little can be done to increase pay by reallocating expenditures, particularly given the increasingly detailed rules of state law and the present conflicts between teacher unions and districts. Districts simply do not have discretion to move much money out of nonsalary accounts and put them into salaries. Thus, if salaries are to be increased, more money must be provided by the state.

How much money will it cost to make teacher salaries attractive enough to pull in and retain highly qualified people? As has been noted, the average K–12 salary in California in school year 1983–84 was $24,000. Increasing it to $32,000 would cost $1.25 billion per year, and moving it up to $40,000 per year would cost $2.5 billion per year.

Efforts to raise teacher pay, of course, must compete with other pressing educational needs in California. For example, new residential and commercial construction in the state is occurring in areas where schools must also be built, and, as has been noted, school enrollments are growing again in California. As a consequence, according to estimates by the State Department of Education, approximately $4.5 billion will be required to construct schools over the next five years.

The money for school construction in California comes from proceeds of bond sales that go into the state's School Building Lease Purchase Fund and from Tidelands Oil revenue. School districts may apply to the State Allocation Board for the use of these funds, and if their requests are approved, their projects must be carried out under detailed standards established in state law.

The approach works reasonably well, but funding adequacy continues to be a problem. The voters authorized $500 million for school construction bonds in the November 1982 election and approved an additional $450 million in the November 1984 election. Existing law also commits $200 million a year from Tidelands Oil revenues, though only half this amount is budgeted in some years. But compared to the almost $1 billion per year that is required, these amounts are small. Consequently, pressures on the legislature to deal with the problem of funding school construction can be expected to increase.

The fiscal impact of dealing just with teacher pay and school construction will be severe. California in 1984–85 spent roughly $12.3 billion on approximately 4.1 million public school students. Thus, if California were to spend an extra $1 billion per year to increase teacher salaries and $1 billion per year to build schools, these two items alone would increase the budget to about $14.3 billion in 1985–86. The state also needs to set aside several hundred million per year to finance a $6 billion shortfall in its teacher retirement plan which was not funded properly during the recent era of fiscal austerity. Other programs, including categorical aid, must also be supported with increased funding.

One possibility would be to take money from other state programs, but it is quite unlikely that politically acceptable savings could be made in other programs to produce anything near the amount of money needed to satisfy large scale increases in the education budget. Another option is to raise taxes. Though California ranks only at the average among the states in per pupil expenditures on K–12 education, it stands near the top in per capita income. These facts suggest that the state can well afford to spend more on education. But California also ranks high among the states in per capita taxes collected; it recently experienced a taxpayer revolt in the passage of Proposition 13, and many political and business leaders worry that high taxes already have eroded California's ability to attract and hold industry. Governor Deukmejian has pledged not to impose any new taxes on Californians.

Economic recovery beginning in 1982 increased greatly the sales tax and income tax revenues received by the state under its already existing tax laws. The 1984–85 state budget contained more than a $1 billion increase in expenditures for schools. In January 1985 in his proposed budget for 1985–86, Governor Deukmejian recommended that the legislature increase the entire K–12 budget by an additional $1.3 billion, which includes an estimated $243 million of income from a new state lottery approved by the voters in November 1984. Both Republicans and Democrats expressed their general pleasure with the proposed budget; thus something on the order of this level of funding can be expected.

This proposed budget, however, still leaves California at only about the national average among the states in K–12 expenditure per pupil. Inflation plus a growing enrollment leave per pupil expenditures in constant dollars virtually unchanged from recent years (see Table 2). Yet California should spend more per pupil than the national average. First, because California is a high cost of living state, it must pay higher than average salaries to attract and hold good teachers, principals, and support personnel. Second, providing quality education for the state's higher than average incidence of disadvantaged students, particularly ethnic minorities and students with language difficulties, will require special financial commitment.

Moreover, because a large fraction of the proposed $1.3 billion increase in the 1985–86 proposed budget is directed to specific

Table 2

California Public School K–12 Revenues

(dollars in millions)

Year	Local Property Tax Levies[a]	State Property Tax Subventions	State Aid	Federal Aid	Miscel- laneous[b]	Total Funding	Total Funding Per Pupil[c]	
							Current Dollars	1976–77 Dollars[d]
1976–77	$4,256.1	$494.0	$2,764.6	$644.4	$495.6	$8,654.7	$1,834	$1,834
1977–78	4,728.6	516.0	2,894.9	891.5	485.6	9,516.6	2,045	1,904
1978–79	2,337.1	241.5	5,333.4	962.3	551.3	9,425.6	2,207	1,897
1979–80	2,000.0	180.0	6,998.5	1,100.4	702.7	10,981.6	2,611	2,046
1980–81	2,166.2	243.6	7,696.0	1,102.1	909.5	12,117.4	2,875	2,056
1981–82	2,674.1	259.5	7,567.1	1,002.1	821.9	12,324.7	2,934	1,946
1982–83	2,675.3	266.5	7,786.1	969.3	792.1	12,489.3	2,953	1,837
1983–84[e]	2,886.5	98.5	9,229.9	1,014.6	792.1	14,021.6	3,292	1,928
1984–85[e]	3,289.1	98.5	10,345.1	1,071.4	792.1	15,596.2	3,596	1,990
1985–86[f]	3,459.9	98.5	11,128.8	1,123.3	1,035.1	16,845.6	3,807	1,991

[a] Includes local debt.

[b] Includes lottery revenues, combined state/federal grants, county income, and other miscellaneous income.

[c] Based on Average Daily Attendance (ADA).

[d] Adjusted by the GNP deflator for state and local government purchases.

[e] Estimated.

[f] Proposed budget.

Source: *Financial Transactions of School Districts, Governor's Budget* (various years).

programs, districts will not be allowed much discretion in allocating it to raise salaries or to restore program cuts they were required to make during the recent period of budget austerity. Taken as a whole, the proposed budget falls far short of what will be required if California is serious about maintaining the momentum now under way to improve its schools. Ultimately, the quest for excellence will require substantial infusions of money, something on the order of $2.5 to $3 billion per year more than current levels of funding. The hope for education in the state is that the success of its reform movement already under way will convince Californians that their schools deserve that support.

IV

The Teaching Profession: Problems and Prospects

11

BERNARD R. GIFFORD AND TRISH STODDART

Teacher Education: Rhetoric or Real Reform?

Since the early 1970s, we have been caught in a downdraft of confidence in the public schools. The system that once had been the core of the American dream became identified as the institution most likely to lead to a national downfall. These concerns are overstated but not without cause. There is well justified concern about student achievement test scores that have been declining for so long that they now hover at the bottom of the scale, and about students who are semi-literate and non-numerate when they leave school. In response, a number of recent reports state that education professionals and the general public alike believe that the public schools should re-dedicate themselves to focusing on improving academic standards.[1]

Proponents of the school reform movements are equally concerned about the numbers of teachers nationwide who, themselves, have not mastered the basics.[2] This has raised a question that is both legitimate and controversial. How can a teacher who cannot pass a test of basic skills in reading, writing, and arithmetic effectively guide students toward achieving high standards of literacy and mathematics proficiency? Yet such concerns focus so low that we are in danger of losing sight of where our aim should be: at the very top—on achieving and maintaining excellence.

The questions of quality bring under scrutiny the current system of teacher education. This close examination should be welcomed by all, since there is no other way to identify and strengthen that which is good or to identify and diagnose the problems within the system so that they can be rectified. One major set of concerns centers on the need for adequate screening procedures for teacher education candidates. Another centers on the inadequate opportunity for teachers to develop high levels of professional skills before or after assuming regular classroom duties. The concerns continue, as both low salaries and the absence of a teaching career lattice serve as disincentives for able individuals to assume teaching as a long-term career. There are, indeed, many excellent teachers currently in classrooms. But there are not enough. And those who are there can attribute their excellence far more to their personal dedication and talent than to the system that trained them.

Teachers are the linchpin of education, and student learning depends on effective teaching. Two recent studies, one of elementary schools and one of high schools, provide evidence that classroom teacher skills largely account for differences in student attainment.[3] Aside from student ability, the kind of teaching a child receives is the best predictor of his or her progress in reading and mathematics in elementary school.[4] Students who make the most progress are those whose teachers emphasize academic goals, accurately assess students' level of skill and provide appropriate learning tasks, evaluate and discuss student work, and carefully design lessons and give clear directions on assigned tasks.

Such findings prompt us to argue that the way to improve the quality of learning in schools is to improve the academic and professional skills of the teachers as well as the conditions under which they work. Education is now at a critical juncture, both in terms of needs and opportunities. It has been predicted, for example, that California alone will need between 90,000 and 190,000 new teachers between 1984 and 1991.[5] Thus, the state will need to replace a minimum of 50 percent of the teaching force and perhaps as much as 75 percent. These new teachers will teach an estimated 77 million students during their teaching careers.[6] Thirty states report that they presently have shortages of secondary teachers, especially in mathematics, science, and foreign languages. Seven states are experiencing shortages of elementary teachers. In five years, these states project that they will be short of teachers in all subjects, at all levels, with the heaviest need remaining at the secondary level.

Because of the magnitude of both the need and the turnover rate, we are in outstanding position to make the best possible impact on public education in a relatively short time. If we raise professional standards and improve teaching career opportunities now, we ensure the best possible teaching for all of the nation's students in a relatively short time.

In this chapter, we will examine ways to improve the quality of public schooling suggesting changes in three main areas: teacher certification, professional education, and career structures for classroom teachers.

Educating and Certifying Teachers

Report after report indicates changes in traditional recruitment and retention patterns of the teaching force nationwide. Many assert that the quality of those entering teaching has declined commensurate with the decline in the attractiveness of teaching as a profession. Today, as the most highly educated segment of the teaching force is preparing for retirement, taking its many years of experience with it, the most talented of the young teachers are leaving for other occupations. Few would argue with the statement that most new teachers entering the field have weaker academic credentials than do exiting teachers. The condition is exacerbated as the number of new entrants is insufficient to meet the increasing need for teachers and the most academically able of those entering the field are also the first to leave it. The need for teachers of mathematics and science is already critical and is still growing. Over the next five years, school enrollments will increase and the supply of prospective teachers will continue to shrink.

A recent survey conducted by Louis Harris and Associates polled teachers nationwide on issues relating to their profession, ranging from the need for computer literacy to the desire for reform and improvement. The teachers responded overwhelmingly in favor of improving the quality of those recruited for teacher education programs and tightening the requirements for teacher certification. Ninety-four percent of those polled indicated that they favored special incentives to bring outstanding students into teaching. Ninety percent indicated that they favored apprenticeship as a requirement for certification. Half indicated that they would favor a differential pay scale for mathematics and science teachers as a means of ameliorating the acute shortage. However, these teachers sounded a strong note in favor of professionalism and stated, by a margin of 61 percent to 37 percent, that they strongly oppose the hiring of talented people who are *not* certified teachers.[7]

This indicates that, while teacher education programs are currently under fire from many groups—including teachers themselves—such programs have the core of something identified by practitioners as valuable or are seen as having the potential for providing knowledge and experience that cannot be gotten as efficiently in other ways. It is worth our while to examine the current state of teacher preparation and to offer recommendations for program and system improvement.

There has been little lasting innovation and even less substantive improvement in teacher education for several decades. A variety of circumstances have conspired to bring about such stagnation: schools of education hold low status on their home campuses. Consequently, they are frequently denied not only prestige but also much needed resources that currently go to more esteemed departments. This situation is part of a self-perpetuating cycle. For many years, there was an over-abundance of teachers, which meant that there were few jobs for new teachers. A dramatic drop in the birth rate brought fewer students to the public schools. Soon there were no jobs for new teachers and many experienced teachers lost the jobs they had. The most able from the pool of potential teachers went elsewhere. Those who did not enter other professional schools entered other jobs. For almost two decades, schools of education vied for students who were too frequently not suited to the challenges and demands of teaching. This brought the prestige and the resources of the schools of education to increasingly new lows.

With so little impetus for improvement, there was no pressure for change and updating of curricula. Rather than bringing pedagogy up to date, programs were cut. Consequently, as other professions advanced, education failed to move toward becoming a substantive discipline. This, of course, brought the problem full circle: a field that is not developing and honing its base of knowledge, said the universities, is not deserving of support. Some schools of education responded that malign neglect was not likely to bring program improvement or provide the nation with high-quality teachers. Evidence to support this view can be found in the Smelser Report of the University of California, Berkeley, which found the university administration had subjected the School of Education to a policy of "punitive starvation", by lowering budget allocations and students' financial aid and failing to appoint a permanent dean for seven years.[8]

Harry Judge and Gary Sykes both observed that programs of teacher education frequently function to the benefit of other departments in the university system, but not to their own benefit, by becoming "the dumping ground for the weakest students in the arts and sciences".[9] Recent efforts to provide access to higher education for a greater proportion of the population has meant that public universities admit students with wide ranges of academic ability. Departments that admit the less traditional students relieve other departments from having to admit students without demonstrated abilities. Schools of education are opposed if they try to change this situation. Donna Kerr found that "faculties in arts and sciences have been known to object to attempts by education faculties to raise their entrance requirements". Sykes said teacher education has become an "intellectual ghetto" at many universities and that this is "higher education's dirty little secret".[10]

Education, viewed on most university campuses as neither a profession nor an academic discipline, is placed in an ambiguous position in the academic community. Applied research and a focus on developing professional skills have a low priority in education schools. Educators disagree as to what should constitute the basis of a teacher's professional knowledge. Hence the objectives and programs of schools of education vary greatly. Tenured faculty with neither experience nor interest in the teaching profession are frequently drawn from academic disciplines other than education. The result is the creation of a mini-university within the larger university, with schools of education employing people with doctorates in psychology, sociology, political science, economics, anthropology, statistics, operations research, physics, computer sciences, history, and philosophy.[11] The teaching and research carried out by such faculty is often indistinguishable from that undertaken by faculty in their home departments. Most of the *applied* teacher education, however, is undertaken by non-tenured faculty, lecturers, and supervisors who have little voice in the development of courses or program requirements.

Needed: Appropriate, rigorous teacher education programs. While there is almost universal agreement about the depth of problems besetting the teaching profession and the need to begin correcting these problems through teacher education programs, there is a danger that facile pseudo-solutions will continue to be accepted by those in need of solutions. A case in point is the current movement for teacher basic competency testing. The stated goal for the use of standardized tests of reading, writing, and computational skills is to provide assurance that the quality of those entering teaching is elevated. Such tests are necessary, but certainly not sufficient. In fact, they are unrelated to the educating of teachers.

Using California as an example, the California Basic Educational Skills Test (CBEST) is a testament to the failure of colleges and universities to guarantee that their graduates are literate and numerate. The need for such examinations is a commentary on the decline of standards. These tests should in no way be accepted as "teachers' examinations." Because of failings in the schooling of test takers, large numbers of them do not pass the simple competency tests. So much public attention has been attracted to the issue that the point is lost of a need for good selection criteria for entry into teacher education programs and for good tests of *professional* proficiency.

Admission to programs. The range and variety, nationwide, in admission standards and criteria for entry into teacher education programs is mind boggling. Some colleges and universities accept students directly into programs as incoming freshmen; others accept only post-baccalaureate students. Some require minimum scores on the Scholastic Aptitude Test (SAT) or the American College Test (ACT); others do not. Some few programs tied to a Master's degree in conjunction with the basic teaching credential require a basic competency examination, the Graduate Record Examination (GRE), and the appropriate sections of the National Teachers Examination (NTE), with passing scores on all. Some programs insist on a grade point average appropriate to graduate school work; others do not. Some programs require proof of satisfactory experience working with children, letters of recommendation, and interviews prior to acceptance. There are a number of institutions that require none of the above. The mean grade point average required for entry into a teacher education program in 1984 was 2.29, or just below a C+, with the majority of institutions requiring college rather than high school grades as an admission criterion and with the vast majority of programs requiring the completion of at least one year of college prior to acceptance.

In addition to the presence, or lack, of institutional requirements for admission, most states now require the passing of a standardized test either prior to entry into the program or prior to the granting of the teaching credential. The majority of these examinations are of the basic skills and subject matter competency variety and still do not meet the need for tests of *teaching* proficiency.

The programs. Once admitted to teacher education programs, student teachers do not receive a complete professional education, i.e., in sufficient courses such as theory, principles, and methods of teaching and learning. Their preparation does not compare in length or rigor with that of most of the recognized professions. When the time allocated to professional training by various professions is compared, teaching is at the bottom, devoting the lowest proportion of credit hours to specifically professional facets of the training.

Nationwide, more professional education courses are required in all teaching categories prior to credentialing than were required a decade ago. On the average, this translates to five more semester units (seventy-five hours contact time) of clinical experience, such as directed observation and student teaching, and four more units (sixty contact hours) of professional courses. In terms of distribution of requirements, there is less variation nationwide than in any other aspect of teacher education: the average elementary school credential program requires sixty-two semester units of general undergraduate studies, thirty-six semester units of professional studies, which include seventeen semester units of clinical experience. The average secondary program requires sixty-four semester units of general undergraduate studies, twenty-five semester units of professional studies, including fifteen semester units of clinical experience. The California State University report *Excellence in Professional Education* emphasizes that, even though this indicates an increase, it is simply not enough. The report presents a growing body of literature making the case for extending the length of teacher preparation.[12]

An analysis of current methods of teacher training shows why more extensive professional training is essential for the development of effective teachers. Teacher preparation in most states, including California, follows the "Competency Based Model", which assumes that the teaching function can be broken into discrete activities — such as question/answer strategies, map-reading skills, use of specific reading tests, etc.—that can be mastered by student teachers and applied in all teaching situations. This is an appealing assumption because discrete skills can be taught quickly and cheaply, but it is also a faulty one. Without knowledge of theory, discrete skills do not provide an adequate basis for the complex decision making required of teachers. Just as lawyers need to be good questioners, but would not be considered professionally competent without a sound background in the law, so teachers with a set of discrete skills are not professionally competent without a theoretical framework enabling them to apply the skills to complex subjects and teaching situations. Since our schools serve diverse populations, teachers need to be prepared comprehensively to accommodate the needs of children with wide ranges of ability, background, and interest.

Even while evidence continues to mount in favor of increasing professional education, thirty-two states are examining the feasibility of implementing alternative, non-college-base paths to certification. Eight states report that they are currently implementing alternative credentials, eight others have drafted such plans, eleven are in the process of considering such plans. In the eight states reporting the implementation of an alternative credentialing route, approval would be provisional, requiring additional college work in professional education courses within a specified time. Florida and New Jersey, however, currently have proposals before their state houses that would completely sidestep teacher education courses.[13]

These actions, which go against professional opinion and evidence, come in response to pressures based upon the folk wisdom that teaching is a craft best learned on the job. Such proposals assume that, if the individuals know the subject matter, they can teach it. We argue that, while academic competence is of vital importance, alone it is insufficient to ensure effective teaching. The effective teacher must also have a high level of professional skill, and this must be developed and evaluated in its own right. If the goal is to upgrade schools, elimination of professional training (inadequate as it may be at present) is a step in the wrong direction and is likely to bring worse consequences than the current training programs. Elimination of teacher preparation programs would perpetuate the very problems now decried—as practical teaching experience in isolation from other academic experience is counterproductive, socializing student teachers into the prevailing school culture, rather than expanding their horizons and awareness of a range of teaching environments.[14] If teachers enter the profession without any professional training, they are likely to adopt and perpetuate many current, yet ineffective teaching practices that should be eliminated.

Rather than trying to circumvent teacher education, we must focus on developing a common core of professional skills that are related to improved student achievement.[15] The characteristics of successful teachers include the ability to: 1) diagnose student skill level and prescribe appropriate learning tasks; 2) vary instructional style and methods to match the characteristics of the learner as well as the subject matter; 3) evaluate and discuss student progress with students and parents; 4) structure lessons and give clear instructions. These findings suggest that teachers need a thorough understanding of child development, learning, and ways of assessing individual learning status, as well as the ability to translate such information into effective methods for instructing children.

A proposed pedagogy. Psychology has reached the stage where knowledge of development and learning can form a basis for pedagogy. The way individuals process new information and the methods they employ to learn, depend on specific ways of knowing, which are related to the learner's developmental status and individual characteristics.

A teacher's primary task is to bridge the gap between the child's world and the adult's world. Children and adolescents are not simply less experienced versions of an adult, they are different in kind. Children do not experience the world as adults do. Moreover, as children develop, their ability to reason also develops. Each level of reasoning represents a different way of organizing experience, information, and knowledge. Children transform what they are taught in ways they have developed for making sense of the world. The effective teacher views the classroom through the eyes of the child to design instruction that will be interpreted appropriately by each student. The teacher must be able to assess the needs of individuals and teach accordingly. In short, a teacher must understand how children develop.

Knowledge of child development is not sufficient by itself, however. A science of instruction requires that knowledge about learning and development be combined with an understanding of the subject matter being taught. To develop effective teaching programs in mathematics, for example, the teacher must perform a sophisticated integration of both psychology and mathematics.

We do not suggest that a fully elaborated set of pedagogical practices has already been developed, but that a body of knowledge exists from which it can be developed. Upgrading the professional education of teachers and raising standards in American schools require that schools of education focus their energies on this task, giving much stronger emphasis to applied research. A radical reform of schools of education is essential. The following recommendations would permit schools of education to perform their jobs:

- Schools of education should be fundamentally restructured. Their primary mission should be instruction in pedagogy — including practical experience — and developing new knowledge of the teaching and learning processes, with both theoretical and applied programs of research.

- Programs of teacher preparation should be longer, permitting time to develop a thorough understanding of children's learning and development and of the requirements of a given subject matter, as well as the skills to apply this understanding to classroom instruction. A program of teacher preparation should help student teachers develop and apply knowledge and understanding of 1) child development and learning; 2) the characteristics and demands of specific subject matter; 3) the interaction between specific subject matter content and the development of children's thinking; and 4) the relationship between learners' characteristics and instructional strategies and subject matter.[16] Student teachers should demonstrate the ability to apply such knowledge to classroom instruction.

- Two years of post-baccalaureate study should be required, perhaps culminating in a Master's degree. Adequate fellowships and forgivable loans should be available to attract the most talented and dedicated students to these extended programs.

Too Much Too Soon: The Life of the New Teacher

Setting new standards and revising the certification process. Effective teachers must not only understand child development and learning processes and the complexities of the subject matter. They must also integrate this knowledge into their teaching methods. The successful transfer of teacher training into classroom practice requires study of theory, observation and demonstration, and teaching practice with feedback and coaching.[17] Educating effective student teachers takes time and requires extensive classroom training and supervision. In California, for example, the current method of teacher preparation defines professional training as complete in one year, after which the student teacher is considered fully qualified and capable of handling all the responsibilities of classroom instruction.

No other profession allows novices such great responsibility with so little practice and on-the-job supervision. No other profession expects beginners to work at the same tasks and levels as their more experienced colleagues.[18] Most professions—medicine, social work, and clinical psychology, for example—require new entrants to undergo a period of supervised internship after graduating from a professional training program.

It ordinarily takes several years to develop the skills needed to deal effectively on a daily basis with the learning and social needs of a group of developing individuals. Teachers must not only plan and deliver appropriate instruction but also organize the classroom, manage student behavior, and interact effectively with school administrators and parents. What neophyte could be prepared to deal with so much, all at once? It is no wonder that most new teachers go through their first few weeks in a state of near panic.[19]

Many new teachers report feeling inadequate to the task of teaching, a feeling that is exacerbated by working in relative isolation. Such factors contribute to the high turnover rate in the teaching profession. Except where special arrangements are made within individual schools, there is little help forthcoming. Yet, intensive supervision during the first difficult months of teaching is the best way to ease new teachers into the job.[20]

Studies of supervised internship programs support this view. The University of Oregon Resident Teachers Masters Program provides each new teacher with a full year of intensive supervision and support by an experienced teacher in the same school.[21] This program has been effective, and 75 percent of its teacher trainees were appointed to permanent teaching positions in the districts where they initially interned. An independent follow-up study indicates that, at the end of three years' teaching, the teacher interns were more competent in diagnosis, planning, and instruction than a similar group that had not benefited from a supervised internship.[22] A similar program at the University of New Hampshire reported that 90 percent of graduates were employed as teachers. Fewer teachers trained in these programs left the profession, in contrast with the higher dropout rate reported throughout the rest of the United States.[23] Consequently, we recommend two innovations.

First, beginning teachers should be assigned a mentor teacher, preferably in the same school, who will provide daily or weekly supervision and assistance. The mentor teachers should have these duties included as a regular part of their work load and not as an add-on function, performed gratis.

And second, the university and school district personnel should cooperate to help beginning teachers to adjust efficiently and effectively to the change from theoretical study to practical application. An internship model should be designed through collaboration between the school districts and the local universities, and resources of schools of education and other university faculty should be available to supervising mentor teachers and teaching interns. The relationship should be reciprocal: outstanding mentor teachers should be appointed as clinical professors in schools of education—in joint appointments between the school district and the university—to organize the internship program and collaborate with university faculty in problem-focused seminars for the beginning teachers. The schools of education, in turn, should provide training in supervision and evaluation for mentor teachers and members of the state evaluation team.

Revising the Certification Process

All prospective teachers should be required to demonstrate both academic and professional competence before being certified. Academic competence, including subject matter competence, should be demonstrated before admission to a program of teacher preparation. Professional competence should be evaluated after completion of a program of teacher preparation. We recommend a two-stage teaching credential consisting of 1) a temporary credential and 2) a long-term credential. On successful completion of a program of teacher preparation, teacher candidates would take a professional teachers exam, modeled after the first part of the Certified Public Accounting Examination, which places great emphasis on substantive knowledge and codes of professional practice and standards. Candidates who pass this exam would be granted a temporary teaching credential and allowed to seek employment as teachers. A long-term credential would only be granted after successful completion of a one-year supervised internship.

Improving Teaching as a Career

WANTED

College graduate with academic major (Master's degree preferred). Excellent communication and leadership skills required. Challenging opportunity to serve 150 clients daily, developing up to five different products each day to meet their needs. This diversified job also allows employee to exercise typing, clerical, law enforcement, and social work skills between assignments and after hours. Adaptability helpful, since suppliers cannot always deliver goods and support services on time. Typical work week 47 hours. Special nature of work precludes fringe benefits such as lunch and coffee breaks, but work has many intrinsic rewards. Starting salary $12,769, with a guarantee of $24,000 after only 14 years.[24]

Given that the hypothetical ad accurately characterizes the job of the typical secondary school teacher, we are left with the question, "Why on earth would anyone ever willingly teach?" Why indeed. Ninety-six percent of the respondents to a 1984 Louis Harris survey said that they teach because they love teaching.[25] One teacher said, "There is no better feeling, after you have worked hard at home to put together a lesson, and then you present that lesson, and the light bulbs go on, and the kids go 'I got it!'"[26] When listing the reasons for remaining in teaching, most items are highly affective and closely tied to student accomplishment: love of the subject taught and strong, supportive peer relationships. Typical lists include: seeing students grow, meeting constant challenges and changes, helping, sharing an appreciation of knowledge, the joy of performing, working as part of a teaching team toward common goals and sharing within the teaching community.[27]

But there is a down side that frequently over-shadows the positive. Some of the items are tied to particular teaching assignments in particular kinds of schools. Others are universal: isolation, sameness of the teaching assignment, poor physical environment, distance between administrators and teachers, lack of support in handling problems, lack of time to reflect and share, low salary, little adult interaction, constant interruptions, stress of constantly being "on stage", the public perception that anyone can teach, lack of opportunities and encouragement to grow professionally, lack of mutual respect among teachers, very low public esteem, inadequate materials, and the unrelenting load of paperwork.[28]

When we combine the down side of teaching with the drive to raise certification standards, we can see that increasing one side of the equation without improving the other side creates a condition that results in the opposite of the desired effect. Now that most states require the passing of the National Teachers Examination, the Scholastic Aptitude Test, the CBEST, or other standardized examinations as a minimum requisite either to entry into a teacher education program or for certification, they are guaranteed that their future teachers will, at a minimum, possess a mastery of the basic academic skills. With the inclusion of teacher competency examinations, we will put to an end the criticism that teachers do not know enough to teach satisfactorily. The quality of new candidates entering the profession would be elevated, but these potential candidates would be unlikely to remain in teaching as a career.

This is indeed the case. Those who score high in mathematical reasoning on standardized examinations will also be the first to leave teaching. In other words, in the present situation, those who are most acutely needed are also the first to leave.[29] In fact, of those placing in the top decile of the National Teachers Examination, over 67 percent leave teaching within seven years, whereas under 33 percent of those scoring in the bottom decile leave during the same period.[30]

Given these figures, we are not surprised to learn that parents dissuade their children from becoming teachers; and even teachers who love teaching advise others against entering the profession.[31] Predictably, enrollments in schools of education are down. Teaching has suffered a greater loss of prestige than any other profession during the last decade. With the gains made by the women's movement and changes in demographics in general, the profession has even lost its historical mainstay—women and minorities, who now have many other career options.

While we wish to work to change this trend, we must also take into consideration the understanding that teaching, like the military and nursing, is a mass profession with a high turnover rate that is inherent in any profession grouping so large a number of individuals. Both teaching and the military have approximately three million members in their ranks. The range and variation of

ability and talent within any group of that size is so large that
turnover per se should not be discouraged. Rather, as with the military, there must be sufficient opportunities for mobility within
the system so that the talented will feel encouraged and rewarded.
After a process of mutual selection at the bottom ranks, those who
remain in teaching as a career will have exhibited the competence
demanded of "career" teachers and will be eligible to earn
advancement and rewards commensurate with their performance, duties, and experience. At present, there are a number
of issues that impede the development of a true core of professional teachers. The most urgent of these are discussed below.

Low salaries. Teachers' salaries compare unfavorably with those
of other professions. The average California teacher earns approximately $22,755 per annum, which approximates 80 percent of a
social worker's salary and 60 percent of an engineer's.[32] Until the
recent salary increase mandated in California's Senate Bill 813,
the average starting salary for a public school teacher was
$13,000. On entering industry, an individual with an undergradu-
ate mathematics or science major is likely to be offered a starting
salary of $20,000, and with a Master's degree in engineering or an
MBA he or she could expect as much as $25,000-$30,000.[33] In
1986, three years after the passage of SB 813, entry-level salaries
for California teachers will be $18,000. But the real dollar value of
this improved entry-level salary will still be below the average
beginning pay received in 1970. Teachers' salaries have declined
12 percent in real purchasing power between 1971 and 1980 and
the decline appears to be continuing and accelerating. Worse still,
the salary structure offers no incentive to stay in teaching. Incomes are "front-loaded." Entry-level salaries are high in relation
to the long-term financial rewards of teaching. Over the years,
each pay increase represents a smaller percentage of the base salary, thus the rewards actually decrease with experience. Teachers
reach the top of the salary scale after only fifteen years experience. The California Roundtable states that:

For approximately 63 percent of California's teachers . . . there is no
opportunity for salary growth, other than inflationary increases and
periodic tenure bonuses provided by a limited number of school districts,
unless they leave the profession or go into school administration. After
ten years of moving up, many of them move out.[34]

No career development structure. As it is structured now, a career in teaching provides no incentive to keep competent, experienced teachers in the profession. The classroom activities and responsibilities of a twenty year veteran are indistinguishable from those of the raw recruit. Talented young teachers see relatively little opportunity for long-term professional development. Teaching is one of the few professions in which the work does not change as a function of experience. There is little in the system to give the teacher a sense of advancement. For a classroom teacher, the door to advancement is marked "exit." Presently, the only route for teachers who wish to become educational leaders is to leave their classrooms and enter administration.

Classroom teachers, regardless of experience, feel they have little influence or control outside of their classrooms and are generally excluded from the school's decision-making processes.[35] Indeed, in recent years, there have been increasing attempts to take away the control the teachers exercise within the classroom. "Legislated learning" has brought into use "tests to ensure teacher accountability, the development of 'teacher-proof' curriculum, instructional management systems, competency-based teacher education, management by objectives, and the like."[36] All of this erodes teachers' images of themselves as competent professionals.

In recent years, teachers have not even had job security. It has become common practice for school districts to send layoff notices to large numbers of teachers in the spring. Although many are rescinded by the end of August, teachers must spend months uncertain about having a job the following year. Moreover, these teachers are not given new job assignments until the new school year has begun. Thus, they have no time to prepare to teach the classes assigned them and are once again caught in a struggle to make do when they could be working to achieve excellence. Toward this goal we make the following recommendations:

Teacher salaries. Each state should develop a structure of salary increases and career advancement levels to reward both excellence and experience and retain the ablest teachers in the classroom. To demand greater rigor in professional preparation without also offering career enhancement would defeat the drive for greater teacher competence. Teacher salaries should be increased annually, to levels at which neither talented entry-level candidates nor experienced teachers are driven to seek other kinds of work solely for financial reasons.

Career structure. A structure for advancement of the careers of classroom teachers should be established, using the academic or civil service models. Progress should be based on qualifications, experience, and demonstrated teaching excellence. Each level should have its own salary increment and professional development requirements, but additional salary raises and increased professional responsibilities and privileges would depend on promotion to the next higher level. We suggest four levels or grades: intern, teacher, specialist teacher, and mentor teacher. The career ladder should allow the more able and more experienced classroom teachers to play a more influential role in the profession.

1. *Intern.* The nature of the position has already been described above. Internships bring the preparation and development of the teacher's skills into the work place. Upon successful completion of the internship, a long-term teaching credential is awarded.

2. *Teacher.* This is the first fully certificated stage of a teacher's career. Persons are expected to accumulate experience in this category before applying for qualification as a mentor teacher or specialist. Teachers are responsible for the day-to-day conducting of classroom activities, aside from types of instruction requiring a specialized authorization.

Further promotion opportunities for outstanding teachers should be patterned after the process through which an accountant can become a Certified Public Accountant. Teachers who wish to work for advancement to master levels in their profession should serve further two-year "mentorship" under the tutelage of a master teacher. During this time, as in the case of accountants, the teachers should work to develop exemplary skills in each of a number of designated areas. The master teachers with whom they worked would certify their attainment of the various competencies.

At such a time, and after a minimum of four years of full-time teaching, the teachers could sit for a national master teacher examination. The test would be entirely voluntary, of course. Like the Certified Public Accountant's Examination, it would consist of a theoretical and a practical portion. Since the examination would be national, outstanding teachers would have the opportunity to seek advancement not only in their home district or state, but anywhere in the nation where their talents as master teachers were sought. With this added leverage of mobility, master teachers would be paid commensurate with their proven skills. Depending upon the particular interest and talent of the master teacher, they could take one of two career routes described below—specialist teacher or mentor teacher.

3. *Specialist teacher.* The specialist teacher would be based in a school and play a leadership role in the instruction of designated subjects. Specialist teachers would act as agents of change and initiate program improvements within a school. They would be appointed in subject matter specialties, such as mathematics, science, or writing, and would assist teachers to upgrade instruction in these areas. In addition to some teaching responsibilities, specialist teachers would work with individual teachers in planning and teaching lessons, act as resource persons for other teachers in keeping up to date on academic and professional developments, and serve as a liaison with outside agencies, such as academic departments in universities, museums, and governmental agencies.[37]

4. *Mentor teacher.* Mentor teachers should be professional leaders, involved in pre-service and in-service teacher education and in monitoring professional standards. Mentor teachers should participate in the teacher certification process, scoring the Professional Teachers Exam, supervising teachers during their internship prior to permanent certification, and participating in the intern evaluation team described earlier. Mentor teachers should also participate in teacher training programs. The most outstanding mentor teachers should be offered short-term (e.g., three-year) appointments as clinical professors in schools of

education. Such appointments would be jointly funded by the universities and school districts.

Conclusion

Raising standards for teachers is the key to improving students' academic performance in public schools. A radical restructuring of the current teacher preparation and certification system is necessary if this goal is to be achieved. Current certification practices neither assure that teacher candidates meet minimum levels of competence nor encourage candidates to excel in the classroom.

Before they are granted teaching credentials, we recommend that prospective teachers be required to demonstrate 1) academic competence, 2) pedagogical knowledge, and 3) the ability to apply both to classroom instruction. All three are essential.

Academic competence (including reading, mathematical computation, written and spoken English) and knowledge of the subject matter to be taught are basic. All teachers need to be academically prepared. We recommend that academic competence be demonstrated prior to admission to a program of teacher preparation. Such competence should be ensured by requiring strict admission standards of education schools.

Academic competence alone, however, does not ensure effective teaching. Effective teachers also need a high level of professional skill. They need to be able to help students to understand the materials and subject matter offered, while stimulating students' thoughts and holding their attention. This involves diagnosing the levels of students' skills, prescribing appropriate learning tasks, varying instructional styles to match the characteristics of the subject matter, and monitoring and reporting student progress.

Professional skill has two main components: pedagogical knowledge and the skill to apply such knowledge regularly in classroom instruction. We recommend that both components be evaluated as part of a two-stage certification process. Pedagogical knowledge involves an understanding of learning and development and of the complexities and demands of specific subjects. The effective teacher constantly makes decisions based on a sophisticated integration of knowledge from both fields. The application of pedagogical knowledge to classroom instruction requires extensive teaching practice with feedback and coaching. We recommend that a full teaching credential be granted only after a new teacher has successfully completed a one-year internship, supervised by a mentor teacher and evaluated by a team. Teachers wishing to work for further professional advancement would work toward master teacher status. The master teacher exam would measure pedagogical knowledge and the ability to make instructional decisions and test abilities of leadership.

We firmly believe that measures to improve academic competence, pedagogical knowledge, and classroom teaching ability, taken together, will substantially raise the standards of teaching in classrooms and elevate teaching to its rightful place among the most esteemed and vital of the professions. In the absence of these reform measures, we will, indeed, be a nation at risk.

12

ROBERT E. DOHERTY

Teacher Bargaining: Teacher Quality, Student Achievement, Public Control

Although the jury is still out on the effect of teacher collective bargaining on the quality of education, we have evidence that bargaining has engendered some tensions while it may have exacerbated others. Transplanting private-sector principles and practices into the public sector, particularly into the public schools, has worked, but only to the extent the new organ has not been rejected. It would be difficult to show that the transplant has improved the health of the patient. On the other hand, the medical analogy may not be apt. For while it is true that, in the teaching profession, employer unilateralism in determining salary levels and other conditions of work has been replaced in most instances by the bilateralism collective bargaining requires, the connections between bargaining and the health of the enterprise are not so clear. Few have suggested that once teachers were allowed to bargain collectively the schools would improve. Bargaining in the public sector was proposed for other reasons, the most compelling being that there were no good grounds for denying to public employees the rights that had long been granted to employees in the private sector. It took the ferment of the 1960s (when most state enabling legislation was passed) for these "rights" to become apparent to state legislatures. American Federation of Teachers (AFT) president Albert Shanker may have made the most telling point on the possible connection between bargaining and quality when he stated in 1977:

> It's possible in the bargaining process to negotiate things that are good for children, and it's possible to negotiate things that are bad for children. The chances are that most things that are negotiated don't have much to do with children at all. They have to do with whether teachers are going to have a better standard of living.
>
> The justification for collective bargaining in the auto industry is not that there is a better car. It is that the auto workers ought to have a decent standard of living. It's part of our democratic values. . . . That's the reason for it, not that it makes education any better.[1]

Effects of Bargaining

What are those bargaining outcomes that are good for children, bad for children, or that seem to have no effect one way or the other? Let us speculate. To begin with, one positive outcome bargaining advocates hoped for was that bargaining would improve salaries to such an extent that the more able college students who had eschewed a teaching career because of the all too modest economic rewards would then be wooed into the profession. The thinking and the evidence to support it are that there is a positive correlation between the intellectual quality of the teacher and student achievement. The learning level of public school students, as measured by SAT scores and other standardized tests, began its precipitous decline in the early 1960s. Many thought that since bargaining would increase salaries, better qualified teachers would be attracted to the profession, and the learning problems would therefore be remedied. For many it was that simple.

Well, it was not really that simple. First of all, the effect of bargaining on salaries was nowhere nearly as dramatic as many had hoped. Clearly, as we shall see, the increase has not been sufficient to woo large numbers of bright and energetic college graduates away from other pursuits.

The standard method of calculating the influence of bargaining on compensation levels is to compare salaries and salary schedules of bargaining districts with districts that do not bargain but are otherwise similar. The trick, of course, is to locate comparable districts (they tend to be in different geographic regions) and to control for all the relevant variables. It is no wonder that scholars who have attempted to calculate the influence of bargaining on salary levels have produced mixed results. The best estimate after analyzing dozens of these studies is that salary gains attributable to bargaining are in the 1 to 5 percent range—and even then the major gains are realized by teachers with several years of experience and many graduate credits.

Improvements such as these are hardly calculated to encourage bright college students to choose teaching as a career; they are at least bright enough to understand that whatever economic gains bargaining brings about will not be realized for several years. One piece of evidence supporting this notion is the decline in recent years of the test scores (SAT, ACT, GRE, NAEP) of students who plan to become teachers. As Linda Darling-Hammond has pointed out, while in the early 1970s education majors' SAT scores exceeded the national average by several points, a decade later education majors' scores had fallen below the national average.[2]

Another disturbing trend that bargaining seems to have been unable to reverse is the inability of school districts to hold those more able teachers they do recruit. At least that is the finding on retention rates in North Carolina. Teachers do not bargain in North Carolina, but they do work under salary schedules similar, if not identical, to the "lock step" schedules negotiated by unions. According to attrition rate figures in North Carolina, female teachers who scored highest in the National Teacher Examination were much more likely to leave the profession within seven years than those who scored the lowest. Of those who scored in the top decile in 1973, almost two-thirds had left teaching by 1980 whereas only one-third who scored at the bottom decile had left.[3] This suggests that after almost twenty years of collective bargaining in the schools, unions have not been able to reverse, or even make a dent in, the downward trend in both teacher and student performance that began about the same time bargaining began to get established.

Teacher unions have been particularly unreceptive to two salary related proposals recently advanced by several educational leaders—proposals designed to bring about some improvement in the learning environment—premium pay for teachers with skills and training that are in short supply (math and science, for example) and salary advancement based on performance or assuming additional responsibilities. The shortage of math and science teachers has become acute; fewer than one-half of the newly hired teachers in those areas in 1981 were certified in the subjects taught. Moreover, only about 1400 math and science teachers were certified in 1981, although a total of 18,000 math and science teachers left teaching the following year.[4] Yet attempts to persuade teacher unions that salary differentials must be provided to lure individuals qualified in those fields to enter and remain in teaching have in most cases been received with hostility. It is not surprising that unions should take this approach. Not only would the acceptance of pay differentials violate the egalitarian and majoritarian principles of trade unions, it would be contrary to the wishes of a substantial majority of union members. Only 21 percent of the teachers questioned in a 1984 Gallup Poll favored paying a differential in subject areas where there were teacher shortages. The public, on the other hand, favored a differential scheme by 48 percent, with 43 percent opposed and 9 percent undecided.

Many plans to grant higher rewards to teachers with certain subject matter specialties have been ill conceived. Thus, in many instances, both teachers and their unions have every right to be skeptical. What the union reaction demonstrates is that proposals designed to improve the quality of education, ones that affect traditional personnel and compensation practices, will not sit well with either unions or their members. The concept of equal pay for equal work is as firmly held by teacher unions as it is by unions in the industrial sector.

Whether the proposals to build more flexibility into salary arrangements irrespective of subject matter specialty are in the form of merit pay, master teachers, or career ladders, teacher unions and the teachers themselves do not take kindly to the plans. According to the 1984 Gallup survey, only 32 percent of public school teachers favored merit pay as contrasted with a 76 percent approval rate by the general public. The unions have for the most part been quite successful in either defeating or watering down flexible salary schemes proposed at the state level and even more successful when proposals originate with school management at the local level. Of the two major teacher organizations, the National Education Association (NEA) and the AFT, the NEA appears to be the most adamantly opposed to greater flexibility. "To designate a small number 'master teachers,'" opined one state NEA leader, "is to denigrate the others."[5] Although the AFT seems to have taken a more cautious, wait-and-see approach, it is a long way from endorsing any scheme that would replace the current salary system that rewards teachers purely on the bases of experience and graduate training.

None of the above is meant to presume that absent union intransigence school districts would have necessarily adopted salary arrangements allowing a more efficient use of human resources. Indeed, there is no assurance that the kind of flexibility some scholars and school officials are proposing would actually make it easier to recruit or retain more highly qualified teachers. It is possible, for example, that the very act of making subjective judgements on teacher performance will cause such morale problems among those not singled out for reward or advancement that the whole exercise would turn out to be counterproductive.[6]

With respect to the notion that the only reason we do not have greater flexibility is because of union resistance, very few master teacher or merit plans were advanced by districts in all the years prior to unionization, and most of those failed within a short time. Nor, for that matter, has there been much success—or even interest—in introducing such plans in those states where teachers do not bargain.

It may be that the need for flexibility is now both greater and more apparent than heretofore. It is also possible that research has revealed the means to introduce such plans without causing lower morale or other forms of disruption. If this is the case, then surely unions and the collective bargaining process itself have been something less than a positive force. There is no gainsaying, however, that unions have in this instance reflected the interests of those they represent. One of the most important purposes of bargaining, Al Shanker reminds us, is to make teachers feel better about their circumstances. And who can deny that in this narrow respect the unions have succeeded?

Scope of Bargaining

We turn now to another issue where the interests of teachers and their unions may be at odds with the interests of the public: the scope of bargaining. Most collective bargaining statutes require that the parties negotiate "terms and conditions of employment." The problem is that unions and employers frequently disagree about what that elusive expression means and what circumstances it encompasses. There is no question about salaries, a health plan, a grievance procedure, length of the work day, etc., and conditions of employment. But what about curriculum, student placement, class size, teacher assignment, and student discipline? These are clearly matters that affect a teacher's working conditions. It makes a substantial difference to a teacher whether the curriculum is innovative, relevant, comfortable, or what have you; whether classes are large or small; whether one's teaching station can be changed by administrative fiat; whether one has to suffer disruptive students in one's class. Yet these are matters that also make a difference to the public and school administrators who tend to see them as being more closely related to school policy than to conditions of employment. Even though no statute mandates an employer to make a concession on any issue the union proposes, there is the tendency that in the pressure cooker atmosphere engendered by bargaining some of these vital interests will be traded off.

Collective bargaining statutes and, behind them, administrative agencies and the courts differ as to what constitutes a condition of employment and what is an educational policy. In New York State, for example, the agency administering that state's public employment law has ruled that the setting of numerical limits on class size is a matter of policy rather than an appropriate subject for negotiation. "Underlying this determination," the Public Employment Relations Board decided, "[is] the concept that basic decisions as to public policy should not be made in the isolation of a negotiating table, but rather should be made by those having the direct and sole responsibility therefor, and whose actions in this regard are subject to review in the electoral process."[7]

But across the border in Pennsylvania, where the administrative agency and the state's budget court have concluded that primacy should be given the collective bargaining statute, class size is thought to be unquestionably a condition of employment. In California, to use still another example, class size is a mandated subject of bargaining.

Probably the most persuasive argument for making clear distinctions between conditions of employment and educational policy can be found in the New Jersey Supreme Court's *Ridgefield Park* decision. The immediate issue in that case was whether the local board had illegally delegated its authority when it agreed to a provision concerning voluntary and involuntary transfers and reassignments of teachers. But the court didn't stop with a consideration of the transfer issue. It ruled that a school board and a teacher organization must confine the subject matter of bargaining to those issues mandated under the statute. For the parties to agree to matters beyond that narrow scope would tend to undermine the democratic process. The court reasoned as follows:

> Since teachers possess substantial expertise in the education area, negotiations between teachers' associations and boards of education present a situation where an agreement which effectively determines governmental policy on various issues is especially likely. The impropriety of permitting such educational policy matters to be determined in the forum of collective negotiation—just as if they pertained to the terms and conditions of employment—is every bit as strong as it is in other areas of public employment. The interests of teachers do not always coincide with the interests of the students on many important matters of educational policy ... boards are responsible to the local electorate, as well as the State, and may not make difficult educational policy decisions in a forum from which the public is excluded.[8]

What *Ridgefield Park* demonstrates so poignantly is the tension between the legitimate and frequently laudable aspirations of teachers to influence their work conditions and the equally legitimate and laudable concerns of citizens to exercise control over the most precious of their public enterprises. Legislators, administrative agencies, and the courts in the various states have differed widely over which issues ought to be resolved at the bargaining table and which issues can better be dealt with in traditional forums. As matters stand, one can expect that teacher unions will press to bring more policy issues to the bargaining table and that school officials will begin to demand that policy issues be excluded from discussion. Indeed, many school boards, recognizing that they have perhaps made too many concessions in this area during the early days of bargaining, began in the 1980s to attempt to recapture many of the prerogatives they so innocently had given away. Most found that these so-called "givebacks" or "takebacks" were not readily forthcoming.

Bargaining Impasses

Probably the most controversial issue associated with transplanting collective bargaining from the industrial sector into the schools is the question of the appropriate means of resolving bargaining impasses. Although the National Labor Relations Act grants and protects the right of employees to strike in their endeavor to secure better worker conditions, most states have not taken kindly to the notion of granting similar rights to teachers. As of 1985, only eleven states had granted public employees the right to strike, and even in those cases the rights are circumscribed. The parties are obliged to exhaust certain impasse-breaking devices, such as mediation and factfinding, and a strike may be enjoined if a court of proper jurisdiction holds that a strike may jeopardize the community's health, safety, or welfare.

Still, in spite of the illegality of teacher strikes in most states and even though many such strikes have been enjoined, there have been a substantial number of strikes in school districts. Of the 502 public-sector strikes in 1980, for example, 57 percent were in education, accounting for 54 percent of workers involved and 63 percent of days idle due to strikes.[9] Many of the strikes were illegal, either because the statutes did not authorize the strike or, as in one case in Pennsylvania, because injunctions were ignored.

It is a puzzle why teachers should be more prone to strike than other public employees. Perhaps teachers feel more intensely about their rights, possibly the issues they deal with at the bargaining table (professional and policy matters) are more volatile.

On a more mundane level, it could be that teachers are more prone to strikes because they know that in most instances (except, as in New York State, where there are heavy fines for striking) the strike is cost-free. For although teachers are not paid while they are on strike, days lost are often made up, and they are paid for those made-up days. Salaries are not lost, only delayed.

Another possible explanation of the high incidence of teacher strikes is that school districts are more willing to take a strike than are county or municipal employers, believing, perhaps, that a teacher strike would not necessarily do all that much mischief. Certainly it would be less troublesome than a strike by police, firefighters, sanitation workers, or nurses.

Still, most Americans disapprove of teacher strikes (over 52 percent in 1980) and, not surprisingly, those who have felt the effect of a strike oppose them even more strongly.[10] Though a poll in 1977 showed that while upstate residents in New York disapproved of granting the strike right to teachers by 57 percent, in New York City where teacher strikes had been an all too common occurrence, residents opposed granting that right by 63 percent. It also might be instructive that according to the Gallup Poll mentioned above, 58 percent of Easterners opposed granting the strike right while only 51 percent of residents of the Southwest, where teacher strikes are rare, were opposed.[11]

The reasons for the public's attitudes on the strike are no doubt mixed, and in many instances only dimly held. Some are opposed because they see children as innocent cost-bearers of the strike, others because of the damage the reputation of a strike-happy school district would have for the community. Still others resent the coercive power a strike brings to bear on school officials, sometimes forcing them to allocate resources in a manner that in their judgement is not conducive to a sound educational program.

Obviously strikes will take place no matter how much the public objects to them. No penalty can assure complete compliance. This does not mean that the public must condone behavior it deems undesirable but cannot eradicate completely. It is certainly possible to keep teacher strikes to a minimum if the penalties for strik-ing are not too severe (then rarely imposed) or, as in the eleven states that grant the strike right, there are no penalties. New York State may have hit upon the optimum penalty. There strik-ers are fined two-day's pay for each day lost due to the strike, the union loses dues deduction privileges for an unspecified period of time and is subject to a fine if an injunction is ignored. To be sure, these penalties, first enacted in 1969, did not have an immediate effect on curtailing strikes, but they seemed to become quite effec-tive as the years wore on. Although New York has over 3,000 bar-gaining units, there were but eight public-sector strikes in 1981, three in 1982, none in 1983, and two in 1984.[12] Given the large number of contracts that come up for renewal each year in New York, that strike record is indeed an enviable one.

In summary, although the public disapproves of legalizing teacher strikes by a narrow, though presumably growing, margin, legislatures in eleven states have seen fit to grant that right. Two states, Ohio and Illinois granted the strike right in 1984, after having the opportunity to observe the effect of strikes in other ju-risdictions for several years. It is also possible, or so it would seem, that if public opinion is opposed to teacher strikes, they can be controlled and the prohibition will not necessarily cause a death blow to the bargaining process.

Public Access

Public-sector bargaining is a form of lawmaking. It is at the bar-gaining table where decisions are made on the allocation of funds and personnel practices. In many instances, public policies are for-mulated, at least indirectly, at the bargaining table. Bargaining also tends to be a closed system, with both the union and the employer agreeing to carry out discussions in private until agree-ment is reached. Probably, privacy is essential if the process is to succeed, since it is unlikely that either side could make the neces-sary compromises if their constituents were looking over their shoulders; it is not possible to satisfy the interests of all groups represented. Older teachers may be concerned about increased sick leave and an improved health plan while younger teachers de-mand salary improvements and greater job security. By the same token, some citizens are concerned only about the tax rate while others demand changes in, say, the length of the school day. Inevitably the desires of some groups will be sacrificed in order to obtain advantages for others. At best, the negotiators will seek an acceptable mean. Thus the advocates on both sides attempt to insulate themselves from scrutiny, both from union members and from the public.

Is it possible to reconcile bargaining with traditional democratic processes? To what extent does bargaining blunt the ability of the public to influence the conduct of its public enterprise? Although it is easy to romanticize a past where virtually all citizens were keenly interested in the public schools and were active in school affairs, it is likely that even with the level of interest shown today there is a certain degree of blunting and frustration. Deals are made in secrecy, and the public finds out about the nature of those deals, the new "law," so to speak, when it is too late to do anything about them.

It is arguable, of course, that since the public delegated its lawmaking authority to the school board, just as school employees have delegated a similar responsibility to the union, the democratic process has been carried out. And just as employees can unseat a union leader who agrees to an unsuitable contract, the public can remove board members who do not, in the public's view, protect and advance the public interest. That's the control, that's all the public participation necessary. The difficulty with that argument, of course, is that the role of the union and the role of the employer are not symmetrical. Union members must in most instances ratify a contract, and if they find the new provisions not to their liking they can send their bargainers back to the table. The public, on the other hand, does not ratify a contract. Once the school board agrees, that's the end of the matter. The "law" is in effect for the next one, two, or three years, depending on the length of the contract. More realistically it is there forever since it is extremely difficult to remove a contract provision favorable to the union or the employees once it has found its way into the agreement. The so-called concession bargaining characteristic of so many bargaining arrangements in recent years has been primarily confined to the private sector.

The fact that there is no public input after the door to the bargaining room has been closed means that the union has a monopoly on getting the message across to the employer. To illustrate, a proposal affecting teacher transfers, teacher evaluations, or the length of the school day may be matters of real importance to members of the community, particularly parents of school-age children. But since the school board rarely polls its constituents, it has no way of knowing what the public's position on these issues might be. Nor is the board subject to the constant pressure of public groups while the "lawmaking" is in process, a circumstance that distinguishes school boards in this instance from most other legislative bodies. Thus we have issues affecting the public interest being decided absent the customary public debate. To permit "one side of a debatable public question to have a monopoly in expressing its views to the government," the U.S. Supreme Court opined in a slightly different context in 1976, "is the antithesis of constitutional government."[13]

The issue in 1976 *(City of Madison Joint School District No. 8)* was whether a member of a rival teacher's organization could speak at a public board meeting on a question currently being negotiated by the board's agent and the majority union. To be sure, the Supreme Court did not speak directly to the question of the public's role in the bargaining process. But in holding that the teacher had the right to address the board on a matter that was under discussion by the parties, the Court did concede "that any citizen could have presented precisely the same points and provided the Board with the same information. . . ."[14]

None of the above argues that greater public access to the bargaining process would necessarily result in settlements leading to improvements in teacher and student performance, although that is the hope of many of its advocates. Rather, the question of public access demonstrates only that tensions can, and sometimes do, exist when a procedure for resolving labor and management disputes in the private sector is transplanted into the schools and other public-sector enterprises. It is public policy in forty of our states that conditions of employment for teachers and other school employees should be determined at the bargaining table. In 1980, 65 percent of all public school teachers were covered by collective bargaining agreements. Currently that figure is approximately 70 percent.[15] It is also public policy in all our states that citizens' influence in the conduct and direction of the schools should not be severely frustrated. It is difficult to get these two notions to mesh neatly.

There have been several attempts to provide greater public access to the bargaining process. In Florida and Kansas, for example, open bargaining sessions are mandates under law; in California and Minnesota bargaining proposals from both sides are made public prior to the actual bargaining. In Rochester, New York, a parent representative sits on the board's bargaining team, and in Philadelphia dissatisfied parents formed the Parents' Union for Public Schools in the early 1970s to pressure the district to modify several provisions during upcoming negotiations. A handful of jurisdictions in Colorado began in the late 1970s to submit the final union and employer positions to the public to decide which of the two positions was more meritorious. There have even been proposals that the agreement itself be put before the public for ratification, similar to the ratification procedure followed by unions.

Have any of the developments described above made the parties to the negotiations more responsive to the public's wishes? It is difficult to tell. Part of the difficulty is that one doesn't know for certain what would have happened without public pressure. Another difficulty is that it is not always possible to identify those who truly speak for the public. In fact, there are several publics, and sometimes boards confuse the most vocal group with the group that might really represent the interest of the majority.

Still another difficulty is that since both parties to the bargain sometimes have strong incentives to maintain a closed system, it is not unusual for both union and management negotiators subject to open meeting laws to meet privately (though illegally) to settle their differences and then play out their prepared script before an unsuspecting public. Procedures that require the public to be informed of each side's opening bargaining proposals may have caused an initial flurry of interest, but that interest seems to have flagged. The public referenda and the formation of parents' unions seem to have caught on barely at all. One must conclude, therefore, that neither has the new form of lawmaking taken hold under collective bargaining, nor have the "laws" emerging from that process sufficiently inconvenienced the public to cause it to take a very hard look at the process.

Conclusion

Is it possible after almost two decades of collective bargaining to make an assessment? What has it done for the welfare of teachers, and what consequences has it had for students? It is probably fair to say that the effect of bargaining on teacher salaries has been minimal, certainly salary gains have not been sufficient to encourage the more able college students to enter the profession. Indeed, negotiated salaries have not even been great enough to maintain the pre-bargaining level of teacher quality. There are, of course, many reasons for the decline in teacher quality, not the least of which is the greater opportunity for many capable women who heretofore may have entered teaching now to pursue more lucrative and prestigious careers. Perhaps the greatest obstacle to substantial salary increases, however, is the unwillingness of local citizens to re-order their priorities and provide the schools the resources they require if they are ever to recruit and retain the teacher talent our children deserve. The power of unions is limited by an indifferent, sometimes antagonistic public. It is unlikely that collective bargaining will shatter their indifference or reduce that antagonism.

The important point is that unions and collective bargaining were not established to improve the educational climate. The hope was that through bargaining teachers would have a stronger say about the matters affecting their working lives. And indeed they now have that. Although bargaining seems to have had little effect on raising salaries, one cannot look at a typical teacher union contract without being struck by the number of provisions that benefit teachers. It is doubtful whether teachers would have grievance procedures ending with binding arbitration, transfer and promotion policies so effective, health and dental plans so generous, or personal leave policies so liberal had they not bargained for them. It is also worth noting that these provisions tend to become even more generous from the teachers' perspective with each negotiation.

If certain contract provisions are antithetical to a good learning environment, one must recognize that these provisions were also agreed to by school officials. Sometimes concessions were made under duress, but in most instances they probably were not. It is perhaps the supreme irony of modern education that at a time when so much was being learned about effective resource allocation through the several educational production function studies, that resources, both financial and human, are still being utilized in such an unproductive manner.

There is bargaining power in knowledge. A board spokesman ought to be able to demonstrate that some union proposals, a rigid class-size provision, say, would not, if implemented, necessarily promote student achievement. Unions, particularly teacher unions, can be persuaded by persuasive factual arguments. It is not enough for school officials to argue that certain improvements cannot be made because the contract ties their hands. They were parties to that contract. If the transplant has worked less than perfectly, and it clearly has, the problem is not due entirely to the operation.

13

ALBERT SHANKER

Collective Bargaining with Educational Standards

From the very beginning there have been two sides to teacher unionism. First, because of perennially low salary levels and deplorable working conditions, teachers continually have had to struggle to maintain a decent standard of living. At the same time, they have never confined themselves exclusively to narrow self-interest. As teachers, they have also felt an obligation to work for a better world, a more just society.

This duality appears in the earliest union efforts. For example, in Chicago, in 1897, Margaret Haley, "the spiritual mother of teacher-unionism in the United States,"[1] spearheaded the formation of the Chicago Federation of Teachers. That year, during the Christmas holidays, the Board of Education claimed that the city was broke and asked teachers to take a cut in salary. Thereupon, the energetic Miss Haley embarked on a personal investigation to discover untapped sources of city revenue.

What she found was a scandal involving government officials and business executives. Huge corporations, she revealed, had been granted franchises to city land free of taxation. As a result of her efforts, the courts forced a number of companies to pay back-taxes to the city treasury.

Undoubtedly, Miss Haley's primary motive was to protect teachers' salaries. But what she did was also part of the grand muckraking tradition of Lincoln Steffens, Upton Sinclair, and Ida Tarbell, and, as such, it had a lofty ethical dimension aimed not only at improving material conditions but at elevating civic morality and heightening public awareness. Later she and the union joined another crusade and helped defeat a bill to establish a dual education system that would have perpetuated class distinctions by barring the children of blue-collar workers from college preparatory courses.

This social consciousness was an intrinsic part of the nationwide teachers movement. An early editorial in *The American Teacher,* the official organ of the American Federation of Teachers (AFT), expressed what must have been an article of faith:

> We believe that teachers owe it to themselves, as well as to the public, to study the relation of education to social progress, and to understand some of the important social and economic movements going on in the present-day world.
>
> We believe that with an intelligent outlook upon life, teachers will be able to contribute from their experience in teaching the best ideas for the adjustment of education to the needs of human living.[2]

This social commitment was not limited to high-sounding abstractions. Some of the earliest demands of the AFT were for low-cost, nutritious lunches for students, improved sanitary conditions in schools, and dental clinics for all school children.

Underlying the teacher's vision of his or her role in society was John Dewey's idea that "education is the fundamental method of social progress and reform," and that the "teacher is engaged, not simply in training individuals, but in the formation of the proper social life."[3]

Schools, therefore, represented the instruments of realizing a utopian ideal. And, since it seemed clear that administrators and politicians continued to mismanage and shortchange these institutions, it was inevitable that teachers would conclude that they alone would mend what others had spoiled. They would save the schools, and, in so doing, would save the future.

Thus, by the time the United Federation of Teachers (UFT) in New York City became the first municipal union to win the right to bargain collectively in 1961, this tradition of teacher activism and commitment to principles of social reform had been firmly established and had become a given of the movement. As Sandra Feldman, secretary of the UFT, wrote of the early union a decade later, "Most of its leaders and much of its activist membership were social reformers, people whose lives are devoted to progress, to whom teacher unionism was a 'cause,' a movement which, in achieving economic dignity and job security for teachers, would improve education for children and further, would be a leading force in the struggle for progressive social change."[4]

In the light of this commitment, it is ironic that critics of teachers' unions continue to maintain that collective bargaining and other union activity are incompatible with adherence to principle and to the maintenance of standards. In a crunch, they say, self-interest must prevail, often to the detriment of students and the community.

This is an over-simplification of a complex process. In negotiations, both sides will usually be pulled by conflicting tendencies. There are generally no villains, simply human beings trying as well as they can to reconcile what is right with their best interests.

But one does not have to claim that teachers are plaster saints to argue that they have often shown a willingness to go a long way to maintain a principle or uphold a standard, often in opposition to their own material interests.

A dramatic example of this occurred shortly before the election that named the UFT as bargaining agent for New York City teachers. A group of black parents decided to keep their children out of school in violation of the state's compulsory attendance laws. When the Board of Education brought them to court, the parents argued that they were justified in keeping their children at home. The neighborhood schools were intrinsically inferior, they maintained, since they were largely staffed by substitute teachers who, for one reason or another, had not qualified as regular teachers. The judge ruled that the parents were justified in their action and ordered the Board to remedy the situation.

The Board's "solution" was to petition the state legislature to pass a bill making all substitutes instant regular teachers regardless of their credentials. This, of course, was immensely appealing to the regular substitute teachers, who numbered between ten and twenty thousand. However, the leadership of the union vigorously opposed this trifling with professional standards in spite of the fact that nearly one-quarter of the city's teachers were in a position to benefit from the proposed legislation. At a dramatic delegates' meeting teachers voted to oppose the Board's action. Therefore, facing a life or death collective bargaining election, the union stood on principle when there was considerable pressure to yield to expediency.

This incident, a mere footnote in the history of education in New York City, is significant primarily because of the insight it offers into the imperatives of teacher unionism. Without standards and principles there is no profession.

Standards in the Marketplace

The teachers who won the right to collective bargaining back in 1961 must have felt something of Gatsby's exhilaration when he stood on his dock looking at Daisy's light beckoning to him from across the bay. Life was full of possibilities; the world, or at least schools, could be re-made. And they were eager to get on with the job.

Both major teacher organizations were quick to claim broad objectives in collective bargaining. In its *Guidelines for Professional Negotiations*, the National Education Association left no doubt about what its leaders expected: "The professional group has responsibilities beyond self-interest, including a responsibility for the general welfare of the school system. . . . Negotiations should include all matters which affect the quality of the educational system."

When asked what the line between what was negotiable and what was not, David Selden, president of the AFT, was more terse but no less emphatic: "There is no line. Anything the two parties can agree on is negotiable."

What followed can best be described as a period of testing. Teachers were flexing their newly-acquired muscle, and school boards and administrators were groping to develop strategies and postures to deal with the new challenge of teacher power. Both parties were sailing in uncharted waters. There was confusion about the limits of authority and the interpretation of legal guidelines.

This lack of clarity made a power struggle inevitable. A good example of this is the conflict between the Flint, Michigan teachers' union and the local school board in 1966. According to state law, the board was obliged to "bargain in good faith" with the recognized union's representatives. The same law limited negotiations to "conditions of employment." But these "conditions" were not spelled out. Almost anything the board did could be construed as fitting this category.

Early in the negotiations, the board agreed to a pay raise for teachers that would be funded by a tax increase submitted to the voters for approval. As the election drew near, the union decided that the proposed tax increase would not be sufficient to fund both the salary increases and other education services. Therefore, it demanded a higher tax and the right in the future to join with the board in recommending tax increases to the public.[5]

Understandably, the board balked at this, viewing the proposal as an effort by the teachers to usurp its power and to undermine the rationale for its existence. Therefore, quite early, the lines of contention were drawn.

Traditionally, collective bargaining has been confined to the questions of salary schedules and working conditions. Teachers, naturally, interpreted the latter broadly even to the point of including, we've seen, the power to recommend the level of taxation; those opposite them at the negotiating table held quite a different view. A fundamental question was: How far can or should a duly elected or appointed agency representing the public go in relinquishing its lawful authority or in modifying its mandate?

The interplay of forces over that last two decades, often involving judges, arbitrators, and high-level public officials, has by no means yielded a definitive answer. But what is clear is that teachers have not taken over the public schools as some critics feared they would. The far-reaching goals that characterized the early days of collective bargaining have been modified, of necessity, by the give-and-take of a democratic society. If, as some have charged, teachers confine themselves in negotiation to matters of "self interest" it is only because they have been forced into that position by forces beyond their control.

Sometimes a sympathetic, forward-looking board of education would bend and appear to be ceding some of its policy-making power. What happens on such occasions is an illuminating example of the fate of teachers' efforts to implement their vision of what schools should be like.

In the mid-1960s the UFT (New York City) developed a comprehensive More Effective Schools (MES) plan to upgrade education in disadvantaged areas. The New York City Board of Education agreed to put the program in place in selected districts. In the preamble to the 1969 contract, the Board committed itself to continuing the program: "They [the Board and the UFT] have now moved toward further advancement of their mutual goals by continuing present programs of demonstrated benefit . . . etc."

Was the preamble part of the contract? Had the UFT won the authority to take part in policy-making decisions? The answers came a few years later. In 1971, because of budget cuts, the Board of Education discontinued the MES program. The union considered this a violation of its contract and went to arbitration. Thomas Christensen, the arbitrator, ruled against the UFT on the ground that although the programs were included in the preamble, they were not subject to the arbitration clause of the contract. Therefore, what appeared to be a victory for the teachers in introducing an innovative and effective program through collective bargaining was shot down in arbitration and later in the courts.

The New York City experience offers another illustration of how the negotiating power of unions has been carefully kept within narrow limits. On the question of class size, the Board will only discuss the matter to the extent that it involves what it construes to be a "working condition." That is, the Board is willing to concede that a high school class of more than forty students represents an onerous "condition." But it will not enter into any discussion of what constitutes an "ideal" class size. That is education policy, their domain.

One commentator has described the current status of teacher collective bargaining as being in its second generation, where "everyone involved tacitly agrees that contracts are primarily concerned with working conditions."[6] Another observer has predicted that as school management and teacher unions grow more comfortable in their relationship, matters of education policy will become a greater and greater part of the negotiating agenda.[7] Others feel that we have already thoroughly entered into this "third generation." In a recent study, Steven Goldschmidt and his associates examined the provisions of eighty contracts from all over the country. They concluded that "the impact of collective bargaining is much greater than previously believed, especially on governance, school organization and administrative work, and student educational programs."[8]

At any rate, the total picture is not clear. What can be said with assurance is that from the teachers' point of view collective bargaining had brought them to a plateau where, though significant gains had been made, their visionary ideals of re-making schools were thwarted. But the special status as official spokesmen for teachers along with the significant revenues from dues check-off gave unions the opportunity and power to promote their agendas in the political arena on all levels.

This was done with such skill and energy that, by 1975, A.H. Raskin, a less than sympathetic observer, could write in the *New York Times* that the national election of 1974 "saw teachers move out in front of doctors, milk producers, and all the rest of the traditional big spenders as possessors of political clout. In money, campaign manpower, and vote coralling effectiveness, organized teachers—only a few years ago strangers to politics—outdid every other interest group."[9]

This political option, as I've said, is often an effective way of bypassing the dead-end of collective bargaining. But that is by no means its exclusive function. It can also be a way of establishing a productive partnership between teachers and the local school board. For example, in a recent article, Chester Finn pointed out that after a decade of negotiations the relationship between the Dade County (Florida) teacher union and the board of education was so comfortable "that the lobbyists of each group would sometimes speak on behalf of both in Tallahassee.[10]

Political activity is not, of course, limited to legislative halls and executive mansions. Teachers have developed a highly effective public relations voice, not only for themselves but for parents and children. Public schools have gotten an undeserved bad image. There are ominous signs that support for them is waning. Voucher plans or schemes for aid to private schools have eloquent and powerful advocates. Under 25 percent of the population now have children in the public schools. And parents' organizations, often eloquent defenders of the system, have, unfortunately, a structural weakness, a relatively rapid turnover of leadership and membership as children graduate and move on out of the schools. They too, of course, suffer from the general weakening of the family structure. In such a situation, the teachers' unions may often be the only major voice to effectively articulate and defend the interests of those whose only hope for advancement is the local public school.

Some of these efforts are naturally concomitant with the bargaining process. All citizens obviously have a stake, one way of another, in the agreements worked out between their representatives and the teachers' union. Therefore, the teachers perform a valuable civic service in taking their case into the public forum. The public needs to be informed about the realities of school life.

There are recent examples of how this can work. Not long ago, the Cincinnati Federation of Teachers (CFT) made public the findings of its task force studying the district's grading policies. The report showed that requirements for passing courses were so low that, in effect, the school board has a policy of "social promotion." The revelations were an "education" for the public and they caused an uproar. The *Cincinnati Enquirer* praised the union in an editorial that said, in part, "The CFT has proved that it is an organization of real education experts. Its conclusions . . . are a big step toward giving Cincinnati the kind of schools it pays for."[11]

Another instance of the effectiveness of a union's public relations role occurred in Oklahoma City in 1983, where the local AFT affiliate conducted a series of public hearings on school discipline. The action so embarrassed the school board that it yielded to public pressure and adopted the teachers' "assertive discipline" program.

Since most of the activity of the current education reform movement sweeping the country is centered in state legislatures and governors' mansions, teachers' political activity will undoubtedly intensify, and their authority, built on the base of collective bargaining, will be a major influence in shaping what our public schools will be like into the twenty-first century.

Setting the Record Straight

For one reason or another some observers of the education scene were quite upset at the idea of teachers sitting down with management and hammering out a collective bargaining agreement. It was undignified, or unprofessional or projected what *Newsweek* once called "an unseemly blue-collar image." More recently a commentator remarked, "... the highly adversarial nature of collective bargaining in public education, including strikes, picketing, and name calling is hardly designed to enhance the reputation or attractiveness of the teaching profession." And when some teachers grew more militant and, in some cases, actually went on strike, a host of critics looked into their crystal balls and saw the imminent downfall of public education done in by hordes of pedagogues brandishing their lethal contracts.

These children of Cassandra saw all sorts of dire consequences flowing from negotiated settlements. For one thing, school administrators, they said, would forever lose the authority they needed to run the schools effectively. Presumably, contractual provisions would turn them all into faculty lackeys. Also, the pundits predicted, school operations and possibly classroom practices would become standardized, written in stone in a decalogue of union rules and regulations. Initiative would be dead. School personnel would become automatons or even worse—factory workers! And perhaps the greatest fear of all was that unions, with their newfound power, would make it impossible to remove incompetent teachers from the classroom. Mr. Ineptitude would run amok in Room 202 in perpetuity.

In reality, nothing of the sort has happened as the result of more than two decades of collective bargaining. In fact, I would like to argue that the process has promoted rather than diminished the quality of professional life in our public schools even on the very issues raised by the critics.

First, let's take the question of administrative authority. There's no doubt that collective bargaining has reduced a good deal of a supervisor's former power. And I assume that there are some old-timers still around lamenting the passing of the good old days, which is another way of saying that many superintendents or principals still fantasize about arbitrarily dismissing teachers they don't like or bouncing them from school to school at whim. One remembers that teachers were once dismissed in New York City for holding "certain views."

In short, the teacher's deep concern for job security and retention rights is an outgrowth of past administrative abuses. And those who think that teachers have far too much protection should at least be historically accurate and not fault teachers' contracts. The fact is that most tenure rules are part of state law and ante-date the advent of collective bargaining. However, negotiated settlements often give added protection by spelling out grievance and appeal procedures. Equally important, the bargaining agent offers the teacher a well-trained, experienced advocate to defend his interests. Often this function is also mandated by state law. That is, the union is legally obliged to defend any member, however culpable.

This raises the question of the extent to which collective bargaining helps maintain incompetents in the teaching profession, thereby putting unions in opposition to the best interests of parents and children. Admittedly, this remains a thorny issue. But we should keep in mind that, by any estimate, we are talking about a very small percentage of the entire teaching staff. I also believe that there is a kind of purging process built into the profession. A bad teacher usually leads a miserable life in the classroom. If a teacher can't control the class, the kids will give him or her all kinds of grief, as only kids can. Therefore, most ineffective teachers throw in the towel on their own. They don't need as much as a hint to leave.

Obviously, there are still some bad apples around, and, yes, their rights to due process are protected by state laws and union contracts. But this does not mean that they are immune from dismissal for just cause. The machinery for dealing with incompetent teachers is in place in every community and has not been compromised by any negotiated settlement. If a poor teacher remains in the classroom, it is more likely the result of his supervisor's inertia and/or ineptitude rather than the protection of the union contract.

But such provisions do have the salutary effect of forcing other supervisors to be more scrupulous in the preparation of their "briefs," more conscientious in "going by the book" lest their cases fall apart because of procedural violations.

One cannot deny that this is often an unwieldy, time-consuming, thankless process. And the truth is that most teachers are as troubled by the situation as are supervisors. Incompetent teachers reflect badly on the profession and their fecklessness usually ends on the back of their colleagues.

To their credit, teachers are in the vanguard of efforts to solve this problem. For example, in Toledo, Ohio, the teachers' union (TFT) has negotiated a problem of peer involvement to aid teachers who are floundering in the classroom. The aim is to strengthen weak teachers and, if necessary, weed out incompetents. An experienced "consulting" teacher is assigned to work with a colleague who's having problems. Help is given on lesson planning, materials development, disciplinary problems, or whatever is needed to improve performance and head off an unsatisfactory rating. If this intervention fails, teachers continue to be involved on the school level in a review process that could lead to dismissal. Inspired by the Toledo plan, the Cincinnati Federation of Teachers and the city board of education have recently negotiated a faculty evaluation system that also uses experienced personnel to train and evaluate beginners.

Though these programs are too new to have produced definitive results, they do show that teachers are prepared to use their negotiating power to attempt to police their profession and maintain high standards.

It would be unfair, of course, to suggest that teachers exclusively bear the burden of reform in this area. We also have to re-evaluate current hiring procedures and supervisory practices that allow incompetents into the classroom in the first place and permit them to remain, often for years, with satisfactory ratings. Intelligent management seeks to prevent problems rather than let them develop until they become insupportable.

Another charge leveled against collective bargaining is that, by instituting rotation and seniority rules, it limits the discretion of administrators in filling desirable positions in the schools, like deans and grade advisors. The obvious answer is that choices are limited to those who are qualified, and there is never a problem about dismissing a person who is not doing the job. What contracts have done generally is eliminate or at least modify the abuses of politics and patronage, elevate the schools' ethical tone, and, by so doing, improve teacher morale. A few years ago, in a letter to the *Phi Delta Kappan*, a teachers' union official described the alternative in Arkansas, where collective bargaining is "considered un-American, undemocratic, and communistic":

A law preventing nepotism was repealed by successful administrator lobbying in 1977, so that nearly half of the staff members in some of the smaller rural schools are composed of pals and relatives of school board members and administrators. It is not a pretty scene educationally or professionally where there is no collective bargaining."[12]

Admittedly, teachers' unions and collective bargaining have made life more complicated for administrators and supervisors. But the complications are just the sort of things that inspire the better executive qualities. Now, for example, the effective principal can no longer rule by fear or intimidation or political patronage. He has to strive, instead, for collegiality with his staff and recognize their partnership in their joint enterprise. This does not mean that hierarchy has been leveled. As Susan Moore Johnson concludes in a recent study of the effects of collective bargaining on the functioning of schools, "Principals even in the strongest union districts retained sufficient formal and informal authority to manage their staffs effectively."[13]

If the collective bargaining process has not fatally diminished the authority of supervisors, it has also not turned teachers, as some critics predicted, into assembly-line workers locked into an automated, inflexible process turning out standardized products. If anything, increased job security and freedom from arbitrary supervisory reprisal have given teachers a greater opportunity to be their own people, to develop methods and materials of instruction more in harmony with their own personalities and the needs of their students. Traditionally, teachers have been on the side of flexibility. Pressures for conformity, for lock-step lesson plans, or for prescribed teaching methods have almost always come from on high. Classroom teachers know better.

Evidence shows that, at the school level, teachers are remarkably flexible regarding the terms of their contract. The general rule, as the Johnson study shows, is that when school administrators are rigid, teachers respond in kind, insisting on the letter of the agreement. But if a principal is reasonable, teachers are likely to work out informal agreements to solve local problems, bending the contract to fit school conditions. Where a good, collegial atmosphere prevails, the teacher's first loyalty is to the welfare of his or her school. Teachers, as Johnson points out, want to be part of a "winning team," and she cites a number of cases where the provisions of the contract took second place to the interests of the schools.

Lessons

In *The Shame of the Cities,* Lincoln Steffens points out that we Americans are inordinately fond of systems. Our dream, he says, is to develop the perfect political order that would run by itself so that we can go about our other business with a good conscience. But, he concludes, even good systems depend on people to make them work. Citizens can't afford to be disassociated from the functioning of government.

The brief history of teacher collective bargaining teaches us a similar lesson. Critics have spoken of the process as a system that is inherently adversarial and destructive, as though all parties were prisoners of an unyielding fate. But the opposite is true. There is simply not just one kind of collective bargaining. Where good will and the spirit of accommodation prevail, effective compromises are made within and beyond the framework of contracts. Principals still do set the tone of their schools. Personalities dominate over systems. Teachers and supervisors still can choose the nature of their relationship and can opt for confrontation or cooperation. The education reform movement sweeping the country will soon force all of us to make weighty, far-reaching choices. The burden of freedom is never light, but it is a burden that the true professional gladly shoulders.

V

The Impact of New Technologies and Techniques

14

RICHARD SIMONDS & JAMES WIEBE

Electronic Technologies and the Learning Process

The recent history of education in the United States has been checkered with "quick fixes" designed to radically improve the quality of instruction. Typically, these new teaching techniques are:

- proposed by an individual or group;

- received with the widespread support of educators;

- implemented without much planning, development research, or considerations of the consequences of the innovation;

- used with varying degrees of success; then

- abandoned.

This is especially true of innovations related to technology. In the recent past we have seen the appearance and disappearance of panaceas such as instructional radio, teaching machines, and classroom response systems. Other instructional technologies, television, and language laboratories are no longer touted as panaceas and continue to have a minor impact on our educational system.

Enter the new technologies—the electronic calculator, video recordings, and the personal computer. Consider, also, the emerging technologies, such as satellite communications, interactive video, voice recognition and synthesis, and robotics. Surely some form of these technologies will be allied to education and training. Finally, we should not forget the broadcast media—so all-pervasive in our society. What impact are they having on our educational standards? Are the hours spent by children in front of the television partly responsible for declining test scores? Will computers in the home and in the schools have an impact on educational standards? On the other hand, if we decide that computers, calculators, video recordings, and television do belong in the classroom, how can we assure that standards are applied to these media so that they are used to their maximum potential?

As sociologist Wilbur Schramm pointed out, it took 500 million years to move from oral to written communications; 5000 years for writing to evolve into printing; 500 years to move from printing to television.[1] In the past fifty years we have seen broadcast television—and video—have a major impact on how we live. In the past fifteen years electronic calculators have made their way into virtually every home. In seven years microcomputers have entered all segments of our society, creating the "computer revolution" that was foreshadowed twenty-five years ago with the advent of mainframes. This acceleration of the acceptance rate for innovations in our society has made it difficult to have standards for their use. It is not easy to develop standards for using innovations in the midst of the change process. Yet, it seems that we must at least attempt to define, implement, and maintain standards, no matter how much or how often we need to change them, or how interactive the process may be.

The discussion that follows considers the impact of technologies on educational standards. It also makes a case for the development of standards relevant to the use of these technologies in our schools and businesses. The technologies considered are television, video, film, electronic calculators, computers, and the techniques of instructional design and development. Some emphasis will be placed on the role of *computers* in education and training.

Television and Education

The issue of television in our society and its impact on education has been hotly debated for years. Some estimates are that the average child spends more time watching television than being in school.[2]

Although many studies involving the impact of broadcast television on children have been completed, the efforts have been neither directed nor orchestrated. The findings, thus, are spotty and inconclusive. For example, research that examined the relationship between the amount of TV viewed and other variables like sharing behaviors have resulted in low or nonsignificant correlations.[3] Other research has shown that children learn from television: the most extensively documented finding of television researchers is that when children watch television aggression, they become more aggressive.[4] Whether or not this aggressiveness has a negative impact on school achievement or discipline, however, has not been determined. Another well-documented finding is that when children witness pro-social themes or behavior, such as altruistic behavior, sharing, and cooperation, those behaviors are increased. These findings have been in short-term behaviors rather that in long-term or transferred situations.[5]

Even though studies have been limited to a few, select programs, there is some evidence that children can learn academic skills from television, although several studies have shown that watching too much of the wrong kind of television can have a negative effect on IQ scores and reading achievement.[6] There is evidence that "Sesame Street" teaches school readiness skills and "Electric Company" teaches reading-related skills when elementary children watch them in school. Results of these studies were rather limited and differences between treatment and control groups were small.[7]

A major problem with research about television learning is the discrepancy between what children *can* learn and what they *do* learn. Programs like the PBS science program, "3-2-1 Contact" have the potential to teach important concepts but are watched by comparatively few children.[8] Comstock concluded that television influences behavior most strongly when it reinforces attitudes of society or when it defines situations for which information is not available from other sources.[9] In addition, research gives evidence that even when a child is viewing television, he may not be processing the information. Often times young children tended to remember noncentral information rather than what was important, while older children remembered the relevant information.[10]

A great deal of research has been conducted about instructional television—television designed to teach. Chu and Schram, after reviewing the research done on instructional television, concluded that children can and do learn from instructional television in the classroom—about the same amount that is learned when the material is presented in more traditional ways. However, they found that variables such as the use of animation, humor, color, etc., had little impact on the amount learned.[11]

A question that educators have asked since television became a dominant force in our society is whether the passive learning provided by television is appropriate for children, especially in the large doses many get from broadcast television. John Dewey, Jean Piaget, and many other educators and learning theorists stress the importance of activity in education: children learn by manipulating their environment, not just by passively observing it.

At present, based on research findings, one cannot categorically say that broadcast television has had a negative impact on standards or achievement in our schools except in instances where children are spending virtually all their free time watching certain types of programs. On the other hand, there may be a link between the highly-produced, visually-rich "entertainment" programming to which children are exposed at home and a perceived need felt by many teachers to entertain while teaching—or entertain instead of teaching.

It has been shown that television *can be* a positive force in education. With a few rare exceptions, however, this positive force is not being used to its potential. Commercial children's television is dominated by the attempt to capture children's attention through action and sound: there is rarely any attempt to educate or train. Virtually no positive, educationally-oriented standards are applied to this type of programming.

In terms of instructional television programs and film, we need to apply rigorous standards to their selection and use. Only programs of solid educational content, free of sexual and racial bias, should be purchased for use in the classroom. More important, once a film or television program has been selected by a school or district, it should be used appropriately. No matter how educationally sound a film is, or how well it has been produced, its value will be untapped if central ideas it presents are beyond the comprehension of the audience or if it repeats materials that have been mastered long ago. Well-produced and educational films like *Donald in Mathemagicland* can be of educational value if shown once to students at the appropriate level. Little educational value is gained when it is shown several times during a year as a time filler, or several years in a row to the same group of students. Teachers need to take the responsibility to assure that film or television programs, from any source, are properly used.

School administrators need to have the courage to set and enforce standards for using instructional films and television programs. In addition, they need to have the courage to allow teachers to show films that do teach and shape and train; that give moral values in a positive direction despite the objections of a vocal handful of opponents. Teacher training institutions need to encourage prospective teachers to address the issue of integrity when using such films and television programs in school.

Calculators and Learning

When pocket-sized electronic calculators first appeared several years ago, many parents and educators expressed fear that their widespread presence would cause a decline in mathematics achievement. The fear was that because of the abundant presence of devices, neither children nor teachers would see the need to master computational skills. Since that time, well over one hundred studies have been completed involving calculators in education. These studies have been virtually unanimous in finding that calculators did not have any adverse effect on achievement, regardless of how they were being used. This included studies where the calculator use was completely integrated into mathematics instruction and used in all computational situations except examinations. Indeed, approximately half the studies found that the presence of calculators in the classroom improved rather than harmed achievement.[12] The types of improved achievement included not only computational skill, but also mathematical understanding and problem-solving creativity.

Uses of Computers in Education

The idea that the computer can and should be used to teach has been with us for more than twenty years. Its potential to accept an answer from a learner, to analyze that answer, and to branch to appropriate instruction has fascinated those who wished to provide individualized, personal instruction—those who felt that the needs of many or most children are not being met in the heterogeneous classroom where many children share one teacher. These computerized instruction enthusiasts envision the use of artificial intelligence to simulate the work of a good teacher working individually with a child. They see computers that understand spoken language, read handwriting, and present ideas through animated or recorded pictures, as well as through written text. But, although computers have been available for many years, these visions are far from reality. The potential impact on education is just starting to be felt. Consider the following: despite dramatic increases in the number of computers available in American schools, on average, there is still less than one computer per 170 students in the fifty largest school districts in the United States.[13] This is hardly enough to make a dent in the way our children are taught and barely enough to make an impact on the way schools are administered and organized, even if computers were used properly in that endeavor. The computers being purchased for use in schools are at the low end in power, memory capacity, and interfacing possibilities (e.g., they do not have built-in capability to tie in with video-discs). Virtually no software is available that can deliver instruction to students in a way that equals, for more than a few minutes, the delivery of a good teacher, and those that come close are very expensive.

When the automobile was first invented, many failed to envision its potential uses in our society and the ways that it would change transportation and our lifestyles. Similarly, early writings about computers in education tend to focus on the potential for emulating the traditional tasks of the teacher—that of delivering instruction, testing, and keeping records. Since the real computer revolution—the personal computer revolution—is so young, it is impossible to determine where it will go. Many of its best current uses were not anticipated just a few years ago, including the generation of music and art, word processing, game playing, and the use of specially-designed programming languages such as LOGO as a tool for learning mathematical concepts and problem-solving strategies.

Given the present level of computer technology, how can computers be used in the classroom? Six possibilities are suggested below.

1. *Computer-Aided-Instruction (CAI)*. In this classroom use of the computer, students use commercially prepared software to learn about specific topics. For example, "Master Type"[14] teaches typing skills to students. Hundreds of other commercially prepared programs are now on the market, designed to teach a wide range of academic topics to students in the classroom or in the home. Although many have questioned the quality of this type of software, good programs are starting to appear.

2. *Computer-Aided-Learning (CAL)*. In this mode, students use the computer as a tool to solve problems. They may write programs in BASIC or LOGO to find the answer to mathematical problems. They may use applications like VisiCalc to help investigate a scientific hypothesis, or they may use "CompuPoem"[15] to help write poems.

3. *Computer-Aided-Testing (CAT)*. Here, the computer is used for diagnostic or achievement testing. With properly developed computerized testing, the frustration experienced by many students at taking tests that have many items they are incapable of doing is minimized. Computerized tests may analyze student input and branch to appropriate items at the student's level. Computerized testing also has the potential to include a variety of stimuli, such as graphics animation or synthesized speech, which are difficult or impossible using paper and pencil tests.

4. *Computer-Managed-Instruction (CMI)*. With CMI, teachers use the computer to help them organize instruction that is delivered in other ways. For example, the computer might keep track of units or objectives that a student has completed, print out worksheets and tests to be completed, grade and correct these materials, and store information about students to be used in future assignments.

5. *Simulations*. Potentially one of the best uses of the computer in education is to give students simulated experiences that would be impossible in real life. In mathematics courses, students can learn to manage household budgets through simulated everyday events and crises, without risking real money or emotions. In social science and business courses, students can practice decision-making skills in political or corporate settings when their age and experience would otherwise never allow it.

6. *Preparation of Instructional Materials*. There are now numerous programs available that allow teachers to store sets of test questions or worksheet items and have the computer print out the appropriate forms. Other programs prepare overhead transparencies, class handouts, and graphics materials for teachers who do not consider themselves artistic.

The few programs mentioned above are representative of the hundreds available. With many companies marketing new programs for use in the schools, and with schools receiving increased budgets for the purchase of computer hardware and software, there is a need to examine our standards in relation to computers in the classroom. We need to ask if the ways teachers are using computers are making the maximum use of this expensive investment. At present, many computers are being placed in classrooms with few controls or guidelines for their use. Some computers are being used for video games (before any research has been completed about the impact of these games), others to teach "programming" for the sake of teaching programming when there is question as to the future of present programming languages. Instruction in programming languages should be oriented toward educational goals beyond simply learning the languages. Some of the computers being placed in schools are being used to deliver instruction with whatever program happens to be available, regardless of quality. This is occurring for several reasons: lack of standards and guidelines in purchasing software; unwillingness to spend money to purchase quality software; and lack of knowledge on the part of teachers regarding what constitutes good courseware. We need to make sure that if teachers are using computers to deliver instruction, the programs have been found by an authoritative group to be of educational value.

States and districts need to become involved in selecting appropriate hardware, in screening software, and in communicating to teachers how and where programs can and should be used. Those entities also need to be thoroughly familiar with software evaluation and with curriculum so that they may guide teachers in the selection and use of computer-aided-instruction.[16]

All teachers should become computer literate. States should require at least one semester of computer literacy, including a survey of computer applications in education for all pre- and in-service teachers. Such courses should include instruction in the use of computers for managing classrooms, the rudiments of programming/problem-solving in a language like LOGO or BASIC, in software evaluation and use, in the use of the computer for managing instruction, and in ethical and equity considerations related to computers in the schools.

Another consideration relevant to computers and educational standards is the increasing use of computers as an alternative source of education. Already, microcomputers are able to deliver supplemental instruction in areas such as mathematics and French at a modest cost in the home. This fact is freeing parents from total dependence on schools. It is a fact that educators would do well to notice.

The Acceptance of Technologies

The record of technology's acceptance in education and training is not good. Some beliefs that have served to inhibit the adoption of technology are that: (1) teaching by any machine violates humanistic principles, (2) courseware (the blending of software and instruction) is of poor quality, and (3) high technology is costly.[17] Any attempt to bring technologies into education or training must contend with these beliefs.

Computer-based-instruction has consistently been found valuable by students, and rated negatively by instructors. The most likely explanation is that it leaves the instructors with an ill-defined role in the education/training process.[18] Innovations that threaten the people who are responsible for their implementation will usually fail. The human component is found time and again to be the most important element in the acceptance of any technology. This is true for the design and development of the technology as well as for the implementation/adoption of it.

Kearsley discusses the decision-making process for selecting and implementing technology-based training and in so doing mentions several key factors that affect adoption.[19] First, the human component is the most important in any electronic technology. The people who design, develop, implement, and evaluate carry a substantial responsibility for the success of a program. Yes, the equipment must work, but the software is a far more important issue. Second, technologies that are used must have a track record. Third, management of technology-based instruction is more important than with teacher-based instruction. The lead times required for development, budgeting, development cycles, and possible organizational changes that may be required to implement a new program require careful management planning. Fourth, the skills of the teaching staff must be equal to the task of implementing the technology-based instruction. And, fifth, the conditions under which delivery or distribution of the program occurs must be considered.

Instructional Design

In the training field, instructional design is often called course design or courseware design. Course design is a far more important issue in the training field than in the education field. In education it is possible to find "off-the-shelf" programs to meet many educational objectives, but in business and industry the objectives are much more specific and unique.

As noted above, instructional technologies bring many benefits to the design of training and education programs. The issues that are having an inhibiting effect on using instructional design in training include:

(1) A lack of trained experts to conduct the instructional design work and often a lack of subject matter experts.

(2) The prohibitive costs of instructional design.

(3) The perception that design time may not be available.

(4) The value of using an instructional design methodology which is just becoming recognized.[20]

One of the benefits of electronic technologies is that they typically allow for learner interaction. When this is the case, it is imperative that the guidelines below be followed:

• control of the program must always reside with the learner. The learner must always be able to choose when to get out of a sequence, to review, to jump up or down a level of difficulty, and to have other options affecting learning.

• responses by the program must always occur when the learner makes any input. This response (feedback) should be timely and appropriate to the learner's activities and level of capability.

• creativity must be built-in to any instructional program. One of the failings of past programmed instruction and some earliest forms of computer-based programs was that they were boring! They lacked spontaneity, humor, variety, and pizazz. Effective instructors use these qualities. So should effective electronic technologies.

• testing and tryouts of any program must be conducted before its release for sale. A recent study found that 80 percent of all educational computer-based training had NOT been tested by even one user![21] It is particularly important that interactive programs be tested thoroughly because there are so many ways in which user interaction could occur.

The software, and in the case of computer-based-instruction the courseware, is far more important than the hardware. It is easier to buy different hardware (and typically less expensive) than it is to write, debug, test, and refine software or courseware.

It is unlikely that educators will create their own software programs because of the amount of time required to design, develop, debug, and test the programs. Depending upon the author's experience with the system and the degree of stability of the course content, each hour of instructional time can require from six hours to 610 hours of development time.[22]

Another concern is that course developers will not move beyond the comparatively simple drill and practice or tutorial methods of programmed instruction and some early computer-based-instruction. There is a richness available in computer-based-instruction with simulations and games, tutorials, and drill and practice if developers use imagination and creativity in planning their programs. This concern was noted in our comments on instructional design. By conducting good instructional design and by testing prototype materials with real users, the possibilities exist for developing entertaining, motivating, and powerful methods of instruction. Crunching them out quickly to get into the market will only replicate the same kinds of dull, mindless, and boring programs that killed programmed instruction in the 1960s.

Implementation and Evaluation of Electronic Technologies

It would seem that any well-designed instructional program would include plans for its implementation. Yet, there are numerous examples where hardware has been purchased and programs have been developed, sometimes at considerable cost, only to have these investments sit idle. It is more obvious with instructional technologies than with lecture courses. With instructional technologies the result is a tangible product with a known development cost—a condition not usually known with lecture courses.

Given the critical examination to which technologies are subjected—far more critical than is typically given to lecture-based, instructor-led forms of instruction—it is important that evaluation be given a very high ranking in the planning for any use of technology-based instruction.

Evaluation should consist of an assessment of the quality of the program, its effect on learning, and any tools it includes for the management of the instructional enterprise. Continual review of the impact on learning, whether delivered by technology or instructor, needs to be built into programs. In addition, cost and its corresponding benefit will need to be considered.

Standards and Technology in Education

In our rapidly changing society, we need to make sure that our standards are in line with the skills our children will need in later life. In mathematics, for example, curriculum and tests should not stress antiquated skills such as dividing six-digit numbers by three-digit numbers by hand or using the square-root algorithm when research indicates that children have a difficult time mastering this process (indeed, many never do) and when we have calculators for this type of task.[23] Although computational skills are important, they are only a part of the total mathematics curriculum. Rather than focusing on computational skills mathematics instruction should stress fundamental mathematics principles (the foundation on which problem-solving skills, mental arithmetic, calculator computation, the use of the computer, and pencil and paper computation are based). Pencil and paper computations should not be abandoned because there will be times when technological devices are not available. However, instruction in computation should stress short, easy-to-remember procedures and mental arithmetic. Mathematics instruction should also focus on applying mathematics and solving problems. Further, our standards in mathematics should include competence in the use of calculators and computers for solving everyday problems and in the mathematical skills relevant to our technological world.[24]

Beyond the skills our students will need for their adult personal lives, we need to train technicians, engineers, and managers for our technological society. In order to compete on an international level, we must produce individuals who have an understanding of mathematical, scientific, and technological principles. From the perspective of future workers, many of those who do not have scientific and technological understandings and skills will be relegated to low-paying, low-prestige, and uninteresting jobs—if they can find work at all. In addition, we need to help people understand the technologies that permeate our society. Many business owners and managers have made bad investments in technology or have not known how to use those investments to maximum potential because of their lack of knowledge and understanding of computers. Those who do not understand the new technologies will be unable to use them to their advantage and will be at the mercy of those who are.

When improving our standards in education with regard to science, mathematics, and technology, we should not ignore the other aspects of education. Many managers complain that the technologically-trained people they hire are deficient in communication skills and the general knowledge needed to be of value to the company. Many companies have had to establish basic skills training to compensate for deficiencies in writing, communicating, and human relations. Computers have not lessened the need for people who can communicate verbally and in writing.

In addition, computers and other new communications technologies are creating an increased need for people who understand other cultures and who speak languages other than English. If we smugly refuse to learn foreign languages and cultures, our worldwide markets will continue to be lost to countries with more diverse and sophisticated educational systems. Our increased standards should include foreign language training and cultural awareness beginning in the elementary grades. Here electronic teaching devices can be very helpful.

The Promise of Electronic Technologies

One of the major challenges facing educators is how to create programs that meet the diverse learning styles of students in heterogeneous classrooms. Electronic technologies offer at least one answer. It has been predicted that programs soon will be available that can be tailored to preferred learning styles (e.g., visually rich, aurally stimulating, in didactic or game format) so that even the most reluctant learner will be motivated.[25] It is reasonable to hope and expect that private enterprise will become involved in offering children computer-based-instruction for use after school. Imagine a McDonald's-type franchise in shopping malls that provides instruction in any area the student or parent wishes. These centers will not require huge outlays for paying trained teachers, only the initial outlay for equipment and software, and small amounts for maintenance. Public schools will be forced to cope with this challenge. No longer will they be able to ignore whole groups of bored, unmotivated students, or students who are not learning. Schools will fear losing students to programs that better satisfy their needs.

The recent advances in artificial intelligence and robotics have the potential for making an impact on education, especially in the area of computer-aided-instruction. Typically, however, computers or other innovations are adopted and utilized in business and industry first. Much later, educators begin to look for their uses in the classroom. Let us hope that the potential of the current and future technologies will not be bypassed because of a stubborn and short-sighted educational establishment.

Possible Future Development

One of the most exciting possibilities of electronic technologies (and especially computer-based-instruction) will be in helping students to "learn how to learn." In the field of education we spend nearly all of our time teaching "content" and precious little giving students the skills to become self-sufficient with their own learning processes.

The basic skills needed for learning are reading, writing, speaking, listening, studying techniques, memorization, organization, problem-solving, decision-making, and conceptualization. By providing these skills we can develop lifelong learners: "when I give you a fish I feed you for a meal, but when I teach you how to fish I feed you for a lifetime."

Electronic technologies, such as interactive videodisc, simulations and games (used with computers and as separate printed materials), and computer-based-instruction offer a new possibility that these basic skills can be taught effectively. The drill and practice needed in some areas as well as the tutorials can be handled easily by electronic technologies.

This methodology would free teachers to work with learners in one-on-one situations. On the other hand, nearly fifteen years ago we talked about using technologies to do basic instruction and having teachers become "facilitators of learning." That has not occurred! Perhaps it gets back to the fundamental point made earlier in this chapter that the human elements of any instructional setting must be considered. Just having the technology does not mean it will be implemented. When instructors find that a technology will help them to do their job without threatening them, we will see the implementation of electronic technologies in education and training.

Conclusions

From some of the concerns expressed earlier in this chapter, the reader might assume that the authors are against the use of electronic technologies in education and training. Nothing could be further from the truth. However, we are concerned with the number of times that technologies have been poorly planned, haphazardly implemented, and weakly evaluated, leaving a feeling that "those technologies are no good!" In fact, our criticism of that situation is that the new technologies are most often *very* capable of meeting the needs of students, but human resistance to utilize them optimally has given all technologies a bad name. So, our concerns actually come from a belief in the promise of electronic technologies and from a realization that if we are to get beyond the *promise,* the principles of instructional design and implementation must be followed. Instructional standards must both exist and be rigorously applied.

There is a confluence of capabilities that puts us closer to the critical mass that will make it possible for electronic technologies to play an important role in education and training. The key element is the human element. If we choose to participate in these capabilities and to become more effective as instructors, by helping our learners in the most powerful human way, i.e., one-on-one tutoring and interactive responding, then the electronic technologies can help us to succeed. Will we rigorously develop and apply standards for the use of electronic technologies in the learning process? That is the question.

15

GEORGE BUGLIARELLO

Educational Standards and the Technological University

A fundamental question for education has been that of the proper balance between looking at the past and anticipating the future. How much weight, that is, should be given to historical knowledge and the values and standards derived from it, versus the weight to be afforded to future-oriented knowledge, which by necessity can only partially be based on experience, and be certifiable through standards? The intrinsic tension between change and stability is being exacerbated today throughout our educational system by a rapidly shifting social and technological environment, and by the demands for quality control in education.

Of all institutions involved in education, the technological university is probably the one in which the tension between change and standards is most pervasive and presents both the most immediate dilemmas and the greatest opportunities for creativity. The ethos of the technological university is manifest by its strong focus on science and technology. This strongly differenti-

ates the technological university from the general one in which
science and technology are but two of many thrusts.

The technological university represents a coexistence of education for values and for know-how. Thus, the tension between
change and standards has a direct impact not only on its liberal
arts program but also, and most urgently, on its professional
curricula.

In formalized technological education—the kind provided, for
instance, by engineering schools—the balance between change
and standards tends to tip towards standards. This is why it remains so difficult to move away from traditional curricula such as
electrical engineering, mechanical engineering, or civil engineering, which reflect the *Weltanschauung* of the end of the last century and early this century. The achievement of a more effective
basis for dealing with the technological needs of the next century
would suggest their replacement with new, more fundamental
curricula centered around concepts such as information, materials, or energy.

Engineering education, which is at the core of the technological
university, is more directly affected by declines in educational
standards in the high school than other kinds of major professional education. Whereas law and medicine build on four years
of college, engineering builds directly on high school education. In
its four-year undergraduate curricula, it must remedy deficiencies
of that education (increasingly glaring not only in mathematics
and the sciences, but also in the liberal arts), provide additional
college-level education in the liberal arts, give a sufficient foundation in mathematics and the sciences, and achieve an adequate
level of professional education to enable its graduates to perform
as engineers. Thus, the weaker the educational attainment in the
high school, the greater the burdens on engineering education, in
a four-year curriculum that, even under the best conditions of
high school preparation, faces the ever more difficult challenge of
preparing for the growing complexity of technology.

Sociologically, the engineering curricula in the United States
have performed the unique function of transforming in four years
bright high school graduates from usually modest socioeconomic
backgrounds, coming from the farms or the great immigration
waves into the cities, into professionals with substantial immedi-

ate earning capacity. For this reason any attempts to lengthen engineering curricula or to transform them into graduate ones, like medicine or law, have been unsuccessful.

Although a well-articulated and successful system of graduate education for engineering complements the undergraduate curriculum by providing the necessary depth for specialization and research, the pressures of a credential-oriented society are placing increasing strains on its flexibility.

Tension between professional knowledge and teaching content and methods is being heightened. That tension occurs in all professional fields, as the extremely rapid rate of change of professional knowledge makes it difficult for the educational system to respond. As a result, frequently the subject matter and teaching methods in the educational systems are obsolete in comparison to what is being practiced in the field. Quite simply, in a professional school those teachers who do not practice at the forefront of their profession can only provide somewhat obsolete knowledge. Even the process of writing books has a time constant such that when a book appears in a cutting edge technological or professional subject, it tends *ipso facto* to be obsolete.

The tension between liberal and professional education, the latter primarily technological education, is being exacerbated. Typically, students engaged in technological institutions are characterized by lower verbal scores and operate in an environment in which the engineering faculty, like most other professional faculties, does not exhibit a strong interest in emphasizing the humanities. This leads to a tension that should be of increasing concern because of its implications for the whole question of societal understanding and control of technology.

Direct learning by a student without enrollment in institutions—and therefore without necessarily the need to satisfy certain standards—is beginning to be a significant factor in education. Such learning has always been possible in one way or another, through reading or attendance at lectures, etc., but now can be greatly enhanced by telecommunications and information technology.

Need and convenience are leading many large employers to establish substantial in-house training efforts for their employees. These efforts have become a very major component of the U.S.

post-secondary and, often, post-graduate educational system, with which the formal educational system has not yet fully come to terms. A number of colleges and universitites may feel threatened by the rapid growth of such a large and potentially competing educational system, and yet they have done very little to develop an intelligent strategic plan for collaboration and integration with that system. In the absence of such a plan, the formal educational system often finds itself under what it feels to be severe pressure to modify its standards to provide credit for industry in-house programs.

Standards for the Future

There will continue to be a need for effective educational standards, because without standards it becomes impossible to build in a realistic and effective way the complex system for imparting and transmitting knowledge, skills, and values that must guide us into the next century. To achieve this goal it becomes imperative for the technological university to address the specific issues and factors of tension just outlined.

Given the tendency that the balance between change and standards tips towards standards, the standards, particularly in professional education (the domain of the technological university), will have to be far more flexible than is the case today. *There needs to be planned,* in effect, a *constant change of standards.* There also needs to be developed the ability to integrate subjects around emerging new themes, such as information, energy, or sociotechnology, in order to counteract the growing compartmentalization of knowledge. This disaggregation results today more from the dynamics of standards and the sociology of educational institutions, as well as professional societies, than from a response to what our society will increasingly demand from the people it educates. Furthermore, the quest for flexibility leads inevitably to greater emphasis on performance standards rather than on standards rigidly prescribing courses and curricula. Performance standards make it possible, for example, to accept and to certify the educational achievements of students learning directly from a network.

The engineering accreditation process will need to move from today's primary focus on minimal standards—important as they are—to one on standards oriented toward the future, to force a greater pace of innovation. (It should be a matter of concern, for instance, that many engineering schools have not participated in the genetic engineering revolution.) The accreditation agencies, the engineering schools, and the engineering profession will need great courage to cut the many Gordian knots that make it appear so difficult today to move to a new approach.

The tension between professional knowledge and teaching content in a period of rapid change is probably best resolved through heightened standards of performance for teachers. To enhance teaching performance, the technological university must insist that its faculty be involved at the cutting edge of research or professional experiences.

Better integration of professional and liberal arts education must be a key goal in engineering education. Given the stringent time constraints of the undergraduate engineering curricula, it can be achieved only by a determined effort to factor, in teaching and in the assessment of performance of technical subjects, a consideration of the relations between such a subject and pertinent historical, philosophical, and sociological factors. This interdisciplinary approach is needed, rather than merely adding to a traditional engineering curriculum a sprinking of liberal arts courses. The integration should not be limited to the undergraduate level, but should extend, with greater depth, to graduate courses as well. Clearly, better integration is not achievable without commitment by faculty members across the board and a major effort by institutions for its support.

A set of flexible, performance-oriented standards needs to be established for in-house training by employers, to open to their employees greater options for training at the university. This would also lead to a better integrated national training system involving employers and universities. Such a system requires that the university be more open to recognizing and utilizing in-house educational experiences at the place of employment. We must also facilitate the combination of teaching and research duties at the university and cooperate with industry research or related tasks useful to the latter. Such collaboration becomes increasingly essential in order to remedy the paucity of new faculty members in selected disciplines. At the same time, industry should endeavor to enhance the interaction between its research efforts and the university pursuing longer-range objectives (pure research for research's sake), and should adopt more liberal policies to encourage and support a greater number of its employees to do graduate work at the university beyond the master's level.

Achievement of more balanced educational standards to prepare the whole man, rather than just the technical knowledge expert, is undoubtedly the most profound challenge. At present, no such standards exist or are being proposed to assure society that its engineers have not only the knowledge but also the fortitude to do what is right rather than merely what is required of them. The very establishment of such standards, difficult as they may be to articulate, prepare for, and uphold, would be a major act of courage by a university. It would demand value judgments, substantial curricula modification, and the willingness to abandon reliance on the acquisition of knowledge and professional skills as the only touchstone of professional education. Thus, we must pay far more attention to the intangibles of education than has been the case to date. The holistic impact of education cannot be obtained unless the whole array of new educational technologies is complemented by a determined emphasis on values and character building. To reinforce an earlier point, the electronic classroom and other new technology-based teaching media need to be designed to encourage three-way interactions among students, teachers, and other members of the community who have relevant feelings, values, knowledge, and experiences to contribute to the educational process. Indeed, any discussion of academic standards and of the actions needed to strengthen education—technological or any other kind—would be futile without stressing this broader context of the educational mission.

In this context we must stress the effects of scientific research and its engineered applications on our ecosystem in general and our population in particular. While recognizing the contributions of innovative technology to our standard of living, scientists and engineers must anticipate the often harmful by-products of their handiwork. The technological pioneers of tomorrow must learn to prevent harmful phenomena rather than seek cures for a condition long after it has severely damaged vitally important natural and human resources. Only if it succeeds in responding to these crucial pragmatic needs of the community can the technological university hope to acquire the credibility that would cause the community to lift its sights and support with this vision the conscious building of our future.

Toward a Technology of Flexibility

There are at least three key aspects for the technological university to consider in order to design into our technology the flexibility we need for the future.

The first is to focus on alternate technological designs using the inspiration of biology. The creation of living systems follows an approach radically different from a technological design. It yields an immense variety of designs, characterized not only by self-adaptiveness and a very sparing use of natural resources in their realization but also by two other most significant factors of flexibility: the acceptance of imperfections and the mass production of individuality. Both of these characteristics need to be viewed not as an involution but as an evolution, indeed a revolution, in our ability to design flexibly.

A second aspect is the need to focus on sociotechnology to further enhance our range of possibilities. Sociotechnology is the still embryonic discipline concerned with improving the interaction between technological systems and other kinds of social systems or, more generally, the interactions among all sorts of social systems. Since social systems are ensembles of biological entities of human beings we must master the ability to decide when something could be done through social organizations or processes, or done technologically, or even biologically.

Third, we need to focus on the potential offered by a sharper conceptual distinction in technological designs between structure and components because their separation offers us a practical chance of mass producing individuality. The example of biological organisms is quite significant, with their immense differences built out of assemblies of cells having remarkable commonalities.

In brief, we need to rethink the philosophy and curricula of the technological university and establish new, far more flexible professional standards for technological education.

VI

Special Problems

16

GLENN DUMKE

A Ministry of Education for the United States? The Problem of Accreditation

The question of maintaining standards and holding both lower and higher educational institutions to them has been a continuing problem with all modern societies. In most parts of the world, the job has been assumed by government, both through direct controls and the process of licensure, and in many countries this supervision has been assigned to a cabinet post, either a ministry of education or a ministry of culture. In the United States, which is unique educationally in several respects, this task has been assumed by a voluntary procedure, that of accreditation.

What is accreditation? At the higher education level it is a procedure organized by colleges and universities, whereby they hold
themselves to minimal standards and in the process engage in
mutual self-help activities. In secondary education the process is
equally formalized in many areas. In California, as an example, a
kind of accreditation was achieved very early by having the
University of California keep lists of high schools in the state and
comparative records of student accomplishment. More recently
the Western Association of Schools and Colleges (WASC) has
developed a careful and thorough process of accreditation for secondary schools. In Los Angeles, for example, twenty-eight of the
forty-nine senior high schools in the district are involved in accreditation each year. In groups of seven, one group is having a
visitation by the WASC committee, another is preparing for the
visit the following year through much committee activity, another
group is preparing a three-year followup report, and a fourth
group is preparing for its next year's followup. Preparing for a
WASC visit is a lengthy and complex process, and the report of the
accrediting commission is taken seriously and suggestions are
carefully implemented. Private schools, and public too, for that
matter, have in addition depended on membership in institutional
associations to present to the public some assurance of educational quality.

Higher educational accreditation is organized in two main
parts: six regional associations (New England, Middle States,
Southern, North Central, Northwest, and Western) that devote
themselves to accrediting the entire institution and its degree programs, and a large number, continually increasing, of professional
associations devoted to approving curricula in certain specialized
fields, such as chemistry, music, etc. College and university presidents willingly support the accreditation process insofar as it attempts to control the number of professional and specialized
accrediting bodies. But their reluctance to strengthen accreditation as a whole works against this goal.

The regional associations now have developed in some cases
accrediting commissions to review public school standards,
although this process has not moved as far as similar efforts at the
higher education level because of the strength of local control in
K-12.

If the present enthusiasm for reform in education is to bear permanent fruit, some attention must be paid to the accreditation process, which is not, at present, doing the job it should be doing. And because educational bureaucrats, like Nature, abhor a vacuum, if accreditation does not rise to its responsibility within the foreseeable future, government will move in. This has already begun. When that happens, sooner or later the United States will emulate most other countries and establish a ministry of education that will end forever the voluntarism that has characterized American education for many years. One of the paradoxes of the situation is that college and university presidents, staunchly defending "local autonomy" against the inroads of the accreditation process and keeping that process weak in so doing, are by that very act inviting government takeover. As resentful as they are of tightened accreditation standards, their resentment will be as nothing to their feelings when licensure replaces accreditation, federal standards replace the voluntary ones now in existence, and state commissions move into control of curriculum.

Problems of Accreditation

One of the chief problems of accreditation is the manner in which it has defined itself. In the regionals an institution is deemed to be accredited if it lives up to its own statement of mission and purpose. This presents a serious problem, because many weaker institutions have statements of mission and purpose that are, to put it mildly, so loose as to be worthless. Yet if a college or university states that its mission is to offer educational opportunity to all persons, no matter what their intellectual abilities, and to offer degree credit for "life experience," however defined, there is no way in which an accrediting association can legitimately deny them the accolade on that basis.

Richard Millard, in his excellent article on accreditation, insists that "Accreditation does not determine institutional or program quality," and he also, in a carefully reasoned statement, strongly defends the principle of judging an institution on its own declaration of mission and purpose.[1] He accepts the stipulation that such a statement must be clear and appropriate, but how to determine clarity and appropriateness is left to the various associations and their committees. There is certainly an argument for this point of view, for rigidity of demand could lead to unrealistic standards for certain institutions, and might well overemphasize quantitative rather than qualitative criteria. But reliance upon "achievement in kind," as Millard expresses it, has led to lessening of rigor and demand and to amorphous and inconsistent decisions by accrediting bodies. Certainly the university's or college's own goals and objectives must be considered, and seriously, but evaluation of the declaration of mission and purpose should also be a responsibility of the accrediting team.

Another problem of the accreditation process is the way it is financed. Regional associations depend on institutional dues for their support. Professional and specialized accrediting groups depend on both departmental and individual dues for sustenance. Regional accrediting commissions therefore find it difficult to be too hard-nosed about enforcement of the rules. As long as their policies do not offend the majority of dues-paying members, they can afford to be occasionally rigorous with a lone campus, but if their policies begin to work against the interests and comfort of the majority, then their own boards, composed of representatives of the institutions themselves, will object and change the approach. As a result, regionals find it quite difficult to discredit, or fail to credit, an institution that has gone through the motions of following a set of none-too-difficult regulations.

Professional associations have a less troublesome task. Members of a profession, whether it is chemistry or art, are consciously or subconsciously aware that the more people who enter their profession or discipline, the more competition they will face as individual practitioners. There is consequently an inherent urge on the part of members of professional associations to keep entrance requirements rather high. This tendency, to keep requirements rigorous, often clashes with campus positions and attitudes. A president of a small college, trying to run a particular department with only two Ph.D.'s, facing an accrediting association that says it will not accredit his department unless it has three Ph.D.'s, obviously wishes some pressure could be put upon the accrediting association to change its rules. Periodically, professional accrediting groups, in response either to an oversupply of practitioners or a desire to upgrade their occupation, will establish extremely rigorous, and often unrealistic, requirements. This has a dual result, that of reducing the number of graduates in the field, and raising a hue and cry on the part of harried administrators. The two years of graduate work requirement for social case workers was an example of this problem, as was the stern insistence by the American Association of the Collegiate Schools of Business (AACSB) on a minimal number of higher academic degrees in a department.

These problems—having to do with professional accrediting groups—led, in 1949, to the establishment of the National Commission on Accrediting (NCA), a watchdog organization promulgated by college and university administrators for the purpose of accrediting the professional accrediting groups. The NCA admirably served this purpose, by establishing a system whereby professional and disciplinary accrediting organizations would not be recognized unless they were first approved by the NCA, which then published a list of recognized professional accrediting bodies. The NCA had the full support of college and university administrators, who constantly urged it to keep the number of recognized professional associations limited. The NCA was later merged with the association of the regionals to form the Council on Postsecondary Accreditation (COPA), about which more later.

The problem of the regionals is lack of ability to enforce rigorous standards; the problem of the specialized is that they are in a state of constant tension with campus administrators.

A further problem of accreditation is the myth of "autonomy." For some reason, not easily explained except through historical development, colleges and universities in the United States have a strong fixation that they are autonomous units in our society, and that external controls of whatever nature, are anathema. This attitude is the more paradoxical when it is held by public institutions depending for their subsistence on local taxpayers or state legislators. To the credit of American government, it can be said that political interference with universities or schools is an exceptional phenomenon, although control of financial management is quite common. Academic freedom, of course, is the catchword that is constantly resorted to when such intrusion, or supposed intrusion, occurs. Presidents can make many brownie points with faculties by staunchly defying state regulations or systemwide bureaucracies.

Gradually, in the second half of the twentieth century, the notion became common that faculties were the controlling influence in higher educational operation, and that the faculty of a college or university was supreme in establishing admission requirements, grading standards, graduation requirements, and even the mission of the institution. This concept, of course, ignored much of higher education's history, with its emphasis upon church, sectarian, individual, and governmental leadership in forming and molding the educational system of the United States. Horace Mann, John Dewey, the Protestant and Catholic churches, President Eliot of Harvard, and the Morrill Act had as much to do with the development of American higher education as faculties. But the myth persists, and obviously it has an effect on accreditation by warning the accreditors they can go so far and no farther without intruding upon the sacred cow of "autonomy."

A few years ago I chaired a task force of the American Association of State Colleges and Universities, which attempted to bring about some agreement among the institutional members as to requirements for the A.B. degree. This project so disturbed many college and university presidents that at the annual meeting secret caucuses were held prior to the task force presentation, and a structured negative vote precluded much debate. One president of a small southern college said, "We cannot by any means have a tighter English requirement. Why, much of our enrollment is frankly illiterate!" The myth of campus autonomy carried the day.

It must be added, however, that in early 1985 the Association of American Colleges published the results of a study which strongly recommended that colleges and universities come to some agreement as to the content of the baccalaureate degree. The attention given this study by the media is evidence that perhaps resistance to this concept is diminishing.

A major problem of accreditation is the inability of educators to agree on basic requirements for the bachelor's degree. The argument supporting this type of intellectual anarchy is, of course, "academic freedom," and local autonomy. A faculty, according to this argument, should be able to define its own degree requirements. But what of society at large? What of employers who assume that a bachelor's degree should mean *something* in terms of ability to speak and write the English language, handle basic mathematics, and possess some degree of competence in the field of the graduate's major? Unfortunately, there are some colleges and universities where not all of these assurances are provided, and in addition, grade inflation, a curse of the campus revolution of a decade ago, still persists and renders many academic evaluations of little value. The rapid growth of training programs in industry to make up for these shortfalls is proof that academe needs some better method of defining its product.

No one expects colleges and universities to have exactly the same requirements for the bachelor's degree, but it is reasonable to assume that such a degree does guarantee that the graduate possesses certain basic skills and abilities that are commonly associated with being an "educated person." The lack of such assurance, coupled with grade inflation, has destroyed in large part the confidence by employers and graduate deans in the output of many institutions of higher education. That lack of confidence will lead eventually to government intervention, particularly with those institutions receiving considerable federal and state assistance.

One problem of accreditation that is being increasingly addressed by the accrediting groups themselves is the qualifications of visiting team members. The accrediting process involves several steps: decision by the accrediting agency as to the acceptability of the applying institution; a careful institutional self-study (which in many cases is the most helpful outcome of the entire process); a visit by a "team" appointed by the accrediting agency and ordinarily including individuals in fields in which the institution specializes; a report by the team; consideration and decision by the agency's board; and, if necessary, an appeals process.

It is highly necessary to have visiting team members go through an orientation program. One of the persistent characteristics of an accrediting visit is that on almost all campuses, dissidents, complainers, and critics of the administration quickly flock around visiting team members to provide them with a warped view of the institution. Unless a team member is warned of this process and is experienced enough to remain uninfluenced by it, serious errors may be made in the team's report and the agency's final decision. And this is only one of the difficulties that occur. Careful training of team members is an absolute essential if fair and impartial judgments are to be made and if serious harm to the institution is to be avoided. Even with the utmost care, errors are frequent, and reputations and institutional viability can both be seriously damaged by inept team reportage.

Alternatives to Voluntary Accreditation

Despite the network of organizations and agencies devoted to carrying out voluntary professional accreditation, and despite its many good aspects and successes, the process is under constant and serious criticism. Presidents and chancellors resent any erosion of "local autonomy." Institutions like the University of California at Berkeley, long the flagship of that university system, are arrogant as a result of perennial superiority and practically ignore the accreditation process. Such elite institutions condescendingly go through the required motions sketchily and with evident lack of interest and concern; this is also true of certain members of the Ivy League, traditional aristocrats of the educational scene, who are so proud of their status that they consider an accreditation visit and evaluation to be presumptuous in the extreme. And yet it is true that even the best of universities have weak departments, and the pattern of strength and weakness varies periodically with the cycling in and out of strong and weak faculty. But the attitude of the aristocrats and of strong presidents toward the accreditation process does nothing to strengthen it in the eyes of its critics.

Its critics are numerous. The federal government, faced with the responsibility of allocating large federal funds to qualifying institutions, is and has been reluctant to depend on the voluntary accrediting process as a basis for its decisions. In the Department of Education (DOE), currently with a Secretary who is frankly supportive of voluntary professional accreditation, the Division of Accreditation and Eligibility still clings tightly to its role of publishing annual lists of institutions that qualify for government largesse. This involvement of the federal government began with the passage of the original G.I. Bill in 1944, which because it had no procedure for distinguishing good from bad institutions, fell into mistaken judgments that aroused much criticism. Another reason for Washington's interest is that federal financing is available to certain types of institutions that are not included in the traditional "higher education" category, which has been the emphasis of the regional associations. Some "proprietary" or commercial type schools are included in the federal government's list, and some members of this category have only recently and grudgingly been admitted to the regional accreditation process.

At a recent meeting of the Advisory Committee for Accreditation and Eligibility of the DOE, a motion was made to the effect that the federal government should limit its listing of at least those institutions within the accepted categories of the regional associations to those accredited by the voluntary process, and that it should abandon its own accrediting procedures in that area. The motion was not enthusiastically supported, but it did occasion considerable heated debate. Meanwhile, the role of the Advisory Committee was moved down three levels of the bureaucracy, so that its counsel to the Secretary will have to be undertaken from a considerable distance.

And yet the officials in charge of the Division in the DOE cannot be faulted entirely, because respect for the regional accrediting process had diminished to the extent that it is often called a mere "mutual backscratching operation." Federal officials must be satisfied in their own minds that quality controls are sufficient to warrant the expenditure of large federal funds. A few years ago a director of the Division openly and aggressively engaged in empire building, which caused the regionals to be suspicious and cautious though current leadership in the DOE and the relevant Division has been excellent and statesmanlike.

There is somewhat of a "Catch-22" aspect to the relationship between the regionals and the Division. Weakness of the regionals has encouraged the Division to assume added responsibility and to defend with some stubbornness its operations. The fact that this situation exists, and that the federal lists are sometimes utilized by institutions that cannot achieve regional accreditation, has led to further weakening of voluntary accreditation and the authority of the regionals.

However, federal involvement in the accreditation process is not the only alternative approach being undertaken. State governments now are becoming increasingly concerned, and several states have already established bureaus or commissions to monitor educational "quality" in public colleges and universities. Even where such commissions do not exist, as in California, the legislature, through its budget process, is exerting similar controls. "Budget language" in California jargon means footnoted statements in state university budgets saying, in effect, "You can have these dollars, but you must spend them in a certain way." This is curriculum control with a vengeance, and although one would like to describe it as a cloud no larger than a man's hand, the cloud is considerably larger already. There have been two attempts made by California legislators to, in effect, "outlaw" voluntary accreditation and substitute state licensure for it. These were presented as bills and went through at least part of the regular legislative process before being killed. But a possible third bill, which may well come out of the woodwork, influenced by current agitation for reform, might well pass. Government control of education is moving ever closer.

Finally, during the administration of President Carter, and at the strong behest of the National Education Association (NEA), a Department of Education was established at the cabinet level. Educators were seriously divided on this issue. Many public school people, representing K–12, understandably favored such a development. Even many university level officials supported the idea, feeling that education needed a platform closer to the President. But there were those who had serious reservations. Eighteen of the nineteen presidents of the California State University system, plus the Chancellor, opposed the idea, on the basis that government intrusion into educational decisions had already gone far enough. Some saw clearly that the establishment of the Department was a massive step closer to a ministry of education and a European pattern of educational management. The possible appointment of an empire-building Secretary at some time in the future would guarantee rapid progress toward federal control of education in the United States.

What would be wrong with federal control? The NEA certainly thinks it would be acceptable, and those who join it in feeling that massive federal funding is an inevitable necessity for education have few qualms about it. There are, however, several aspects of federal control that raise serious questions.

One is the possible abandonment of a long-standing American

tradition—that of local control of education. In a country as large as the United States, conditions differ from region to region, and state to state. To have a curriculum appropriate for mountain regions of the deep South, or for the bilingual culture of the Southwest would be inappropriate for the vastly different problems of inner-city schools in major eastern metropoles. There is reason for localism in educational management in the United States. We would abandon it at our peril.

Another problem of federal control is the possibility of having tightly centralized requirements that would reflect the positions of pressure groups. The French centralized examination system is an example. In a pluralistic society, there must also be some pluralism in educational requirements.

This nation has also been continuously proud of the existence of public and private institutions side by side—another evidence of pluralism. A ministry of education would necessarily depend for its authority on the number of federal dollars spent on the schools and colleges it must supervise. Private education, both K–12 and at the collegiate level, would diminish in importance and might vanish altogether.

Finally, the worst possibility is that education might become politicized and operated at the whim of the party in power. This admittedly seems far-fetched in a country like the United States, but it has happened in countries like Germany that have in the past been very proud of the independence of their educational systems. There has recently been in America great concern exhibited over the possibility that religion might influence education through the agitation over school prayers. This danger, if it is one, would be no greater than the danger of having politics influence education. In fact religion, over the centuries, has been a fairly constructive force in education, from the monasteries of the Middle Ages to the small private church-related colleges of middle America, but politics in education, from Hitlerian controls to Soviet domination of the social sciences, has been mostly bad.

Ministries of education are, however, almost universal in other parts of the world. In West Germany the rector is the ceremonial head, usually (and always in former years) chosen from senior and respected members of the faculty, but the actual management and financial control lies in the hands of a faceless bureaucrat who runs the university from behind the scenes. In France the control is much more open and direct, while in communist and other police states a ministry of education or culture has absolute control over schools, colleges, curricula, personnel, and research. Britain has, as usual, adopted a moderate approach, halfway between direct control and decentralization, in the University Grants Commission. But dependence of British education upon government funds has the authority leaning in the direction of government.

State control has the same drawbacks, and some are even greater and have the possibility of even larger negatives than federal direction. There was a period, several years ago, when government contracts to the aerospace industry in California were sharply diminished, and engineers previously in strong demand were a glut on the employment market and many were walking the streets. The legislature responded by putting pressure upon colleges and universities to abandon their engineering programs. Fortunately this did not happen, because killing a program with tenured professors is not a short-term proposition, and within two years engineers were again in short supply and everyone was glad that the programs had not been abandoned. The same thing happened with regard to teacher education. There was a serious oversupply of teachers in the late seventies and early eighties in view of demographic projections of declining enrollments, and again legislators and other state authorities demanded that schools of education be closed or curtailed. At this writing the demand is up again, and once more there is a sense of relief that the political pressure had little result.

More serious is the possibility of state erosion of academic standards. A few years ago one state assemblyman in California, responding to pressure from ethnic minorities in his home district, called a public hearing to put the president of the local state college on the defensive because he was insisting on rigorous academic standards for his relatively new institution. His argument, that it was most unfair to educationally disadvantaged students to tell them that they were qualified to compete in a competitive society when they actually were not, had little persuasive effect. But, again fortunately, the president and the college were able, with some difficulty, to retain their creditable academic standards.

These narrow escapes by the California educational system are increasing in number, and only because there is no state bureau or ministry with legal authority have serious mistakes been avoided. But a state bureau set up to monitor educational affairs, with authority to enforce, and subject to the whims of a nearby legislature, would inevitably create serious problems.

The reason for such detailing of dangers inherent in government control of education, both federal and state, is that the major shield and buckler that currently defends against it is the voluntary accreditation process. The most telling argument in favor of government intrusion into the educational scene is that the educators themselves are not capable of effective quality controls, and the most evident existing quality control mechanism is accreditation. But if accreditation, as it is currently interpreted, does not, in the words of Richard Millard, "determine institutional or program quality," and if colleges and universities continue to be evaluated on the basis of their own definition of mission and purpose, without monitoring of the appropriateness of that definition, then those who support government intrusion have a genuine basis for their position. And the growing chorus of criticism of the accreditation process, as recounted earlier, is strengthening that thrust.

Possible Solutions to the Problem

If accreditation is education's method of evaluating its own product and, in effect, establishing a kind of quality control, then it must be deemed to be effective, or other forces will move in to replace it. It is currently, as has been stated, under considerable criticism and has several evident weaknesses. As a result, government, both federal and state, is moving in to fill the gap. Educators, in large measure, resent the accreditation process, but they resent and fear even more government control. If government intrusion is to be avoided, and if a ministry of education is to be eliminated from our future, then what must be done? There are several answers to this question, none of them easy.

One answer is to redefine the accreditation process. No longer should a college or university be allowed to be judged solely on the basis of its own statement of mission and purpose. Obviously the institution's wishes in this matter should be respected, but the appropriateness of such a statement, its basic reasonableness and effectiveness, should be adjudged by the accrediting agency, and the agency should have the state authority to make such judgment.

Another answer would be to enlarge the scope of accreditation so that its evaluations would not limit themselves to establishing minimal standards. The educational process itself does not cringe from grading its clients, even though recently many of the grades have erred on the side of generosity. There is no reason why educators engaged in accreditation should not grade their clients. Such grades should not be misused to the detriment of a college or university or school. But they should definitely be used to bring an institution up to speed if it is clearly lagging in certain respects. It is patently unfair to good and sound institutions to have some half-baked little college, existing on the very margin of acceptability in terms of the minima, and without the academic quality of most of its confreres, be able to advertise itself as "fully accredited," along with Harvard, Yale, Princeton, and the Universities of California and Michigan. It is one thing to have a different sense of mission and purpose; it is quite another to have limited ability to produce educated graduates. Accreditation agencies should have the freedom and power to go beyond minimal standards if the occasion warrants.

Another improvement would be to have the financing of accreditation removed from utter dependency upon the institutions it accredits. How this might be done is a real problem. The most evident alternative would be to have state governments finance the accrediting process as they finance the public institutions themselves, but this in itself brings up the bogey of government intrusion and political influence. Probably the best compromise would be to have a foundation, governed by a board of leading and disinterested citizens, manage the financing and assessments of the accreditation process, and in so doing perhaps devise new sources of revenue that have not yet been thought of. Such a third-party control of financial support would have the advantage of being able to report to and appeal to the public if events began moving in the wrong direction. But to continue to have the accreditation process directly dependent upon the institutions it must judge, and to have the governing boards of the accrediting agencies composed of representatives of those institutions, guarantees a degree of softness in accrediting decisions. Until this problem is solved, if only partially, the question of rigor in accrediting procedures will continue to confront us.

If accreditation is to recover the confidence it once engendered among the public, it must do something about degree requirements. There was a time in American history when a person with a bachelor's degree was expected to denote certain abilities, including some competence in written and spoken English, some basis for good taste in the cultural amenities, and some basic skills in mathematics, science, or verbalization. Graduate degrees are much simpler to define; they have always meant competence in a specific field of specialization. Today, however, an employer interviewing a job applicant with a bachelor's degree might confront an individual unable to write and spell effectively, awkward in oral expression, with little or no knowledge of history or the American business system, and no competence in mathematics beyond simple arithmetic or basic algebra, but who has many college credits in courses such as leadership, minority studies, stage production, and the politics of revolution. A few years ago when there was enthusiasm over the idea of students structuring their own curriculum, the situation was often incredible.

It is high time that educators recognized that, much as they hate to admit it, they too have a product—graduates. And, although the analogy is hateful to many, their product is often not meeting the demands of the market. As a result, just as American automobile buyers became dissatisfied with the American product and turned to Germany and Japan for better results, so now employers are starting their own training programs to produce a product in which they have confidence. In addition, their fiscal support of existing institutions now must run a gauntlet of questions that never before have been asked, such as "Can the graduates of College X actually read and write?" and other embarrassing (and up to now, unbelievable!) queries.

Of course, employers are not the only factor to be considered. A liberal arts education has often been defined as having as its main purpose the enabling of men and women to live better and fuller lives as individuals. And perhaps a curriculum limited to ethnic studies, stage production, and the politics of revolution might produce that result for certain people. But that is not the only obligation an educational system has in today's complex world. It is the means—as it has always been—for the society which fathered it to live and prosper and maintain itself effectively, and how to survive economically in that society is certainly a major objective, even though it is not the only one. The "bottom line" of all of this discussion is that those institutions that are doing a creditable job of producing effective graduates—and there are many of them— are being treated unfairly by an accreditation process that lumps them in with marginal performers. And education itself is treating unfairly those elements of society that depend upon its product when the accreditors stubbornly refuse to separate the sheep from the goats.

Even though there will always be screaming and gnashing of teeth among educators when the subject is brought up, there is really no reason—and I speak from the vantage point of having spent a lifetime in higher education—why educators, if they put their minds to it, could not agree upon *some* common ground in requirements for the A.B. degree. My own ideas on the subject are quite simple. A bachelor's degree should include assurance of literacy in written and spoken English, some perspective gained through history and the social sciences, some appreciation of the arts, and some problem-solving ability through acquaintance with mathematics and science. In addition, the graduate should have at least a beginning competence in some field which will enable him to make a living, if necessary. I would be the last to try to impose these ideas upon educators—I have already tried and failed. But *something* of this nature should be thought through and adopted, so that the accreditation process will have more meaning than it now has.

Finally, COPA—the Council on Post-secondary Accreditation— which represents both regional and specialized accrediting agencies, should boldly assume its role of being the accrediting agency for accrediting agencies, and hold its members to standards that will have some meaning. This is not to say that COPA is not doing a beneficial job at present. Considering the constraints under which it operates, it is doing quite well. But many of these constraints should be removed. The definition of accreditation as being subservient to the institution's own view of itself, its limitation as to establishment of minima, the absence of rigorous decision making due to the way it gains financial support, and finally, the absence of any set of agreed-upon achievement levels for the bachelor's degree, all of these prevent COPA from fulfilling its destiny of being an accreditor of accreditors. It is only natural that, under these conditions, of the two major activities of accreditation that Millard discusses, "quality assessment and quality enhancement," the latter should be emphasized. If effective and stern judgments cannot always be made, then let us at least use the accreditation process to improve things where possible—this seems to be the conclusion that many have drawn. But this conclusion does not fulfill the objective of accreditation, and, of equal importance, it does not have accreditation doing what the public thinks it should be doing. If the process is to survive, therefore, and if the rapid advance of government in the process of educational evaluation is to be halted, steps must be taken to restore accreditation to the role it is assumed to have—that of evaluating educational institutions, honestly, rigorously, and openly, so that when a person obtains a degree from an accredited institution, reality will match expectation.

Nearly a decade ago the Education Commission of the States set up a task force to explore the relationship of state governments to higher education, especially relating to quality. Its conclusions, not unanimously arrived at by any means, were that states should establish boards or bureaus to monitor educational quality of higher education institutions within their borders, and that this was necessary because the accrediting process was too weak and imperfect to be completely depended on—although, as a sop to accreditors, the report added that the process should be used wherever possible.

However, a further, more profound examination of the problem of educational quality from a national viewpoint produced some conclusions worth noting and did not limit itself to deploring the inadequacies of accreditation and suggesting a substitute. Rather, it made some recommendations aimed at preserving voluntary accreditation and its role in keeping education out of government control. In 1982 the Carnegie Foundation for the Advancement of Teaching, headed by Dr. Ernest Boyer, formerly U.S. Commissioner of Education, published an essay on *The Control of the Campus: A Report on the Governance of Higher Education.* Prepared with the help of many experienced educators, the study came to some definite conclusions and recommendations about the accrediting process.

The report states that "... accreditation has increasingly lost significance at the very time it is needed most." And it goes on to say:

Among accreditors there is no agreement about the meaning of a college education, and the neglect of undergraduate education is especially disturbing ... accreditation review often is little more than an empty ritual. Most discouraging, perhaps, many campuses downplay the importance of accreditation visits. Higher education leaders frequently decline to participate in the process.

Further, we found that regional accreditation has not responded satisfactorily to the new accountability mandates imposed by government agencies and the courts. Even though public obligations have increased, accrediting officials seem hesitant to accept expanded evaluation responsibilities. One key accreditation office took the following position:

Accreditation cannot, by itself, serve as the basis for determining eligibility for federal funds; neither can it function as an arm of government in policing compliance....[2]

The report continues:

Higher education quite properly opposes any government move to accredit institutions. But this threat can be contained only as regional bodies expand the scope of their authority and hold colleges accountable not only for academic excellence but also for good management, affirmative action, and consumer protection, too. We conclude that the erosion of regional accrediting authority and prestige leaves a dangerous void.[3]

The study then makes certain recommendations, among which are the admonition to senior college officials to support fully the accrediting process, that regional associations should do more than measure a college "against its own objectives," that different categories of accredited status should be devised so as not to lump marginal institutions with preeminent ones, and the COPA should serve as a court of last resort.[4]

In dealing with specialized accreditation, the study deplores the movement of state controls into the accrediting process by means of licensure.

We are especially troubled that at least twenty-one specialized accrediting associations have been linked to occupational licensure by the state. Through such arrangements, they wield enormous power over higher education by controlling entry into the professions, and giving states strong influence over academic matters. The role of the state in occupational licensing should be to certify results, not to control the process of education. . . . State officials should not involve themselves directly in the review of academic programs. Rather, they should call upon higher learning institutions periodically to assess such programs and report their findings.[5]

Finally, in dealing with the role of the federal government, the study praised the now rapidly-eroding tradition of depending on the voluntary accrediting process to determine eligibility for federal funds, and it concluded flatly:

In determining the eligibility of colleges to participate in federal programs, the Secretary of Education should use regional accreditation as the basis for approval. The preparation of an approved list of regional associations should be a function of the Council of Postsecondary Education, not the federal government . . . this important principle—federal support without federal control—has created a need for new procedures. . . .[6]

A ministry of education for the United States? Certainly, if current practices continue and if no major changes are made in the accrediting process. Certainly not, if accreditation once again becomes what it started out to be, namely, an evaluation of institutional quality, and if COPA assumes its proper—and tough and difficult—role, that of being an accreditor of accreditors. Resolving such issues will not be easy, but then, worthwhile solutions to difficult problems never are.

17

KENNETH A. SIROTNIK

JOHN I. GOODLAD

The Quest for Reason Amidst the Rhetoric of Reform: Improving Instead of Testing Our Schools

The thermometer reads 98.6.° Yet the patient feels terrible, looks terrible, and the doctor knows from many years of clinical experience that something is wrong and that much more information is needed to diagnose and treat the illness adequately. The patient could have anything from cancer to the common cold, of course, and the thermometer could still record a normal tem-

We wish to acknowledge and thank several colleagues for their thoughtful comments and suggestions regarding this manuscript: Maxine Bentzen, Paul Heckman, and Jeannie Oakes.

perature. In the next room, another patient is feeling a bit feverish but not too uncomfortable otherwise. Indeed, the thermometer reads nearly 101° and the physician notes a few key signs during an examination of the patient. A couple of aspirin to relieve the symptoms, antibiotics for a week or two, and the patient will be back in good health.

Clearly, the thermometer does not have an automatic relationship to the presence, absence, or diagnosis of the illness; the severity of the ailment; or the prognosis for the patients. If the thermometer were the physician's only tool, contemporary medical science would not have advanced much further than the barbershop practices of bygone eras.

In our view, the rise and fall of standardized test scores is about as valid an indicator of the health of a school as is the thermometer for the health of human beings. But the thermometer is a benign, albeit superficial, indicator. Standardized test scores are not. When used in an accountability framework that is basically punitive in its current form, the statistical consequences of the "normal" curve are not only demoralizing for professional educators, they send insidious and erroneous messages to people regarding the educability of human beings.

We are sympathetic to the recent concern about educational standards, but we believe that these concerns must go considerably beyond the current fixation on standardized test scores alone. We will explain our countervailing view, but we must do so in a broader context since testing, evaluation, and accountability are highly interdependent. In our view, what goes on in the name of testing and evaluation is largely a consequence of the values and ideology implicit in the concepts and practices that presently define accountability. Therefore, we will first defend our claim of the harmful consequences of norm-referenced testing. Second, we will offer an alternative perspective for assessing the health of schools that is grounded in the use of multiple sources of information, *including* measures of student learning, within the context of constructive evaluation and school improvement. Finally, we will propose a view of standards that can form an accountability framework characterized less by punishment and more by responsible people engaged in the activities of their profession.

Morality versus Normality

The debate between advocates of norm-referenced versus criterion-referenced testing is an old one. The competing perspectives can best be summarized by noting that the norm-referenced approach tries to answer the question "Has Johnny learned more than Mary?" while the criterion-referenced approach is concerned more with the question "Has Johnny, Mary, or any other student learned what we have tried to teach them?"

The makers and users of standardized (norm-referenced) tests sort out students on the basis of the bell-shaped distribution or "normal" curve. (See top half of Figure 1.) We see nothing *normal* about this statistical and psychometric invention. Indeed, it represents, in this context, a rather aberrant view of human capability, and it certainly reflects an extraordinarily mediocre educational aspiration—50 percent of our youth can never be expected to be above average! But, this kind of "normalcy" conflicts not only with everything we know about the educability of youngsters but also with the best of our educational intentions.

Two significant statements illustrate our society's moral commitment to democratic education. In 1916, John Dewey stated that:

The devotion of democracy to education is a familiar act. The superficial explanation is that a government resting on popular suffrage cannot be successful unless those who elect and obey their governors are educated... But there is a deeper explanation. A democracy is more than a form of government; it is primarily a mode of associated living, of conjoint communicated experience.... Obviously a society to which stratification into separate classes would be fatal, must see to it that intellectual opportunties are accessible to all on equable and easy terms.[1]

In 1983, the National Commission on Excellence in Education echoed this thought when it stated that those who do not acquire an education appropriate to our technological era will be "disenfranchised" from both material success and even participation in our national life. "A high level of shared education," the Commission concluded, "is essential to a free, democratic society and to the fostering of a common culture, especially in a country that prides itself on pluralism and individual freedom."[2]

Beliefs regarding the human learning potential are connected

Figure 1
Contrasting Views of the Human Education Potential
as Reflected Statistically
in Hypothetical Test Score Distributions

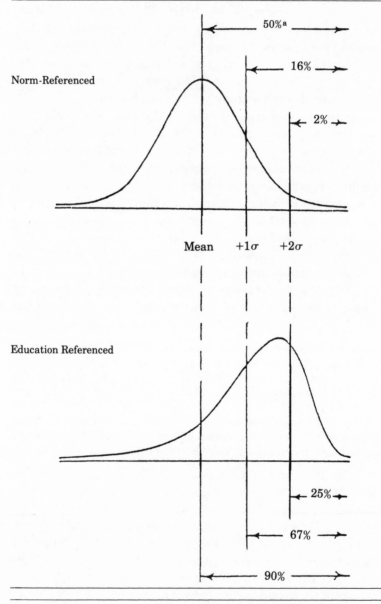

aThese figures are the percentages of students scoring above the indicated points in the distributions.

Source: Authors' calculations.

to democratic values in educational practice. The eminent teachability and educability of human beings is quite well-known and substantiated by everything from the experiences of teachers to the volumes of educational research on instructional practices. Given a context of reasonable and adequate resources, most children can learn almost anything, particularly when instructional practices such as individualization, small group learning, and peer tutoring are in place. Good examples are the mastery learning results generated by Bloom and his colleagues.[3] So what message is really conveyed by the normative image captured in the bell-shaped curve? It is a self-fulfilling prophecy of mediocrity and inequality.

Moreover, norm-referenced thinking, especially as practiced in present-day accountability structures, breeds strange, if not disconcerting, practices. We have known ever since Coleman, et al., about the ubiquitous and unsurprising correlations of test score averages with community demography (particularly with what are essentially economic status indices: limited English speaking, non-English speaking, aid to federally dependent children, etc.).[4] So how can schools be held accountable when they have "inferior raw materials" with which to work? One answer is embodied in the invention of the "minimum competency" test. With this device, schools and their communities can assure themselves that they have done the best they can when enough students can pass tests that are easy enough—tests that reflect minimal survival skills in reading, writing, and arithmetic. The message to teachers and parents implicit in minimum competency testing stands in jarring juxtaposition to that contained in current slogans of "excellence in education."

Another twist on the same theme of lowering expectations occurs in California, for example, where the answer is to "double standardize" the state test score results. Not only do schools compete with one another across the board, they also compete within their own cohort groups, which are based upon economic status indicators like those noted above. A school, therefore, can theoretically end up below, within, or above "expectancy" and yet be anywhere in the statewide score distribution. For example, a school scoring below the statewide average may actually be at (or even above) average when compared only with a small group of schools sharing similar economic status indices. This school then gets back a report saying, in essence, that although its students seem to be generally below average in performance, they are, nevertheless, doing as well (or even better!) than expected.

We used the word "compete" deliberately. In California, for example, the results of the games are printed each year, and tiny score changes become the subject of lengthy articles by education writers. Now the stakes are even higher—believe it or not, up to $400 per student can be won by schools for sufficiently large gains in test score performance.

Nowhere is the "rising tide of mediocrity" more in evidence than in simplistic accountability practices such as these. If we have $400 per student to spend, then let's spend it equitably and in ways that help to promote *maximum competency* for most of our youth. The norm-referenced view and the accountability practices that it generates guarantee only limited success—a kind of "cream-of-the-crop" vision of school effectiveness. We have a different vision. It is related to criterion-referenced assessment, but it is more than just a testing concept that suggests the obvious, that what is tested should match up with what is taught. Our vision might be termed *educationally referenced*—teaching and learning that are referenced to the best of our educational aims and practices. By educationally referenced, therefore, we mean nothing short of a social, political, and economic commitment to educating *all* our youth with a balanced, common curriculum and with the best of instructional practices. For heuristic purposes, we might characterize this view by a very skewed distribution with most of the population centered over the range of success (Figure 1). Rather than success being the outcome of an elite few, this vision proposes success for many. And as noted above, the mastery learning research and practices are one set of examples suggesting that this vision can be the reality.

Constructive Evaluation versus Ritualistic Testing

A major reason for launching *A Study of Schooling* was to find out what goes on in schools.[5] Toward this end, we gathered a great deal of information from many different sources on an extensive array of features of the places we call schools. Some thirty-five technical reports were written, articles were published in numerous periodicals ranging from *Education Week* to the *Harvard Educational Review,* and four books have been published. We and our colleagues did all this when, as planned, not one shred of the data collected included scores on achievement tests!

Did we pull a fast one on the educational research community? Or, perhaps there is more to life in schools than can be inferred from test scores alone. Obviously, we subscribe strongly to the latter proposition. Superficial accountability frameworks fuel a popular misconception that evaluation is synonymous with testing. Testing is only a small part of evaluation. To evaluate is to describe and make judgments.[6] And when what is being described and judged is complex, there are no meaningful quick and easy ways out.

Schooling is a complex phenomenon. Indeed, it is a network of interacting phenomena—workplaces for adults, learning places for youth, child care places for the community, and objects of legislation for state and federal governments, to name a few. The evaluative process will need to be thoughtful, flexible, and responsive to contextual circumstances as well as general educational goals. Much in the way of critical evaluative information on administering, teaching, and learning is barely touched upon by one (or a handful) of superficial indicator(s).

Consider these circumstances that vary from school to school: age and condition of the facility; community demography and geography; school size (number of students); teacher-student ratio; teacher turnover; student absenteeism and transiency; duration of current principalship; daily schedules and period structures; student tracking policies; distribution of teaching FTE to content/department areas; materials and resources. Moreover, consider the array of ongoing, dynamic behaviors and processes that constitute the practice of schooling: the organizational and curricular commonplaces such as instructional practices, learning activities, assessment, problem-solving and decision-making, communication, and so forth.[7] Finally, consider the extensive realm of information not represented in the circumstances and activities of schooling, namely, the phenomenology of the setting—the meanings that people bring to and take from the setting. These are people's orientations, their sentiments (feelings), opinions, attitudes, beliefs, and values that interact with and shape the circumstances and activities of schooling. To ignore these kinds of data is to ignore a fundamental component in the way scientifically or technologically grounded knowledge becomes, or does not become, part of the working knowledge of human beings.[8]

We must emphasize, however, that we are not simply advocating the collection of a wider range of information just to replace an over-reliance on test scores. Instead, what we have in mind is a fundamentally different way of thinking about and using information—a different epistemology regarding evaluation and the roles that people and data play in the process. To our way of thinking, information is not an end in itself, nor is one particular piece of information (like test scores) the ultimate criterion by which all else is judged. Educators must be actively and continuously engaged in the systematic and rigorous deliberation over any and all information seen to be potentially relevant to improving their school. Information thus becomes both an adjunct to and a by-product of a process of critical inquiry—the process of school renewal itself.

Considerable discussion exists elsewhere on the idea and practice of promoting school renewal through the collection and use of comprehensive evaluative information; the details need not be repeated here.[9] Instead, we will try to reinforce this concept with several more examples. It is our observation that with the rhetoric of reform often come simplistic remedies—more time, more homework, more testing, more discipline, more leadership, more courses, and the like—concocted by legislators and educational entrepreneurs who oversimplify the best that educational research has to offer. Findings from research, however, can be dealt with reasonably only in an evaluative context sensitive to the conditions and cultural regularities of the school.[10]

As a case in point, consider our visit to one of the high schools in *A Study of Schooling*. We were unable to see the principal, with whom we had an appointment at 9 AM, until 11 AM. He was on the telephone all morning dealing with the courts. In the meantime, we walked through the school building with the vice principal for curriculum and instruction. When we asked, "How do you spend your time?" he said, "Doing what I do now," as he reprimanded and separated students fighting in the hallway. "My great frustration," he said, "is that I came here because I was going to *be*

Director of Curriculum and Instruction. Now I know why I was invited." We looked at him and also knew why he had been invited.
He was six-foot six, two hundred and thirty pounds, an imposing
figure as he walked through the hallway with another vice principal (for discipline) who was about the same size. As they went
through the hall, almost their entire time was spent in cleaning up
fights. And as we observed behind the classroom doors, we noticed
that students in the industrial arts classes, for example, did not
join other groups of students for their academic classes. They
simply moved as an intact group from working in the shop into
mathematics, social studies, English, etc., and the ambience of
their school environment hardly changed. The disruptive conver-
sation went on, the unruly behavior continued, and one had to conclude that those students were unlikely to learn anything that the
school was trying to teach.

Where do improvement efforts begin in this school? Do you say,
"We're going to have a staff development program to improve instructional methods—teach specific cueing techniques, for example? Do you "implement" the principles of school effectiveness:
strong principal leadership, high achievement expectations, clear
academic emphasis, strong discipline and control, and so forth?
Do you consult the school's average standardized test scores for insight on how to proceed? Of course not! You begin where the
culture of the school is. You bring people together—students,
teachers, parents, administrators, board members—to address
their own problems. And to the extent that these constituencies
can get past the exigencies of the given conditions (granted, a big
"if"), to the extent that they begin to deal seriously with questions
like "What *can* we do?," then they can and must deal with questions like "What *are* we doing?" These queries lead naturally to
the kind of comprehensive data that we suggest can characterize
a school and set the context for school improvement efforts.

As another example, consider Sara Lightfoot's penetrating
analysis of six schools—two private and four public (two more or
less upper socioeconomic class and two urban high schools).[11]
Lightfoot's evaluation of these schools—what she calls the "good-
ness" of a school—centers primarily on the quality of life in a
school's environment. The quality of *educating* in these schools

becomes critical only *after* the quality of living has been raised to a point where instruction and learning can proceed.

The schools in Lightfoot's study are profoundly different. Carver School in urban Atlanta is one of her "good schools." She talks about it as being good "enough"; she does not say excellent, but good enough to be capturing the attention of far more students than was previously the case. As she describes a lot of things about that school, we wonder, on the basis of some criteria like test scores, how in the world Carver could be a "good school" in her judgement. Then we begin to see Carver in historical perspective: the lack of attention to the life of the school before the coming of a particular principal and a supportive superintendent, the conditions in the school that operated against learning, and the progress that had been made during recent years. Schools have immensely different cultures. There is no way to prescribe details in common for them. Indeed, in another high school that Lightfoot describes (Highland Park in Chicago), to prescribe an increase in the intensity of academic life would risk increasing to the point of being detrimental what is already intense in the culture.

For a third illustration, we focus less on the sociocultural aspects of schooling and more on curriculum and instruction per se. More time on academics, for example, is currently a hot issue. Reformers are now adding minutes here and there to the school day. But what do schools do now? How much time do they already have and how is it being allocated? Additional information to shed light on questions like these can provide the appropriate context in which to evaluate the wisdom of the proposed reforms like adding more time. When these data are collected routinely at the local level, they can help districts and schools to evaluate and construct their own, perhaps more relevant and appropriate, reforms.

For example, in *A Study of Schooling* we discovered some children being instructed for only eighteen and a half hours a week while others, in another elementary school with roughly the same length of school day, received twenty-seven and a half hours of instruction per week. When we looked at the data pertaining to practices at the school on the low end of instructional time usage, we found a rather careless environment with respect to the use of time: slow getting started, tardy children getting tardier while they waited to see the principal, recess stretching from fifteen minutes to thirty minutes, lunch hour and good old clean up time dragging on much longer than was intended. The scenarios at schools on the upper end of the time-use continuum, of course, were quite the opposite. There are obviously enormous differences between schools in the use of time, and these clearly reflect cultural differences in the total school environment. In light of such vast dissimilarities, what wisdom can there be in a blanket recommendation to increase the length of the school day?

Problems like these need to be addressed by the parents, teachers, and students at each school, under the leadership of the principal, using data relevant to that school. Analysis of our data, for example, showed that elementary children were instructed during the week for an average of twenty-two and a half hours. When we compared that average with a model of access to the domains of knowledge in the elementary school, it was clear that the average instruction time was not enough. But we did not go on to recommend a longer school day. We recommended instead that the local school work on that problem because they did have enough time if they didn't waste so much of it. With twenty-five hours a week, for example, you can have ninety minutes a day of reading and language arts, an hour a day of math, fifty-five minutes a day of social studies, fifty-five minutes a day of science, three art periods a week, and health and physical education every day. But with only eighteen and a half hours a week, you might have something like ninety minutes a day of reading/language arts, an hour a day of math, twenty-three minutes a day of social studies, thirteen of science, no art, and not much physical education or health. With twenty-seven and a half hours, you can obviously have the twenty-five hour curriculum and a lot more.

We could go on with examples of this nature to drive home the point that normative test score averages tell us nearly nothing about the quality of a school and nothing about what it means to work in the school, learn in the school, and seek to improve the school. Even good criterion-referenced measures of intended teaching and learning would need to be carefully interpreted in light of contextual data.

It must be emphasized, however, that in having a more comprehensive evaluation of the environment of the school, one still does not have a program of improvement. To this body of evalua-

tive data one must also bring the value systems of the professionals in the school, as well as those of interested citizens who are
brought into what Joyce calls "the body of responsible parties."[12]
With a shared body of data, they begin to engage in long-term
planning by asking: What are the most critical areas requiring improvement? These are then arranged into an agenda of improvement for the local school, approved by the superintendent and the
board, and supported by them. In this way, resources are brought
to bear on what those closest to the school see as its greatest
needs. And a constructive evaluative process can help to provide
direction for improvement efforts.

But the care and sensitivity with which we need to evaluate and
improve schooling is not at all apparent in current accountability
practices. Putting schools into competition with one another based
on quantitative reifications of a few basic skill areas does nothing
but increase the reactive stance of teachers and administrators
who want and need to be in control of their professional lives. This
attitude may make sense for competition in the private sector
where the company with the best product does the most business.
In the public sector, however, we want every organization to provide quality service to its constituencies.

To summarize, we have argued that:

- The assessment of student learning is part (not all) of the
  evaluation of schooling. Standardized achievement testing is
  only a small, and not a very informative, part of the assessment
  of student learning.

- Test data must be thought of as but one of many kinds of information that can be brought to bear on understanding what goes
  on in schools and on dialogue, decisions, and actions regarding
  what to do to improve schools.

- Information should be used constructively by the very people
  most responsible for delivering and receiving quality education.
  It is a grave misuse of standardized test scores to hold students,
  teachers, administrators, etc., accountable on the basis of them.

In a nutshell, we need to stop trivializing the educational profession by allowing it to be characterized and judged by superficial indicators. What, then, do we do? What are the standards? How is

accountability to be structured? What, indeed, are the characteristics of a *real* educational profession? It is to these questions that we now turn.

From Accountability to Responsibility

Most people we know would have little difficulty accepting the proposition that our nation's youth are our most important resource. Certainly the value most parents place upon their children goes without saying. These young people spend up to half their waking hours every day, five days a week, about thirty-six weeks a year, in school. In other words, our children spend approximately 1000 hours each year in classrooms.

We entrust these precious resources for this amount of time to people called teachers. In many parts of the nation we pay these adults salaries of less than $20,000 a year. Often, a beginning teacher earns less than the bus driver who brings the children to school. The clash between the rhetoric of reform and the values and priorities reflected in these wages is deafening. In Japan, the average teacher's salary translates to roughly $50,000 a year, and high school teachers spend only fifteen hours per week in total class instruction, leaving the balance for tutoring, correcting papers, preparing new lessons, evaluating old ones—in short, engaging in *professional* development and planning activities. In Scandinavian countries, the teaching profession is similarly conducted; the status of teachers in the community is equivalent to that of university professors.

If a respectable salary, quality work time, and status in the community are among the necessary attributes of professions, then teaching in the United States certainly is not a profession. In our country, we rarely hear of the dedicated engineer, lawyer, systems programmer, and the like; but the "dedicated teacher" is legendary. Of course, dedication is a must to enter, stay, and excel in the "profession." In *A Study of Schooling*, the majority of the 1350 teachers surveyed had primarily altruistic reasons for entering teaching: the desire to teach, the worthiness of the profession, and the wish to serve others. These same teachers also indicated that, if they were to leave teaching, among their primary reasons would be organizational and personal frustration. Befitting these sentiments was the teachers' infrequent selection of money as the major reason for entering teaching, yet their ranking it second as a reason for leaving.

Keeping in mind these "rewards" of teaching, what are the circumstances of teaching and what characterizes the work-life of teachers? In our view, the job more nearly resembles that of a laborer than that of a professional. Elliot Eisner sums it up vividly as follows:

If you were to conjure up a system that would increase the probability that there would be *no* growth in teaching over the course of a career, what features would you generate in your mind to increase that likelihood? . . . [One] of the things that you might do is to create no incentives for being excellent in teaching. You might make sure that teachers got virtually no useful feedback about what they are doing. You might create infrequent, in-service education programs, removed from the school and taught by people who haven't crossed the threshold of the school themselves for a decade. Then you might think you will do your duty to inspire teachers in your district by inviting [a famous educator] to give heartfelt speeches to jack them up in September so that they can carry themselves through June. In other words, I am suggesting to you a hypothesis. The hypothesis is that after teachers acquire the skills necessary to maintain the classroom and cope with the predictable crises that emerge in the classroom, after two or three years in the classroom, growth in teaching is relatively flat. We have not provided the conditions in our schools to enable people to do better at their jobs. Yet we seem to pursue the idea that somehow we can humilate practitioners into excellence by the publication of the performance of their students.[13]

In *A Study of Schooling,* we found that teachers have little or no opportunity to observe and interact with one another professionally on a regular work-a-day basis.[14] They have little or no opportunity to reflect upon and discuss together the meaning and implications of information about their school that could inform improvement efforts. Instead, they are generally isolated from each other as well as from instructional leadership at the school and district levels.

In our view, schooling is organized in a cellular and paternal structure: teachers parent students; principals parent teachers; superintendents parent principals; and the family head resides in the state capitol. It is not surprising, then, that accountability is built into this structure symbolically rather than substantively.[15] Test score averages are passed back and forth between the levels—much like hot potatoes—and, as we have argued, they reflect little in the way of useful information for the evaluation and improvement of practice.

If you look up the word "accountable" in the dictionary, you will find definitives such as "liable," "explicable," and "answerable." You will also find the word "responsible" given as a possible synonym. Reciprocally, when you look up the word "responsible," you find the synonym "accountable." But here, under "responsible," you also find a longer, more layered set of meanings that include words like "moral," "rational," and "trustworthy." Therein lies the subtle but crucial difference between accountability and responsibility, and we propose switching emphases to the latter concept.[16] There is a human relations aspect to this proposed reconstruction of accountability and a recommended agenda of responsibilities. We will deal briefly with both points.

The hierarchical, tightly-coupled view of organizational productivity is quickly becoming an archaic concept and practice. The signs are all around us. A startling view is offered by Naisbitt in his analysis of the implications of society's transition from the industrial age to an age of information and service.[17] Particularly noteworthy for educators are the "megatrends" of short-term to long-term thinking, institutional to self-help, representative to participatory democracy, hierarchies to networking, and either/or to multiple options. In light of these major trends toward increased decentralization, significant changes in traditionally entrenched, top-down societal institutions (like public schools) are not going to occur simply because they are legislated or made the object of political rhetoric. Significant changes are long-term propositions that necessarily involve the very people most affected by the changes and that permit local flexibility in how people can best bring about change given the exigencies of their particular setting. Most important, people with common needs and struggles need the kind of support from one another that networking (not hierarchical isolation) can provide.

Interestingly, significant organizational changes are now underway in many corporations designed to increase both production and the quality of work life. It may have taken another country, Japan, to remind the private sector that these two aspects of the work environment are intimately related, but they have, nonetheless, taken heed. Good examples can be found in Peters' and Waterman's provocative analysis of what some of the more successful and future-oriented companies are now doing in terms of employer-employee structures and relationships.[18]

Our notion of responsibility essentially turns the conventional pyramid of accountability on its head. For the sake of furthering dialogue, we suggest in Figure 2 alternatives to conventional institutional concepts. Our intention is not to replace one set of buzz words with another. Instead, our alternatives are intended as heuristics to suggest the considerable "paradigm shifting" that we believe to be necessary. Basically, the conventional accountability notion suggests authority, manipulation, and control whereas the "new accountability"—responsibility, if you like—suggests leadership, collaboration, and enlightenment.

This is not a proposal motivated out of fuzzy, soft-headed humanism; nor are we suggesting some kind of laissez-faire, everybody-do-your-own-thing type of decentralized structure. There is nothing lackadaisical about quality education. The reconstruction of accountability must include a teeth-bearing

Figure 2
Some Heuristics for Shifting from
Accountability to Responsibility

REPLACE	WITH
Product	Process
Trade (Worker)	Profession (Professional)
Symbols (Explanations)	Meanings (Understandings)
Short-Term	Long-Term
Closure	Ambiguity
Confirmation	Exploration
Uniform	Contextual
Reactive	Proactive
Authority	Leadership
Isolation	Collaboration
Manipulation	Facilitation
External Reward	Internal Motivation
Legitimate Right	Trust
Followership	Working Consensus
Talk/Conversation	Discourse/Communication
Cost-Benefit Analysis	Critical Analysis

agenda of responsibilities at state, district, and local levels that is far more rigorous and demanding than anything currently in practice. It must do more than pay lip service to the schooling goals that we all value (see below) and to the time honored claims for democratic education. We can only outline here the features of this agenda and the more complete discussion presented elsewhere.[19] In essence, authority (as leadership) and accountability (as responsibility) must be differentiated, distributed, and balanced across the entire system. The system must not be held accountable in summative fashion through the quantification of a few student outcomes. Rather, the system must be held *responsible* for articulating comprehensive educational goals, providing resources commensurate with attaining these goals, engaging in the professional practices required to reach these goals, and formatively evaluating these processes in ways that actively involve educators in their own school improvement efforts.

These responsibilities pervade the system from the state to the classroom levels, but different emphases are appropriate at each level. For the purposes of this discussion, we will describe briefly only three general sets of responsibilities, the state's, the districts', and the schools'. First, state officials (the governor, superintendent or commissioner, and Board of Education) must be held responsible for both articulating and encouraging legislation to support a comprehensive and consistent set of educational goals for schools. Current expectations for schools constitute a hodge-podge resulting from accumulations of piecemeal legislation. Yet there really is (and always has been) a substantial constituency for each of our traditional goals of schooling—the basics are here to stay; there is no need to go back to them. But a broader view of what schools are for is required.[20] Boyer concluded, as we did in *A Study of Schooling,* that we—educators, students, parents, community at large—*want it all* when it comes to education in our schools: academic and intellectual development, personal development, social development, and vocational and career development.[21] Moreover, the formal curriculum documents of three-quarters of all the states contain the same endorsement of goal areas.

There is no purpose served at the level of the state in chopping up these expectations into endless lists of objectives. The goals can be subsumed under a limited number of categories, much like Tyler suggested over thirty-five years ago, with the crucial requirement that the curriculum be balanced and accessible to *all* students.[22] These broad expectations for curriculum and instruction must then be endorsed as a composite whole (with revision provisions, say, every four years) and declared off limits to piecemeal legislation. This, then, gives us some hope of evaluating (in the ways we have been talking about) the fit between these goals and the conditions designed for their attainment. And these conditions include not only the curricula and teaching practices but also the necessary resources that must be provided by the state and districts.

The state, then, must hold districts responsible for communicating these educational goals to their schools, developing a balanced curriculum in each school, employing qualified teachers, providing time and resources for improvement efforts in each school, and assuring equity in the distribution of these resources. Thus, instead of monitoring from remote state capitols the activities and performance of individual schools and teachers, the state provides and supports a common and rigorous framework of curricular values and principles that still leaves room for necessary contextual adaptations at the district and school levels. State governments would have virtually no involvement in the specifics of instruction, yet they would have increased responsibility for the basic conditions that can either facilitate or hinder the local development of effective schools.

Given these kinds of responsibilities at the state level, districts must then be willing to genuinely decentralize responsibilities to schools. Each school should be held responsible for developing and implementing a balanced program of studies. Planning documents and budgets, developed by the staff in each school, should be submitted to the superintendent (through the principal) for evaluation. These plans should be long term, say three to five years, with annual updating and review.

The operating principle here is "every tub on its own bottom"— every school taking care of its own business, dealing with chronic problems, communicating with parents, and so forth, while being held directly responsible (under district auspices) for implementing the basic common curriculum endorsed and supported by the state. The essence of the district-school relationship is the review process, in which the principal presents and justifies program plans. The superintendent (and board) should then be free to allocate discretionary funds for unusually creative efforts as well as to deny funds for failure to plan and implement.

Finally, schools—actually, the professional staff members within them—must be held accountable to one another for engaging in the professional activities we have been describing. It is the responsibility of each school to become largely self-directing. School staffs need to develop the capacity for renewal and the structures for doing it. This includes sustained and systematic dialogue, decision-making, action-taking, and evaluation—the identification of problems, the gathering of relevant data, rigorous discussion, formulation of solutions, and the monitoring of actions.[23]

To be sure, executing these responsibilities requires effective leadership abilities in the principal; and it is the responsibility of districts to cultivate and nurture promising candidates for principalships rather than hand out the job indiscriminately for reasons of seniority, political favors, or the like. But it is also the responsibility of society and its representatives to create the conditions necessary to attract qualified people (teachers and administrators) into a quality profession.[24]

There is much more to the agenda of responsibilities for improving public schooling. But what we have outlined here should be sufficient to illustrate and contrast our view of responsibility with current practices of accountability. Indeed, the combination of commitment to a set of curricular and instructional values and goals, strong leadership, quality professionals, and quality professional working circumstances is a powerful force for school improvement. It contrasts sharply, in our view, with an accountability system attenuated in substance and saturated in authority. To operationalize what we are proposing, we must give up the assumption that giving power to others is somehow tantamount to giving up authority and control. We believe that this assumption is erroneous; that instead, the appropriate empowerment of others is itself an eloquent display of leadership.

An example from the experience of one of the authors illustrates this well.[25] Nine years ago, the superintendent of schools

and the board of education in Edmonton, Alberta, introduced a decentralized planning process. Responsible parties at the level of
the local school engaged in assessing their needs (in the usual
"seat-of-the-pants" fashion) and came up with priorities. They
were able to sit down, in a non-confrontational situation, with the
superintendent and the board to review what it was that they
were about and what they wanted to do. They then went about getting the endorsement of the superintendent and the board, getting
differential support, getting funds for what they wanted to do, and
then going about the business of doing it and reporting their
progress the next year. This process became increasingly refined
over the succeeding years.

Two years ago, Edmonton experienced a severe budget cut, comparable to the budget cuts that have occurred in many other districts. One might have expected a terrible morale situation—
teachers upset, principals upset—a real "downer." Instead, a very
positive situation developed. The superintendent and the board
called in all the principals and said, "We have to make a budget
cut of so much percent. Go back and revise your plans and see
what you can do about it." The principals came back several
months later with the requested revisions. Not only had they
effected the budget cut, they then had a surplus. And when they
asked the question, "May we keep it?," the only sensible answer
for the superintendent and the board was "yes." Imagine . . . good
morale while effecting a budget cut!

Concluding Remarks

Our intention has been to provide a strong, alternative view to
conventional standards and accountability practices. It seems to
us that much of the current educational reform movement, like
that of its predecessors, amounts to little more than rearranging
the deck chairs on the Titanic. The idea of replacing standards
with stronger standards in an accountability system that tightly
couples symbols instead of substance has done little but contribute
to demoralizing an already tenuous profession.

We began with the analogy of test scores to temperature readings and the fact that in several serious illnesses the thermometer
would tell us nothing. We conclude by noting that with a serious ill-

ness there is more often than not a long-term cure, a long-term preventative, a long-term correction of the condition. We would like to submit that if the schools are indeed in the condition of health that many reports say they are in, then it is going to require a long period of care and attention to put the schools into the health that we would aspire to during coming decades.

Because of the common tendency to connect achievement test scores with school effectiveness, short-term remedies are often proposed that turn out not to address the health of schools. That is, they do not address the quality of educating in schools. And if the thermometers used do not turn attention to the quality of educating in schools, then the schools are not likely to get profoundly better, even if achievement test scores do go up. And there is no question in our minds that achievement test scores in coming years will go up, particularly if people are monetarily rewarded, in effect, for paying particular attention to the kinds of items likely to be on the tests. In that case, therefore, the scores will go up, particularly in the most mechanistic aspects of learning.

Our concern is that the quality of educating in schools will no more correspond to the rise in achievement test scores than it could be said to have paralleled the decline. We all need to be aware that there are conditions having to do with the economy, with the success of other institutions, and with how we feel about ourselves which become immediately reflected in the schools. We have not yet been very successful as social scientists in interpreting the reasons for the earlier decline in test scores. It is doubtful that we will be very successful in interpreting any increases in test scores in the years immediately ahead. Shifts in test scores are intimately connected to shifts in the larger social press of which we are all part.

As the test scores go up in the years to come, the rhetoric of self-congratulation on the part of those who use those scores to measure successful school reform will increase. That is, the rhetoric will be adjusted to the test scores, not to the fundamental improvement of schooling. We are raising serious questions about such a connection with test scores and seek, instead, more substantive reconstruction and reform. Unfortunately, the magnitude of the effort required leads too many of us to succumb to the easier but unreliable reliance on test scores as the thermometer for determining the health of our schools. Although perhaps naive, our hope is that reason and responsibility will prevail, that educators at all levels of schooling will be provided more professional working environments where information is used constructively to promote understanding of what they do and how they might do it better.

VII

Conclusions

18

ERNEST L. BOYER

America's Schools:
The Mission

"What does the United States want its schools to achieve?" Education for citizenship, job awareness if not job training, self-worth, social values such as respect for other persons, neighborhood and community, patriotism and decency.

Indeed, the history of education in America makes clear that we always wanted all these things for the privileged few and slowly came to want them for all children. We have been willing to struggle and argue, plan and innovate, pay and organize interminably in order to implement these goals. We seek to hold them in balance and realize them more fully. This monumental struggle, relentless, ongoing, is one of the most hopeful features of the American story.

In this chapter, I lay out highlights of the history showing what our leaders and the people have wanted schools to accomplish. The shifts in emphasis are there, the ebb and flow is evident, but throughout that wonderful energy and faith in education are the dominant themes.

Later on, as the story moves into the present time, I turn to the future and suggest a vision of what is needed if the schools are to help the United States achieve a future that will embody the best characteristics of that past in which so much has been invested and from which so much is expected.

Evolving Goals for Education and Schools

The Boston Latin Grammar School, founded in 1635, was more than a random happening. The goal was to prepare privileged young men for Harvard, which, in turn, would prepare them to serve both state and church. Historian Lawrence A. Cremin reminds us that, in the early days of the Republic, schooling "was to be only one part of the education of the public, and a relatively minor part at that."[1] In those days, the family and the church were considered powerful educators, too.

As the nation grew, the mission of schooling was extended. In 1751, Benjamin Franklin established a secondary school in Philadephia to instruct people in more practical skills, such as letter writing and accounting. Franklin's school became the model for "academies" that dominated nineteenth century secondary education. These schools reflected the new nation's growing commitment to "useful learning."

The first *public* high school in America—the English Classical School—opened in Boston in 1821. An alternative to academies, this school was a free, publicly-supported institution. Other public high schools soon appeared in Portland, Maine and Worcester, Massachusetts.

In 1827, the Commonwealth of Massachusetts passed a law requiring every town or village of five hundred or more families to establish a school to teach American history, algebra, geometry, and bookkeeping, in addition to the common primary subjects. Towns of four thousand also were to offer courses in general history, rhetoric, logic, Latin, and Greek.[2]

In 1870 there were about 500 public high schools in the nation with about 50,000 students. During this same period, Calvin M. Woodward, a Harvard-trained mathematician, launched a campaign to persuade Americans that high schools were out of touch with the nation's economic and vocational needs. Woodward claimed that high schools were training students to be "gentlemen" rather than preparing them for work. He wanted more "manual training" in the schools, which, he believed, should be an "equal partner" in the broad general curriculum for all students.[3]

Woodward's campaign gained wide support from the ranks of business. The business community felt that getting job training in the schools was particularly attractive, especially as unions began imposing rules on the management of apprenticeships. In the end, vocational education became firmly planted as a central goal of secondary education, but frequently without Woodward's vision of blending the manual and the liberal arts.

With the industrial expansion of America, education increasingly was valued in economic terms. Many students saw the new vocationalism as a shortcut to better jobs. They turned away from academic subjects, thus helping to scuttle the intended fusion of intellect and labor. In the end, Woodward himself appeared to cave in. "By multiplying manual training schools," he said, "we solve the problems of training all the mechanics our country needs."[4]

By the turn of the century, the number of high schools had grown to 6,000,[5] with an enrollment of 519,000 students.[6] This represented only about 8.5 percent of the youth group.[7] A still smaller percentage—6.3 percent—actually graduated. During this period, presidents of the nation's most prestigious higher learning institutions were distressed by the uneven quality of high school education, even though only a tiny fraction of the nation's youth were going on to college. School people, in turn, were upset by the patchwork of college admissions requirements.

In response, the National Council of Education in 1892 appointed a group of educators, dominated by university professors and chaired by Charles W. Eliot, president of Harvard University, to clarify the goals of secondary education and smooth the transition from school to college.

This nationally prestigious body, known as the Committee of Ten, mapped a core of academic subjects to be studied in the high school. In addition to Latin, Greek, and mathematics, there were the "modern subjects"—English, foreign languages, natural history, physical science, geography, history, civil government, and political economy.

The Committee of Ten stressed "mental discipline." All subjects, the committee said, were to be taught in the same fashion to all students. There was to be no substantial difference between education for higher college and education for work. Preparation for higher education, the committee argued, was the best preparation for life.[8]

Charles W. Eliot put the matter squarely. While rejecting the notion of universal education, Eliot refused to believe:

... that the American public intends to have its children sorted before their teens into clerks, watchmakers, lithographers, telegraph operators, masons, teamsters, farm laborers, and so forth, and treated differently in their schools according to these prophecies of their appropriate life careers. Who are to make these prophecies? Can parents? Can teachers?[9]

With the arrival of waves of new immigrants from Europe, the mission of public education once again expanded. The nation's schools were called upon to "Americanize" the new arrivals, teaching them English, basic lessons in health, sanitation, nutrition, and, most especially, citizenship. One turn-of-the-century writer vividly described how the public school stood as a symbol of hope for the new Americans.

At the corner of Catherine and Henry Streets in New York is a large white building that overlooks and dominates its neighborhood. Placed in the middle of a region of tawdry flat houses and dirty streets, it stands out preeminent because of its solid cleanliness and unpretentiousness. It is the home of Public School No. 1. In it are centered all the hopes of the miserably poor polyglot population of the surrounding district—for its pupils the scene of their greatest interest and endeavor, and for their parents an earnest of the freedom they have come far and worked hard to attain.[10]

In 1913, the National Education Association appointed a blue-ribbon Commission on the Reorganization of Secondary Education. In a report issued five years later entitled *The Cardinal Principles of Secondary Education,* the committee expanded school purposes to include health, citizenship, and worthy home-membership. Almost as an afterthought, "command of fundamental processes" was added to the list. The report said:

Education in a democracy, both within and without the school, should develop in each individual the knowledge, interests, ideals, habits, and powers whereby he will find his place and use that place to shape both himself and society toward ever nobler ends.[11]

Early in the twentieth century, secondary schools also felt the impact of the seminal works of the philosopher John Dewey.[12] Dewey, father of the progressive movement, was alarmed at the extent to which industrialization and urbanization were eroding the traditional American institutions—the home, the community, and the church.[13] Concerned that workers were becoming "mere appendages to the machine they operate," Dewey argued that schools must educate the whole child, filling in where other institutions failed. He looked to the family as the model. "What the best and wisest parents wants for his own child, that must the community want for all of its children."[14] Ironically, while there was much talk about "social learning," this was also a time of increased differentiation in the schools by social class.

The progressive movement that had begun with the perceptive insights of John Dewey soon lost its way. Much of the misinterpretation of Dewey was made by some of his most enthusiastic supporters, and it eventually led to unsound, careless, and even extreme expressions of educational philosophy. In 1913, for example, a Los Angeles superindendent proclaimed: "The principal business of the child is to play and to grow—not to read, write, spell, and cipher. These are incidental in importance. If they can be made a part of the play, it is well to use them; if not, they should be handled sparingly."[15]

A backlash was inevitable. Indeed, as early as the late 1920s a movement called "essentialist" education attacked what was viewed as the neglect of traditional fields of study, an overemphasis on social studies, and thoughtless curriculum revision. The Essentialist Committee for the Advancement of American Education presented its platform in 1938.[16] The aim: to return school "to the exact and exciting studies," to support the "mental disciplines," and to save such courses as Latin, algebra, and geometry.

William Chandler Bagley, a professor at Teachers College, Columbia University, argued for the enduring values:

It is true that the world of today is a different world from the world of
1913 and from the world of 1929 . . . but this does not mean that everything has changed. . . . The winds that blow still follow the law of storms:
Huckleberry Finn and *Treasure Island* still delight youth; and the Sistine
Madonna is just as beautiful as of yore.[17]

Soon the majority of America's teenagers were completing high
school. And the last to be included were young people from
minority populations. Cohen and Neufeld, in a perceptive article,
describe the revolution this way:

Entrance requirements were changed: The admissions exams were
dropped in favor of simple elementary school completion. This marked
the beginning of the high school's transition from an elite to a mass institution. . . . And it marked the beginning of a long struggle for a new
social goal—universal high school attendance.[18]

The high school had, in fact, become the people's college.

In a push for excellence to match access, a cadre of university
professors began to design and test new curricula for the schools.
In 1956, Jerrold Zacharias, Professor of Physics at MIT, developed
a new curriculum to update the content of high school physics.[19] A
mathematics project was launched at the University of Illinois.
National curriculum reform projects in biology and English
received federal support.

But it took Sputnik to push school improvement to the top of the
national agenda. The National Defense Education Act of 1958 provided funds for the improvement of science, mathematics, and
foreign-language teaching. It was subsequently broadened to include support of the humanities and the social sciences as well.
"Rigor" became the catchword of the day.

Soon the nation's schools were caught up in yet another national crusade. Pushed by the historic United States Supreme
Court decision in *Brown vs. Board of Education* (1954), public
education was called upon to serve more equitably the historically
bypassed students—the poor, the underprivileged, and the under-
achieving. Congress and the courts moved, belatedly, to counter
years of scandalous discrimination. Racial balance and compensatory education became urgent new priorities. Schools became
the battleground for social justice.

When the Vietnam War sparked student revolt and confrontation, "relevance" became the new mandate for education. Colleges

dropped requirements and added electives to meet student interest. High schools followed suit. A new group of reformers, including James Coleman and John Henry Martin argued that the road to relevance was beyond the school.[20] Educators were urged to provide more "real life" experiences for the young—work-study programs, "action-learning," cities-as-schools, and the like.

Today's high school is called upon to provide the services and transmit the values we used to expect from the community and the home and the church. And if they fail anywhere along the line, they are condemned.

What do Americans want high schools to accomplish? Quite simply, as stated in the introduction, we still want it all.

Four Essential Goals

A high school, to be effective, must have a clear and vital mission. Students, teachers, administrators, and parents at the institution should have a shared vision of what, together, they are trying to accomplish. But is it possible to serve all students and also find a coherent purpose for our schools?

I am left with the distinct impression that high schools lack a larger vision. They are unable to find common purposes or establish educational priorities that are widely shared. They seem unable to put it all together. The institution is adrift.

I believe every high school should have clearly stated goals and purposes that are understood and supported by the students, teachers, administrators, and parents of the institution. But where do we begin? Do we reach back to the Latin Grammar School, to prepare young men—and women—for Harvard and Yale, or for one of three thousand other colleges and universities? Do we recapture the vision of Calvin Woodward, to prepare young people more effectively for the work place? Do we follow the Americanizing impulses of the new immigrations? Or should high schools continue to take over the work of other troubled institutions—the family, the neighborhood, the church?

In the following section I propose four essential goals and explore the ways these purposes can be achieved.

- First, the high school should help all students develop the capacity to think critically and communicate effectively through a mastery of language.

- Second, the high school should help all students learn about themselves, the human heritage, and the interdependent world in which they live through a core curriculum based upon consequential human experiences common to all people.

- Third, the high school should prepare all students for work and further education through a program of electives that develop individual aptitudes and interests.

- Fourth, the high school should help all students fulfill their social and civic obligations through school and community service.

Today, many proposals for school reform are heatedly debated. But, unguided by a larger vision, they amount to little more than tinkering with an elaborate and complex system. What is needed—and what I believe these four goals constitute—is a clear and coherent vision of what the nation's high schools should be seeking to accomplish.

We have heard much talk about raising academic standards, improving test scores, lengthening the school year. Many school people seem more concerned about how long students stay in school than they are about what students should know when they depart. We also have heard talk about adding another unit of science, another unit of math, or another unit of English to the required core, but we have heard little about the content of a high school education, about what it means to be an educated person.

More substance, not more time, is our most urgent problem. I suggest a course sequence for all students. The goal is not to impose a single curriculum on every school, but to underscore the point that what is taught in school determines what is learned.

A mastery of language. The first curriculum priority is language. Our use of complex symbols separates human beings from all other forms of life. Language provides the connecting tissue that binds society together, allowing us to express feelings and ideas, and powerfully influence the attitudes of others. It is the most essential tool for learning. I recommend that high schools help all students develop the capacity to think critically and communicate effectively through the written and spoken word.

"Human beings combine in behavior as directly and unconsciously as do atoms," John Dewey said. "But participation in activities and sharing in results . . . demands communication as a prerequisite." Only humans communicate in subtle and complex ways. Only humans find meaning in a few squiggly lines or in patterned utterances we call speech. Only humans create sentences that have not been heard or seen before, or describe a tall leafy object by using four abstract symbols: T-R-E-E. It is from this very activity that human society was formed.[21]

Language is linked to thought. Philosophers and linguists have long debated the precise ways the two are joined.[22] I do not propose to pursue that finely-shaded argument here. I do affirm, however, that thought and language are inextricably connected, and that, as students become proficient in self-expression, the quality of their thinking also will improve.

When I speak of language I first mean the mastery of English. The richness of other languages and cultures are essential, and, therefore, I propose the study of a second language for all students. Still, for those living in the United States, the effective use of English is absolutely crucial. Those who do not become proficient in the primary language of the culture are enormously disadvantaged in school and out.

How is the mastery of English to be accomplished?

The process begins early. No school is needed to teach a child to speak. The typical three-year-old has a vocabulary of a thousand words or more. Children, when they are very young, can use complex language that involves an intricate system of grammar.[23] They begin to master, almost miraculously it seems, the symbol system of the culture.

Schools should build on the remarkable language skills a child already has acquired. Unfortunately, reading programs in the primary grades often seem to assume that children come to school with limited language and that decoding skills can be separated from comprehension. An approach to reading that builds on the child's own language experience offers a rich alternative that can at once continue language development and build confidence as well.[24] Once young learners have become actively involved in the writing and reading of their own thoughts, they are ready to consider seriously the ideas and writing conventions of others.

In the early grades, students should learn to read and comprehend the main ideas in a written work. They should learn to write standard English sentences with correct structure, verb forms, punctuation, word choice, and spelling. In elementary school, students also should learn to organize their thoughts around a topic, and present ideas orally, both in casual discussion and in more formal presentations. In one suburban midwestern elementary school, first graders annually write and produce their own collections of poems and stories. They even hold a publishers' tea to introduce their creative efforts to parents and friends.

The language development of each child should be carefully monitored. Records of his or her proficiency in the use of oral and written English should be maintained and passed from grade to grade. If a student is not making satisfactory progress, special tutoring should be provided.

An equally unsettling problem in today's schools, perhaps, is the neglect of writing.

Clear writing leads to clear thinking; clear thinking is the basis of clear writing. Perhaps more than any other form of communication, writing holds us responsible for our words and ultimately makes us more thoughtful human beings.

Specific knowledge is conveyed in specific language, and unless the student communicates clearly what he has learned, thoughts will remain vague and imprecise. Creativity will be lost. Donald Graves, Professor of English Education at the University of New Hampshire, says: "In reading, everything is provided . . . in writing, the learner must supply everything."[25]

Recently, during visits to American high schools, only infrequently did I find writing being taught. Occasionally, writing assignments were given, but often papers were returned late with only brief comments in the margin. One student observed: "A good teacher writes a comment on the bottom of an assignment that shows you she has graded your work as carefully as you have written it."

Teaching students to write clearly and effectively should be a central objective of the school. But this goal cannot be magically accomplished. Time must be provided to assure that the task is adequately performed. Teachers must have time not only to assign writing but also to critique carefully what students write. I suggest that those who teach basic English have no more than twenty students in each class, and no more than two such classes should be included within the regular teacher's load.

A well-taught basic English course will help students become better writers. But, unless the effort is reinforced by other teachers, the gains will be diluted if not reversed. In a recent study of high school writing in the United States,[26] it was found in most non-English courses that writing assignments were rarely given. Students' written responses were restricted to multiple-choice answers, filling in blanks, or short-answer statements on the quizzes. Good writing must be taught in every class.

The high school curriculum should also include a study of the spoken word. As humans, we first use sounds to communicate our feelings. Very early, we combine phonemes orally to express complex ideas. In our verbal culture we speak much more than we write. We use the telephone more frequently than we send letters. Talk is everywhere. Throughout our lives we judge others, and we ourselves are judged, by what is said. We need to be as precise in speaking as we are in writing. Therefore, I recommend that high schools give priority to oral communication, requiring all students to complete a course in speaking and listening.

The one-semester speech course I propose would include group discussion, formal debate, public speaking, and reading literature aloud. Again, the goal is not just effective self-expression; it is also reflective thinking. Students' oral comments must also be accompanied by careful analysis and critique by teachers.

Listening should be included, too. Today's young people are bombarded by messages. They should be taught to evaluate what they hear, to understand how ideas can be clarified or distorted, and to explore how the accuracy and reliability of an oral message can be tested.

All too often, our efforts to speak and listen to each other seem to be a vicious spiral, moving downward. "But we have all experienced moments," Booth said, "when the spiral moved upward, when one party's effort to listen and speak just a little bit better produced a similar response, making it possible to try a bit

harder—and on up the spiral to moments of genuine understanding."[27]

Language defines our humanity. It is the means by which we
cope socially and succeed educationally. The advent of an information age raises to new levels of urgency the need for all students to
be effective in their use of the written and the spoken word.
The mastery of English is the first and most essential goal of
education.

The curriculum has a core. A core of common learning is essential. The basic curriculum should be a study of those consequential ideas, experiences, and traditions common to all of us by
virtue of our membership in the human family at a particular moment in history. The content of the core curriculum must extend
beyond the specialties and focus on more transcendent issues,
moving from courses to coherence. The following are recommended:

- The number of required courses in the core curriculum should
  be expanded from one-half to two-thirds of the total units required for high school graduation.

- In addition to strengthening the traditional courses in
  literature, history, mathematics, and science, emphasis should
  also be given to foreign languages, the arts, civics, non-western
  studies, technology, the meaning of work, and the importance
  of health.

Highlights of the Core Curriculum are as follows:

Literature. All students, through a study of literature, should
discover our common literary heritage and learn about the power
and beauty of the written word.

United States History. United States history is required for graduation from every one of the high schools included in our study,
and it is the one social studies course uniformly required by most
states. I favor a one-year United States history course that would
build on the chronology of the emergence of America, or a study of
the lives of a few influential leaders—artists, reformers, explorers
(including minorities and women) who helped shape the nation.

Western Civilization. Beyond American history lies the long sweep of Western Civilization. I recommend that all students learn about the roots of our national heritage and traditions through a study of Western Civilization.

Non-Western Civilization. All students should discover the connectedness of the human experience and the richness of other cultures through an in-depth study of a non-western nation. I suggest a one-semester required course in which students study, in considerable detail, a single non-western nation.

Science and the Natural World. The study of science introduces students to the processes of discovery—what we call the scientific method—and reveals how such procedures can be applied to many disciplines and to their own lives. I suggest a two-year science sequence that would include basic courses in the biological and physical sciences.

Technology. All students should study technology: the history of man's use of tools, how science and technology have been joined, and the ethical and social issues technology has raised.

Mathematics. In high school, all students should expand their capacity to think quantitatively and to make intelligent decisions regarding situations involving measurable quantities. Specifically, I believe that all high schools should require a two-year mathematics sequence for graduation and that additional courses be provided for students who are qualified to take them.

Foreign Language. All students should become familiar with the language of another culture. Such studies should ideally begin in elementary school and at least two years of foreign language study should be required of all high school students. By the year 2000, the United States could become home to the world's fifth largest population of persons of Hispanic origin.[28] It does seem reasonable for all schools in the United States to offer Spanish.

The Arts. From the dawn of civilization, men and women have used music, dance, and the visual arts to transmit the heritage of a

people and express human joys and sorrows. They are means by
which a civilization can be measured.

Civics. A course in American government—traditionally called
civics—should be required of all students, with focus on the traditions of democratic thought, the shaping of our own governmental
structures, and political and social issues we confront today.

Health. No knowledge is more crucial than knowledge about
health. Without it, no other life goal can be successfully achieved.
Therefore, all students should study health, learning about the
human body, how it changes over the life cycle, what nourishes it
and diminishes it, and how a healthy body contributes to emotional well-being.

Work. The one-semester study of work I propose would ask how
attitudes toward work have changed through the years. How do
they differ from one culture to another? What determines the
status of and rewards for different forms of work?

Independent Project. All students, during their senior year,
should complete a Senior Independent Project, a written report
that focuses on a significant social issue and draws upon the
various fields of study in the academic core.

Transition: to work and learning. Putting students into
boxes can no longer be defended. To call some students
"academic" and others "nonacademic" has a powerful and, in
some instances, devastating impact on how teachers think about
the students and how students think about themselves. We say to
some, "You're the intellectual leaders; you will go on to further
education. You're the thinkers, not the workers." To others we
say, "You will not go on to college; you're not an academic." Students are divided between those who think and those who work,
when, in fact, life for all of us is a blend of both.

Indeed, looking to the year 2000, I conclude that twelve years of
schooling will be insufficient. Today's graduates will change jobs
several times; new skills will be required; new citizenship obligations will be confronted. Of necessity, education will be lifelong.

Therefore, I recommend that the current three-track system—academic, vocational, and general—be abolished. It should be replaced by a single-track program—one that provides a core education for all students plus a pattern of electives, keeping options open for both work and further education.

Eliminating the vocational track does not mean abolishing all vocational courses. Indeed, many of these courses are enriching and useful. They provide excellent options for a wide range of students and should be strengthened, not diminished. What I would eliminate are discriminatory labels and a tracking pattern that assume some students need no further education and that cut off their future options. I would also eliminate the narrow "marketable" skills courses that have little intellectual substance, courses that give students "hands-on" experience while denying them a decent education.

Beyond literacy and the core of common learning, I also propose that all students—through a carefully selected cluster of electives—be given an opportunity to pursue their own unique aptitudes and interests. Specifically, I recommend that the last two years of high school be considered a "transition school," a program in which half the time is devoted to completing the common core and the other half to a program of "elective clusters."

"Elective clusters" would be a carefully planned program for each student. Such a program would include five or six courses that would permit advanced study in selected academic subjects or the exploration of career options—or a combination of both. Clusters might range from health services to the arts, from computers to science, from mathematics or a foreign language to office management. Here is where specialized upper-level academic courses and quality vocational offerings would appropriately fit.

A few high schools may be able to offer a full range of elective clusters—fifteen to twenty perhaps—to match the interests of their students. For most, however, this is not possible today and it will be less possible in the future. Many comprehensive high schools are getting smaller. Budgets have been tightened. Teachers have been laid off, and elective courses in both academic and vocational programs have been dropped. In spite of the talk about the smorgasbord of electives, the truth is that at many schools students will have fewer, not more, elective choices in the days ahead.

Clearly, if high schools are to offer advanced academic study and career exploration, they must recognize they cannot do it all. High schools must become "connected" institutions, creating networks and specialty schools, drawing upon resources beyond the campus. Part-time lecturers from business and industry and other professionals should be used. And students themselves must be given more responsibility for their education. New teachers, new locations, and new technology are important.

Here, then, are my conclusions:

- The school program should offer a single track for all students, one that includes a strong grounding in the basic tools of education and a study of the core curriculum. While the first two years would be devoted almost exclusively to the common core, a portion of this work would continue into the third or fourth year.

- The last two years of high school should be considered a "transition school," a program in which about half the time is devoted to "elective clusters."

- The "elective cluster" should be carefully designed. Such a program would include advanced study in selected academic subjects, the exploration of a career option, or a combination of both.

- In order to offer a full range of elective clusters, the high school must become a connected institution. Upper-level specialty schools (in the arts or science or health or computers, for example) may be appropriate in some districts. High schools should also establish connections with learning places beyond the schools—such as libraries, museums, art galleries, colleges, and industrial laboratories.

There is also an urgent need to help students figure out what they should do after graduation. Therefore, I suggest:

- Guidance services should be significantly expanded. No counselor should have a case load of more than one hundred students. Moreover, school districts should provide a referral service to community agencies for those students needing frequent and sustained professional assistance.

- A new Student Achievement and Advisement Test (SAAT) should be developed, one that could eventually replace the SAT. The academic achievement portion of the test would link it to the core curriculum and to what the student has studied. The advisement section would assess personal characteristics and interests to help students make decisions more intelligently about their futures. The purpose is not to screen students out of options but to help them move on with confidence to colleges and to jobs.

The needs of the student for guidance are matched by the need of the school to be better informed about its graduates. To achieve this, the following is proposed:

- The United States Department of Education—working through the states—should expand its national survey of schools to include a sampling of graduates from all high schools at four-year intervals to learn about their post-high school placement and experience. Such information should be made available to participating schools.

Service: the new Carnegie unit. Beyond the formal academic program the high school should help all students meet their social and civic obligations. During high school young people should be given opportunities to reach beyond themselves and feel more responsibly engaged. They should be encouraged to participate in the communities of which they are a part. I recommend:

- All high school students should complete a service requirement—a new Carnegie unit—that would involve them in volunteer work in the community or at school.

The Carnegie unit, as historically defined, measures time spent in class—academic contact time. This new unit would put emphasis on time in service. The goal of the new Carnegie unit would be to help students see that they are not only autonomous individuals but also members of a larger community to which they are accountable. The program would tap an enormous source of unused talent and suggest to young people that they are needed. It would help break the isolation of the adolescent, bring young people into contact with the elderly, the sick, the poor, and the homeless, as well as acquaint them with neighborhood and governmental issues.

The service program would work like this: During each of their four high school years, students would do volunteer work in or out of the school. They could tutor younger students; volunteer in the school cafeteria, office, audio-visual center; or maintain sports equipment and playing areas. They might also move beyond the school to libraries, parks, hospitals, museums, local government, nursing homes, day-care centers, synagogues, or churches.

The new Carnegie unit would not be bound rigidly by calendar or clock. The amount of time could vary. I suggest, however, that a student invest not less than thirty hours a year, a total of 120 hours over four years, in order to qualify for one Carnegie service unit. Students could fulfill this service requirement evenings, weekends, and during the summer.

The proposed service program will require careful supervision. Jerome Kagan, professor at Harvard University, writes:

Acts of honesty, cooperation, and nurturance are public events that the staff of a school can tally and use to assign individual evaluations that are understood to be essential complements to subject mastery. We do not keep such records as faithfully as course grades, because we do not believe that schools should judge motives and behavioral attitude toward others; that is a task for the home and police department. But judging youth on standards for action and talent would make it possible for many more students to participate in, and identify with, the school community.[28]

In the spirit of this proposal, I recommend that students themselves be given responsibility to organize and monitor student service and to work with school officials in seeing that credit is appropriately assigned.

John Dewey wrote on one occasion: "A society is a number of people held together because they are working along common lines, in a common spirit, and with reference to common aims. . . . The radical reason that the present school cannot organize itself as a natural social unit is because just this element of common and productive activity is absent."[29]

A service term for all students will do much to help build a sense of community and common purpose within a school. In the end, the goal of service in the schools is to teach values—to help all students understand that to be fully human one must serve.

Excellence: The Public Commitment

Finally, school improvement is dependent on public commitment. How we as a nation regard our schools has a powerful impact on what occurs in them. Support for schools can take many forms, and it must come from many sources. Citizens, local school boards, state agencies and legislatures, and the federal government must work together to help bring excellence to our public schools.

No one reform can transform the schools. The single solution, the simple answer, may excite a momentary interest but the impact will not last.

Today, the push for excellence in education is linked to economic recovery and to jobs. We're being told that better schools will move the nation forward in the high-tech race. And, echoing the post-Sputnik era, we're being told that tougher math-science standards are required to keep the nation strong.

Clearly, education and the security of the nation are interlocked. National interests must be served. But where in all of this are students? Where is the recognition that education is to enrich the living individuals? Where is the love of learning and where is the commitment to achieve equality and opportunity for all?

Our schools have adjusted successfully to a host of new demands. They now serve more students from different racial, cultural, and social backgrounds. They have responded to enrollment declines and budget cuts. Experimental programs, such as magnet schools, have been introduced, and public schools are now educating vast numbers of handicapped students who previously were locked out.

There remains, however, a large, even alarming gap between school achievement and the task to be accomplished. A deep erosion of confidence in our schools, coupled with disturbing evidence that at least some of the skepticism is justified, has made revitalizing the American high school an urgent matter. The world has changed—irrevocably so—and quality education in the 1980s and beyond means preparing all students for the transformed world the coming generation will inherit.

And in the debate about public schools equity must be seen not as a chapter of the past but as the unfinished agenda of the future.

To expand access without upgrading schools is simply to perpetuate discrimination in a more subtle form. But to push for excellence in ways that ignore the needs of less privileged students is
to undermine the future of the nation. Clearly, equity and excellence cannot be divided.

I do not suggest that schools can be society's cure for every
social ill. A report card on public education is a report card on the
nation. Schools can rise no higher than the communities that support them. And to blame schools for the "rising tide of mediocrity"
is to confuse symptoms with the disease.

Still, without good schools none of our problems can be solved.
People who cannot communicate are powerless. People who know
nothing of their past are culturally impoverished. People who cannot see beyond the confines of their own lives are ill-equipped to
face the future. It is in the public school that this nation has
chosen to pursue enlightened ends for all its people. And this is
where the battle for the future of America will be won or lost.

19

GLENN DUMKE

Epilogue

It is by now unnecessary to recall the reasons why concern about the decline in educational standards has dominated discussions of American education since publication of *A Nation at Risk* two years ago. Declining test scores, huge percentages of college entrants who need remedial work, college and university graduates who are inept in communication, mathematics, and understanding of science and technology, all testified to the need to "do something" about the problem.

Reviewing the flurry of reports that have appeared and the intensity of reforms addressing the question, this volume has tried to step back and take stock. How are we doing in relation to the most basic problem? And what unintended consequences—which inevitably plague all attempts at reform—have occurred?

After two years of reform, it is clear from several papers in this book that there is still uncertainty about the most basic question regarding educational standards. What standards? This is the issue that Francis Keppel addresses in the beginning of the book—the importance of reaching a consensus on what we mean by standards and deciding what we want our schools to do before we try to fashion solutions—before we begin applying band-aids or performing major surgery.

The only consensus Americans have achieved about education so far has been a commitment to allow everyone an *opportunity* for education. But once in school, what do we want to happen? Do we want an education limited to intellectual training in its extreme form, essentially a preparatory course for college, which is the pattern in many countries? Or do we want a system that will train good citizens—with appreciation of ethics and values, and an ability to get along with others, but with less emphasis on basic academic skills? Do we want our schools to concentrate on traditional education per se, or do we want them to address current problems such as training good drivers, alerting our youth to the dangers of alcohol and drugs, and maintaining the culture and language of ethnic minorities? A price must be paid for each of these alternatives. If you stress one, you de-emphasize the others. There is only so much time available, even if the school day and year are extended.

The sense of debate in the educational profession should be evident from the conflict of views expressed in this volume. Philip Marcus and Bill Honig, for instance, place strong emphasis on teaching academic subjects. On the other hand, although they do not reject the importance of acquiring basic academic skills, Madeline Hunter and Kenneth Sirotnik and John Goodlad express concerns that the current "back-to-basics" movement is conceiving the problem of education too narrowly. Hunter stresses emotional and psychological dimensions of learning in the terms educators now consider them, and Sirotnik and Goodlad focus on limitations in educational testing as part of their broader concern that the educational system should reach out to as broad a constituency as possible. Having noted the disagreements, however, it is also possible to make too much of them. Although the "back-to-basics" movement finds its most enthusiastic supporters among traditionalists, traditionalists also have a long record—going back to ancient Greece, in fact—of commitment to broader concerns of education, beyond narrow academic goals.

The chapters in Part II set forth the very different tasks and burdens of education at different grade levels. At the elementary level, for instance, it is important to stress the three "R's" more than in the past; but to maximize learning, it is also important to adapt teaching to the personalities and character of individual students.

In secondary school, a more academic focus is both appropriate and necessary—increasing academic subject matter, classroom hours required, and amount of work demanded. Colleges and universities were scarred by the campus revolt of the 1960s, which left a legacy of grade inflation and undemanding academic requirements. Since the standards set by higher educational levels have an undoubted effect on the lower levels, no serious effort to improve lower level standards can avoid addressing higher education as well.

Voluntary professional accreditation has traditionally been the means by which institutional quality is judged and maintained, and if this process is not tightened, it will very likely be replaced by government licensure. New educational technology can help, but it has not proved to be the panacea that was hoped for. The two authors writing about faculty collective bargaining have different views of that controversial issue. But whatever small impact collective bargaining has had on improving pay and working conditions, many people believe that the adversary relations implied by collective bargaining have damaged teaching as a profession.

In the search for improved quality, one of the most fundamental issues we face involves the dilemma of choice—a dilemma that also arises in connection with how we look at the many conflicting things we want schools to do. To what extent do we want to allow individual parents and children to choose what they want the schools to be, and to what extent should society make those choices? And in the search for better schools, should we abandon bad schools or direct our effort toward improving them?

The problem of choice is not limited only to the pure voucher system, which Milton Friedman conceived as a means of allowing everybody full choice in either public or private schools. Choice also arises in proposals for relaxing rigid restrictions on attendance at particular public schools. Magnet schools, aimed at very able students, depend on relaxing those restrictions and have attracted a wide following among educators. Relaxing restrictions would in general tend to encourage different schools to specialize more than they do now, with perhaps more magnet schools serving gifted students, and other schools, staffed by appropriate specialists, emphasizing learning problems of the disadvantaged.

All such issues of choice—and others, such as tuition tax credits, which are growing in popularity—finally return us to the problems associated with tensions between basic values in education.

Other problems also affect standards. One is the problem of discipline in the schools. One of the main reasons for teaching's lack of professional appeal and the reason why many able people shun it is the fact that the school's former legal position of *in loco parentis*, with adequate authority to enforce discipline and maintain an environment conducive to education, has been gradually removed by the courts. It is no longer possible for a college dean freely to enter a student's dormitory room to conduct an investigation without running into legal complications, nor is it possible for a teacher or administrator in K–12 to discipline or expel troublesome students without risking harassment by lawsuits, legal expense, and so on. Whatever happens to teaching salaries, public regard and respect, or legislative support, teaching will never resume its former status as a desirable profession until and unless teachers and administrators are given adequate and appropriate authority to maintain order and assure an environment and atmosphere conducive to learning. Legislators must take the first corrective step, but the courts also have an obligation, as do the bar associations.

No serious discussion of the crisis in education is complete without consideration of why it happened. What institutional and philosophic elements pulled us off course and brought forth such a unanimous cry for reform?

One "cause" is the historic tendency of any democracy to respond sympathetically to the requests of its citizens, particularly when they are organized in pressure groups. One reason the Roman Republic collapsed internally was that it built through government largesse a permanent, politically powerful welfare population. In the same way, U.S. citizens yielded over a period of years to claims that "everybody should have a college education," a right they regarded as a natural outgrowth of the nation's early commitment to public elementary education. This attitude, reflecting the egalitarian strain in the American character, pressured legislatures to emphasize equality over excellence in allocating funds to education. This attitude, as a by-product, also exhibited considerable sympathy for permissive educational policies toward the "alienated youth" of the 1960s; and both responses became important elements in producing the decline in standards that is the subject of this book.

The continuing American commitment to equality also leads many citizens to misunderstand the difference between "opportunity" and "guarantee." Americans have always believed that everyone, regardless of background, should have an *opportunity* to progress in an educational system as far as his or her abilities will permit. That, of course, was the reason for publicly supported education in the first place—our determination to avoid the elitist limitations that most countries impose on their youth. But guaranteed access should not and must not also guarantee graduation or a degree. Unfortunately, the high emphasis on "access" has lowered standards everywhere, including the Ivy League and other prestige institutions.

With emphasis on access, pressures to increase educational budgets—which depend on enrollment in both public and private institutions—have also encouraged dilution of standards. The more students, the more dollars! The California State University system has struggled for years to devise a different budget process, which would encourage admission of quality rather than numbers. But for obvious reasons, it is easier to identify the problem than solve it.

A final problem related to issues of equality involves concern about civil rights and the belief by some civil rights leaders that high educational standards are "racist." Any argument that says in effect that minorities cannot achieve high standards is not only insulting to minorities; it is also unfair to people who must ultimately succeed or fail in a society that lives by high standards. To tell a person that he is educationally qualified to survive in a competitive society when he is not is both unfair and irresponsible, if not downright cruel.

One final "cause" of the problem, which is evident in many places besides education, involves the reluctance of professional groups to police themselves. Although the accreditation process is supposed to tell the public whether an institution is worth attending or not, educators have been so wary of stern demands on the part of accreditors that they have refused to permit the process to serve this basic purpose.

All of these issues, however, inevitably return us to the question of how we define what we want our schools to do and be. The lack of consensus on this point is at the heart of many problems discussed in this book.

In considering educational goals, it is important to begin by understanding what schools *cannot* do. They cannot solve all of the problems of a troubled society. They cannot do everything well, all at once. Most importantly, they cannot succeed in their most basic purposes if they are constantly veering in response to the winds of political change. They must be able to operate with stable, firm, agreed-upon objectives. *A Nation at Risk* alerted the public to problems many of us, as educators, were aware of and concerned about for a long time. But until reforms of education evolve from a broad consensus about what to do, uncertain purposes will dissipate the commitment to reform, and all reform initiatives will be subject to the vagaries of changing fashion.

In the past, unfortunately, we have tried to make pluralism the excuse for our failure to confront education with the seriousness it deserves—which means to develop a national philosophy of education. Working for such a philosophy obviously does not mean imposing an inflexible educational system on people everywhere, regardless of background, interest, ability, or circumstance. Decentralization and pluralism *are* important values. But decentralization should focus on tactical application of basic educational values and purposes.

The importance of the issue suggests the value of organizing a Presidential Commission or a series of national conferences to address it. Until we do, we must expect that all reform initiatives will be marked by continuing uncertainty of purpose.

Appendices

Notes

Contributors

Appendix A
Action at the Grass Roots—A National Sampling

The following chart presents a sample of reforms instituted by states and individual school districts since publication of A Nation at Risk *in 1983. The names of the relevant officials are given for the benefit of those who may wish to seek additional information about these programs. They are not intended to represent the full range of measures being instituted.*

Geographical Area	Grade Level	Reforms Adopted
Arkansas		
Little Rock (Bill Collins, Governor)	Secondary	The first state to require testing of already certified teachers. Those who fail have four chances to try again. After June 7, 1987, teachers who fail the 100-question National Teacher Examination cannot teach in the state.
California		
Long Beach (Francis Laufenberg, Superintendent)	Secondary	Established a multi-lingual assignment center to screen and place students with limited language skills.
Oakland (J. David Bowick, Superintendent)	K through 6	Superintendent visits parents at home and commits them in writing to spend at least one-half hour daily with their children on "reading, writing, arithmetic, or just conversation." Eventually, he hopes to get parents of all 50,000 Oakland students to sign such pledges.
San Francisco (Robert L. Alioto, Superintendent)	Elementary	Established 37 "alternative" schools, in addition to regular schools, focusing, respectively, on the basic 3 Rs, a foreign language, or parent participation in curriculum and homework. Parents must select such a school and register their children there. Parent-teacher conferences are held in the native language of the parent.
Florida		
Dade County (Miami Area) (Leonard Britton, Superintendent)	Elementary	Introduced an oral language development program for pupils whose street dialect could inhibit academic and employment opportunities.

Geographical Area	Grade Level	Reforms Adopted
Jacksonville (Herb A. Sang, Superintendent)	All	Broadcasts a daily television program, the "Learning Hour," a live, interactive program providing phone-in homework assistance; science, math, English instruction; and quizzes for which prizes are awarded. Weekend segment aimed at parents, theme being "learning is a family affair." Program able to compete with commercial TV. Started by volunteers, concept gaining strong community backing. District, once very low in statewide comparisons, now scores near the top.
Georgia		
Atlanta (Alonzo A. Crim, Superintendent)	All	Established a coalition between higher education, business, and public schools, called "Atlanta Partnership." Among several programs is the "technology quadrangle" — four magnet schools specializing, respectively, in math and science, applied technology, information processing, and communications. Schools receive benefits of business contacts and university research.
Illinois		
Chicago (Manfred Byrd, Jr. Superintendent)	All	Operates an Incentive Grant Program which encourages teachers and principals to ask for new equipment and materials. 10,000 teachers out of 23,000 in the District made grant proposals and 10% were approved, ranging from $100 to $10,000. Funds paid for items such as after-school tutorials, recording equipment for oral history projects, computers for attendance monitoring and classroom practice.
Indiana		
Indianapolis (James A. Adams, Superintendent)	All	Provides teachers with test data for each class to evaluate individual student strengths and weaknesses.
Massachusetts		
Boston (Robert R. Spillane, Superintendent)	All	Places new emphasis on accountability; appointed new principals for nearly 50% of the schools. Publishes test results for each school.

Geographical Area	Grade Level	Reforms Adopted
Springfield (Thomas Donahoe, Superintendent)	Secondary	To be eligible for sports and other extracurricular activities, students must have a C average with recently raised academic standards. Increased number of courses required for graduation.
Michigan		
Detroit (Arthur Jefferson, Superintendent)	All	Two-year old School Improvement Program created 5-to-10 person teams of staff (in secondary schools includes students) to set measurable objectives for the school year in 3 areas: learning, counseling and guidance, school security.
Minnesota		
Minneapolis (Richard E. Green, Superintendent)	All	Students not meeting academic and attendance standards may not participate in extracurricular activities.
St. Paul (David A. Bennett, Superintendent)	Secondary	Prepares profiles of failing students and develops corrective programs. Encourages parent-teacher conferences, proved to be more effective than teacher/ counselor-student sessions.
Nebraska		
Omaha (Norbert J. Schuerman, Superintendent)		Concluding that reading skills are fundamental to learning, established a Reading Services Department to monitor reading skills and objectives, and to coordinate these within a standard curriculum. Reading specialists are available at each school together with remedial reading programs.
New York		
New York City (James P. Sullivan, Coordinator, Police/School Liaison Program (on loan to N.Y. Board of Education))	Secondary	A police officer and social studies teacher team up to conduct an elective course of the history of the law, focusing on police work. A 13-school pilot program expanded in two years to cover 62 of the city's 110 high schools. Vandalism and criminal activity in and near schools have declined.

Geographical Area	Grade Level	Reforms Adopted
Ohio		
Columbus (James G. Hyre, Superintendent)	Secondary	Started school-business partnership for career development with intern openings, job placement, and workshops. Also, set up business supported tutoring and other measures through Adopt-A-School program.
Oklahoma		
Tulsa (Larry L. Zenke, Superintendent)	Secondary	Initiated special course in critical thinking, vocabulary, and test taking skills.
Pennsylvania		
Philadelphia (Constance E. Clayton, Superintendent)	All	Recently established systemwide standard curriculum, backed by curriculum-referenced tests.
Pittsburgh (Richard Wallace, Superintendent)	All	Installed a system of monitoring achievement resulting in test scores above national averages in math, reading, and language.
Texas		
Dallas (Linus Wright, Superintendent)	All	Began new step-by-step teaching program emphasizing feedback and results. 600 businesses have "adopted" virtually all district schools, providing tutoring, company tours, and financial support.
Wisconsin		
Milwaukee (Lee R. McMurrin, Superintendent)	All	Schools conduct own self-evaluation, with all schools meeting to share and evaluate data, but each school setting its own improvement targets.

Appendix B
Per Pupil Spending and Teacher Salaries, 1984–1985
(Ranking by State, including District of Columbia)

State	$ Spent per Pupil	State's Ranking	Teacher Salary	State's Ranking
Alabama	$2,247	49	$20,209	36
Alaska	6,867	1	39,751	1
Arizona	2,801	40	23,380	20
Arkansas	2,344	47	18,933	46
California	3,291	26	26,300	7
Colorado	3,398	24	24,456	17
Connecticut	4,477	6	24,520	16
Delaware	4,155	7	23,300	21
District of Columbia	4,753	5	28,621	3
Florida	3,409	21	21,057	31
Georgia	2,692	42	20,494	34
Hawaii	3,596	17	24,628	15
Idaho	2,290	48	19,700	42
Illinois	3,517	18	25,829	10
Indiana	2,638	44	23,089	22
Iowa	3,409	21	20,934	32
Kansas	3,668	16	21,208	30
Kentucky	2,792	41	20,100	38
Louisiana	2,821	38	19,690	43
Maine	3,038	33	18,329	49
Maryland	4,101	8	25,861	9
Massachusetts	3,889	13	24,110	19
Michigan	3,434	20	28,401	4
Minnesota	3,408	23	25,920	8
Mississippi	2,205	50	15,971	51
Missouri	2,993	35	20,452	35
Montana	3,968	11	21,705	27
Nebraska	3,128	31	20,153	37
Nevada	2,998	34	22,520	25
New Hampshire	2,964	36	18,577	48
New Jersey	5,220	3	25,125	12
New Mexico	3,278	28	22,064	26
New York	5,226	2	29,000	2
North Carolina	2,588	45	20,691	33
North Dakota	3,249	30	19,900	40

Appendix B Continued

Per Pupil Spending and Teacher Salaries, 1984–1985
(Ranking by State, including District of Columbia)

State	$ Spent per Pupil	State's Ranking	Teacher Salary	State's Ranking
Ohio	3,315	25	22,737	23
Oklahoma	3,264	29	18,930	47
Oregon	3,963	12	24,889	13
Pennsylvania	4,002	10	24,435	18
Rhode Island	4,097	9	27,384	5
South Carolina	2,650	43	19,800	41
South Dakota	2,813	39	17,356	50
Tennessee	2,349	46	20,080	39
Texas	3,287	27	22,600	24
Utah	2,182	51	21,307	29
Vermont	3,783	15	19,014	45
Virginia	3,043	32	21,536	28
Washington	3,437	19	25,610	11
West Virginia	2,866	37	19,563	44
Wisconsin	3,880	14	24,780	14
Wyoming	4,809	4	26,709	6
U.S. Average	$3,429	—	$23,546	—

Source: National Education Association, Research. *Estimates of School Statistics, 1984–85.* Copyright ©1985. Reprinted by permission.

Editor's Note: The figures given above are presented in nominal terms and make no adjustment for important other factors, such as the cost of living, physical environment, and other variables that determine the real standard of living.

NOTES

1. William J. Johnston: "Introduction"

1. Other, more recent studies include Ernest L. Boyer, *High School: A Report on Secondary Education in America* (New York: Harper & Row, 1983); John I. Goodlad, *A Place Called School: Prospects for the Future* (New York: McGraw-Hill, 1984); Task Force on Federal Elementary and Secondary Education, *Making the Grade* (New York: Twentieth Century Fund, 1983); National Science Foundation, *Educating Americans for the Twenty-First Century* (Washington, D.C.: National Science Foundation, 1983); Education Commission of the States, *Action for Excellence: A Comprehensive Plan to Improve Our Nation's Schools* (Denver, CO: Education Commission for the States, 1983).

2. Philip N. Marcus: "Evidence of Decline in Educational Standards"

1. Diane Ravitch, *The Troubled Crusade: American Education, 1945–1980* (New York: Basic Books, 1983), p. 6.

2. Diane Ravitch, "Scapegoating the Teachers," *The New Republic,* November 7, 1983, p. 27.

3. Allen Bloom, "Our Listless Universities," *National Review* (10 December, 1982): 1537.

4. Ben J. Wattenberg, *The Good News Is the Bad News Is Wrong* (New York: Simon and Schuster, 1984), Chapter 30, "War Games."

5. *New York Times,* "Booming Corporate Education Efforts Rival College Programs, " p. A10, 28 January 1985.

6. "Doing Well By Doing Good: Business Philanthropy and Social Investment, 1860–1984," unpublished paper of Program on Non-Profit Organizations, Yale University, January, 1985, p. 10.

7. *New York Times,* p. A10, 28 January 1985.

8. Joseph Adelson, "Why the Schools May Not Improve," *Commentary* (October, 1984): 41–45.

9. Patricia A. Graham, "Schools: Cacophony About Practice, Silence About Purpose," *Daedalus* (Fall, 1984): 44.

3. Francis Keppel: "Standards—By What Criteria?"

1. *Phi Delta Kappan* 66, no. 5 (October, 1984): 104–5.

2. Powell and Steelman, "Variations in State SAT Performance: Meaningful or Misleading", *Harvard Educational Review* (November, 1984).

3. K. E. Young, C. M. Chambers, H. R. Kells and Associates, *Understanding Accreditation* (Jossey-Bass Publishers, San Francisco, 1983), pp. 226–32.

4. Carnegie Council on Policy Studies in Higher Education, *Three Thousand Futures* (Jossey-Bass: San Francisco, 1980), p. 119.

5. Nathan Glazer, *American Journal of Education* (May, 1984): 310.

7. Hobert W. Burns: "A View of Standards in Post-Secondary Education"

1. Lewis Carroll, *Alice's Adventures in Wonderland* (Harmondsworth, Middlesex [England]: Penguin Books, Ltd., 1955), pp. 87–88.

2. National Commission on Excellence in Education, *A Nation at Risk: The Imperative for Educational Reform* (Washington: United States Department of Education, April, 1983), pp. 5–6.

3. There are administrators who remember the hiring of faculty members, sight unseen and credentials unreviewed, in order to get an instructor into the classroom tomorrow.

4. George Will, "The Decline of Education," *San Francisco Chronicle,* undated clipping ca. 1982.

5. David B. Truman, "Foreword" to Daniel Bell, *The Reforming of General Education* (New York: Columbia University Press, 1966), p. xi.

6. Theodore D. Lockwood, "The Rush Back to General Education," *The Chronicle of Higher Education* (XIV: 13), May 23, 1977, p. 32.

7. Martin Trow, "Reflections on the Transition from Mass to Universal Higher Education," *Daedalus* 99, no. 1 (Winter, 1970): 35.

8. Gary A. Knight and Peter Schotten, "Illiberal Education," *The College Board Review* (Fall, 1975): 9.

9. Samuel Hux, "The Laissez-Faire University," *Worldview* 20, no. 5 (March, 1977): 41.

10. Lewis Carroll, ibid., pp. 45–46.

11. Thomas Sowell, "We're Not Really 'Equal,'" *Newsweek,* September 7, 1981, p. 13.

12. John W. Gardner, *Excellence: Can We Be Equal and Excellent Too?* (New York: Harper & Brothers, 1961), p. 15.

13. R. Bretall (editor), *A Kierkegaard Anthology* (Princeton: Princeton University Press, 1946), p. 269.

14. Hobert W. Burns, *Philosophy, Politics, and Public Education* (Syracuse: Syracuse University [The J. Richard Street Lecture], 1963), pp. 8, 11.

15. Richard W. Lyman, "Remarks to the General Session," 1974 Annual Conference of the National [and California] Association of Independent Schools, San Francisco, March 21, 1974. Mimeograph, p. 4.

16. Thomas Sowell, ibid.

17. Ernest van den Haag, "Economics is Not Enough—Notes on the Anticapitalist Spirit," *The Public Interest* (Fall, 1976): 112.

18. Lewis Carroll, ibid., pp. 79–81.

19. "A nation that expects to be both free and ignorant . . . expects what never was and never will be." Thomas Jefferson, letter to Colonel Charles Yancey, 1816.

20. Paul Kurtz, "Excellence and Irrelevance: Democracy and Higher Education," in *The Idea of a Modern University,* edited by Sidney Hook, Paul Kurtz, and Miro Todorovich (Buffalo: Prometheus Books, 1974), p. 191.

21. Buell G. Gallagher, *Campus in Crisis* (New York: Harper & Row Publishers, 1974), pp. 204–205.

22. Geoffrey Wagner, *The End of Education* (New York: A. S. Barnes and Company, Inc., 1976), p. 130.

23. Ibid., p. 128.

24. John R. Silber, "The Need for Elite Education," *Harper's,* June, 1977, p. 22.

25. William E. Vandament, "CSU Plan to Reduce Remedial Activity: 1985–1990," memorandum to Presidents of The California State University (AA 85-05), February 25, 1985, pp. 4–5.

26. Lewis Carroll, ibid., pp. 126–128.

27. Ed Asiano, "Grades Up, Value Down," *Summertimes* (San Jose University) 68, no. 4 (July 22, 1981): 1.

28. The California State University, "Academic Grades, Spring 1974" and "Academic Grades, Spring 1984," memoranda from Office of the Chancellor to campus Directors of Institutional Research (IR 75-06 and AS 84-28), *passim.*

29. George F. Will, "D is for Dodo," *Newsweek,* February 9, 1976, p. 84.

30. In 1962–1963 the average SAT scores, verbal and mathematical, were 478 and 502; a decade later they were 445 and 481; a decade after that they were 424 and 446. Only in 1981 did they begin to level off and, in 1984, showed a slight rise.

31. National Commission on Excellence in Education, ibid., p. 14.

32. Charles J. Brauner and Hobert W. Burns, *Problems in Education and Philosophy* (Englewood Cliffs: Prentice-Hall, Inc., 1965), p. 102.

33. *U.S. News & World Report,* December 4, 1972, pp. 56–58.

34. *The Chronicle of Higher Education,* February 3, 1975, p. 24.

35. Ibid., February 20, 1973, p. 12.

36. *San Francisco Chronicle,* March 2, 1974.

37. *San Francisco Sunday Examiner and Chronicle,* July 13, 1969.

38. *Stanford Daily,* undated clipping ca. March 1975.

39. John W. Gardner, *Excellence,* ibid., p. 74.

40. Daniel Patrick Moynihan, "Can Private Universities Maintain Excellence?," *Change* 9, no. 8 (August, 1977): 8.

41. Lewis Carroll, *Through the Looking Glass* (Harmondsworth, Middlesex [England]: Penguin Books, Ltd., 1951), pp. 99–100. (First published in 1872.)

42. Michael W. Kirst, *Who Controls Our Schools?* (New York: W. H. Freeman and Company, 1984), p. 161.

43. Ibid., p. 157.

44. Ernest L. Boyer, *High School: A Report On Secondary Education in America* (New York: Harper & Row Publishers, 1983), p. 253.

45. Martin Trow, "Underprepared Students and Public Research Universities," in *Challenge to American Schools: The Case for Standards and Values,* John H. Bunzel, editor (New York: Oxford University Press, 1985), p. 194.

46. John H. Bunzel, "Introduction," ibid., p. 7.

8. Sally B. Kilgore: "Educational Standards in Private and Public Schools"

1. The High School and Beyond survey of school administrators is part of a larger longitudinal study of secondary and post-secondary schooling and work sponsored by the National Center of Education Statistics. Students from 1,015 schools—public and private—are included in the sample. The 1982 administrators survey has responses from 892 schools, 121 of which are private secondary schools.

2. The data should be interpreted with caution. Respondents were asked to list the entrance requirements of their schools. Only 3 percent of the public school respondents indicated that they had any academic requirements. It is possible that with the open-ended structure of this item, respondents overlooked the successful completion of 8th or 9th grade as an entrance requirement.

3. National Catholic Education Association, *The Catholic High School* (Washington, D.C.: National Catholic Education Association, 1985).

4. As a reference, the average college or university uses undergraduate tuition fees to meet 50 percent of the undergraduate operating expenses. See R. Geiger, *Private Sectors in Higher Education: Structure, Function, and Change in Eight Countries* (University of Michigan Press, forthcoming).

5. Perhaps those instances where school districts sought to effect desegregation through the creation of schools with only one grade level—the seventh grade—give greatest testimony to the importance of institutional heritage. Teachers were expected to create spontaneously an orderly environment. Seventh graders are a sufficient challenge for educators in institutions *with* traditions and older children to orient student behavior. Dare we imagine the situation without these conditions? Gary Fine provides an excellent review of the growing sociological literature on organizational culture in G.A. Fine, "Negotiated Orders and Organizational Cultures," *Annual Review of Sociology,* Volume 10, edited by R.H. Turner and J.F. Short, 1984.

6. Some data suggest that the application of standards is increasingly restricted to entrance into honors courses. Again, though, the level of performance or achievement expected of the student varies by school, since these programs usually enroll students whose achievement is in the top 10 or 20 percent for that particular school. Thus, many suburban schools may be quite content to allow students to self-select into a pre-college curriculum. Admission standards are limited to specific classes, such as honors English or math. See also M.K. Finley, "Teachers and Tracking in a Comprehensive High School" in *Sociology of Education,* (October, 1984): 233–243.

7. In 1983, I conducted exploratory interviews in 4 school districts in Texas and 2 school districts in Georgia. Using a snowball sampling strategy, I talked to both middle school and high school counselors and teachers.

8. The elite private school sample of the High School and Beyond study includes 12 schools that in 1979 had the highest number of National Merit Finalist seniors attending their school.

9. This variation within the public sector would explain the seemingly contradictive findings of J.E. Rosenbaum, *Making Inequality* (New York: Wiley, 1976); and R. Rehberg, and E. Rosenthal, *Class and Merit in the American High School* (New York: Longman, 1978).

10. Discipline actually tied with value orientation as the second most frequently cited reason for placing a child in a private sector school in the M. Williams, K. Small, and A. Hunter report, "Parents and School Choice," Working Paper of the School Finance Project, U.S. Department of Education, 1983.

11. See J.S. Coleman, T. Hoffer, and S.B. Kilgore, *High School Achievement* (New York: Basic Books, 1982; and A.S. Bryk, P.B. Holland, V. Lee, and R.A. Carricdo, *Effective Catholic Schools: An Exploration* (Washington, D.C.: National Center for Research in Total Catholic Education, 1984).

12. S.B. Kilgore, *School Policy and Cognitive Growth in Public and Catholic Secondary Schools,* unpublished dissertation manuscript, University of Chicago, 1982.

13. Coleman, Hoffer, Kilgore (1982) find that school size negatively affects attendance rates in the public sector. The effect of size on student misbehavior was not explored.

14. The probabilities are obtained by estimating, in each instance, by subtracting the probability that none of the teachers will know a given student from one. In the first case, the probability is $[1-(6/8)^4]$ and in the second case, the probability is $[1-(38/40)^4]$. The example also assumes that the origins and destinations of the students are random.

15. Whether or not student conduct is used as an admission criteria for the academic track has been the subject of numerous debates. Although student misbehavior is correlated with track placement, the causal order remains unclear. Using the HSB sophomore cohort data, my own investigation of students leaving the academic track between the 10th and 12th grades fails to demonstrate any significant role for student behavior.

16. National Commission on Excellence in Education, *A Nation at Risk* (Washington, D.C.: U.S. Government Printing Office, 1983); E.L. Boyer, *High School: A Report on Secondary Education in America* (New York: Harper & Row, 1983); J.I. Goodlad, *A Place Called School* (New York: McGraw Hill, 1984); and Coleman, Hoffer, and Kilgore, 1982.

17. National Commission on Excellence in Education, 1983.

18. S.B. Kilgore, and W.W. Pendleton, "Curriculum Policies and School Outcomes: Unantici- pated Consequences of Education Reforms." Unpublished manuscript.

19. This exploratory research was done using the sophomore cohort of the High School and Beyond survey.

20. S.B. Kilgore, N. Lewin-Epstein, "The pursuit of education: Abandoning educational ambitions in context." Unpublished manuscript.

21. Ibid.

22. Bryk, et al., 1984.

23. Ibid.

24. Coleman, Hoffer, and Kilgore, 1982.

25. Bryk, et al., 1984.

26. D. Resnick, "Minimum Competency Testing Historically Considered," *Review of Research in Education* Volume 8, edited by D.C. Berliner, 1980; and Lorrie Shepard, "Tech- nical Issues in Minimum Competency Testing," *Review of Research in Education*, Volume 8, edited by D.C. Berliner, 1980.

9. Bill Honig: "California's Reform Program"

1. See Patricia Albjerg Graham, "Schools: Cacophony About Practice; Silence About Pur- pose," *Daedalus* (Fall, 1984): 29.

2. Ibid.

3. See *Performance Report for California Schools; Indicators of Quality 1984.*

10.   James D. Likens: "A Preliminary Diagnosis: The California Experience"

1. This chapter draws extensively on a two-year study of K–12 public education in Califor- nia, Project 28 of the Southern California Research Council, *Financing Quality Education in Southern California* (1985). The project, which was coordinated by the author and by Hans C. Palmer, received generous funding from the Haynes Foundation and from more than fifty sponsoring business corporations in Southern California. The core of the project consisted of six symposia at which invited experts addressed pressing issues in California public education; this chapter relies heavily on the views and analysis of the following individuals who spoke at these symposia: Bill Honig, Michael W. Kirst, Harry Handler, Conrad Briner, Claudia Hampton, Charles Carpenter, Marylyn Pauley, W. M. Marcussen, Gerald D. Foster, Kevin McCarthy, Gerald Kissler, Charles Kerchner, Lorraine M. McDonnell, Daniel Mazmanian, J. David Bowick, Robert Cervantes, Kenneth Hall, Eugene Tucker, and James W. Guthrie. Mem- bers of the project's Business Executives Research Committee also played a key role in shaping the conclusions of the study. While the contributions of these people are gratefully acknowledged, they must be absolved of any responsibility for errors that may be found in this chapter, or for its overall point of view and conclusions.

2. Ernest L. Boyer, *High School: A Report on Secondary Education in America,* The Car- negie Foundation for the Advancement of Teaching (New York: Harper & Row, 1983), Chapter 3.

3. Michael W. Kirst, "Improving Schools in an Era of Fiscal Constraints," presentation to the California Coalition for Fair School Finance, March 1982.

4. Berman, Weiler Associates, *Improving Student Performance in California, Recommenda- tions for the California Roundtable,* R-101/3 (Berkeley, CA: November, 1982).

5. A summary may be found in California State Department of Education, "Hughes-Hart Educational Reform Act of 1983: Summary of SB 813 and Related Legislation." See also two publications by the California Coalition for Fair School Finance, "Senate Bill 813: The Hughes-

Hart Educational Reform Act of 1983" (October, 1983) and "Provisions of Senate Bill 813" (November, 1983).

6. James W. Guthrie and Michael W. Kirst, "Conditions of Education in California: 1984," Project PACE, 1984.

7. For example, The College Board, *Academic Preparation for the World of Work*, (New York: College Board Publications, 1984); National Academy of Sciences, National Academy of Engineering, Institute of Medicine, *High Schools and the Changing Workplace: The Employers' View*, Report of the Panel on Secondary School Education for the Changing Workplace (Washington, D.C.: National Academy Press, 1984).

8. For example, the College Board report cited in the previous footnote; and Welford W. Wilms, *Technology, Job Skills, and Education: A Reassessment of the Links*, study prepared for the Education Committee, Los Angeles Area Chamber of Commerce, January 25, 1983.

9. John I. Goodlad, *A Place Called School: Prospects for the Future*, (New York: McGraw-Hill, 1984), Chapter 4.

10. Much of the data on performance of California students reported in the remainder of this section come from Gerald R. Kissler, Vice Provost, Planning and Administration, College of Letters and Science, University of California, Los Angeles. Some of this information is found in his paper, "The Educational Crisis in California: Can the Catastrophe Be Avoided?" presentation to the California Coalition for Fair School Finance, March, 1983. See also Guthrie and Kirst.

11. Lorraine M. McDonnel provided the ideas for this and the following two paragraphs. See also Allan Odden, "Financing Educational Excellence," *Phi Delta Kappan* (January, 1984); Michael Cohen, "Instructional Management, and Social Conditions in Effective Schools," in Allan Odden and L. Dean Webb, eds., *School Finance and School Improvement* (Cambridge: Ballinger, 1983).

12. In 1985 State Senator Hart has introduced a bill to reduce class size in California high school mathematics, social studies, English, and science classes from their present average of about thirty students to twenty students per class over eight years. The bill, which would eventually provide an extra $200 per student for high schools that meet the enrollment goal, would cost more than $1 billion per year by the time it was in full effect after eight years. The bill does not include other high school subjects such as foreign language or electives. Nor does the bill propose lowering class sizes in elementary schools. If one were to do so following the formula of Senate Bill 1210, its cost would also exceed $1 billion per year, not counting the cost of new facilities; reducing class size from the present 30 per class to 20 per class would also require building one new classroom for every two now in place.

13. Quoted in Gerald Holton, "A *Nation at Risk* Revisited," *Daedalus* (Fall, 1984): 18.

14. Ibid., p. 18.

15. Ibid., p. 22.

16. For a good discussion of vouchers see John E. Coons and Stephen D. Sugarman, *Education by Choice: The Case for Family Control* (Berkeley, CA: University of California Press, 1978). Excellent analyses of attempts to conduct voucher experiments in California and elsewhere are found in Elliott Levinson, *The Alum Rock Voucher Demonstration: Three Years of Implementation* (Santa Monica: Rand Paper Series P-5631, April, 1976) as well as in David K. Cohen and Eleanor Farrar, "Power to Parents?—The Story of Education Vouchers," *The Public Interest*, No. 48 (Summer, 1977): 72–97.

17. Henry Levin, "Reclaiming Urban Schools," *IFG Policy Perspectives* (Winter, 1983).

18. Boyer, pp. 233–236.

19. In the 1970s the state very nearly broke up the gigantic Los Angeles Unified School District, which has an enrollment in excess of 500,000. Through the years some organized pressure has come from the San Fernando Valley, which is largely comprised of Anglo, middle-

class suburbs, to permit it to leave L.A. Unified School District and become a separate district; in 1985 a bill has been introduced in the legislature to achieve this objective. Some consideration is also being given in heavily Hispanic East Los Angeles to asking the legislature to authorize it to leave L.A. Unified School District and form a new district.

20. For a general discussion not specifically directed to California, see Linda Darling-Hammond, *Beyond the Commission Reports: The Coming Crisis in Teaching*, (Santa Monica: Rand Paper Series, July, 1984).

21. Guthrie and Kirst.

11.   Bernard R. Gifford and Trish Stoddart: "Teacher Education: Rhetoric or Real Reform?"

1. National Commission on Excellence in Education, *A Nation at Risk: The Imperative for Educational Reform* (Washington, D.C.: U.S. Department of Education, April, 1983). Ernest L. Boyer, *High School: A Report on Secondary Education in America* (New York, N.Y.: Harper & Row, 1983). George H. Gallup, "The Fourteenth Annual Gallup Poll of the Public's Attitude Toward the Public Schools", *Phi Delta Kappan* 64 (1): 37–50 (September, 1982). Hereafter, *A Nation at Risk, High School,* and Gallup "The Fourteenth Annual Gallup Poll."

2. Memo to members of the Planning and Research Committee from David P. Wright, Coordinator, Planning and Research, California, Commission on Teacher Credentialing, "Report on Results from the July Administration of the California Basic Educational Skills Test (CBEST)", Sacramento, CA: California, Commission on Teacher Credentialing, November 14, 1983.

3. California Commission for Teacher Preparation, Carolyn Denham and Ann Lieberman, eds., *Time to Learn* (Washington, D.C.: National Institute of Education, 1980), and Michael Rutter et. al., *Fifteen Thousand Hours: Secondary Schools and Their Effects on Children* (Cambridge, Mass.: Harvard University Press, 1979).

4. Denham and Lieberman, eds., *Time to Learn.*

5. Ralph Brott, "Teacher Testing" (unpublished paper), Berkeley, CA: School of Education, University of California, 1983. See also *Improving the Attractiveness of the K–12 Teaching Profession.*

6. This figure was calculated by multiplying the maximum number of new teachers, 190,-000, by the current pupil-teacher ratio, 20.6 by 20 years of teacher experience.

7. Louis Harris and Associates, *The Metropolitan Life Survey of the American Teachers: A Summary* (New York: Metropolitan Life Insurance Companies, June, 1984).

8. University of California, Commission on Education, Neil J. Smelser, Chair, *Report of the Commission on Education* (Berkeley, CA: Office of the Chancellor, University of California, May 13, 1981).

9. Harry George Judge, *American Graduate School of Education: A View from Abroad* (New York, NY: The Ford Foundation, 1982); Gary Sykes, Contradictions, Ironies and Promises Unfulfilled: A Contemporary Account of the Status of Teaching", *Phi Delta Kappan* 65(2): 87–93 (October, 1983); See also Donna Kerr, "Teacher Competence".

10. Gary Sykes, "Contradictions, Ironies and Promises Unfulfilled".

11. William H. Drummond and Theodore E. Andrews, "The Influence of Federal and State Governments on Teacher Education", *Phi Delta Kappan* 62(2): 97–99 (October, 1980). Hereafter, Drummond and Andrews, "The Influence of Federal and State Governments".

12. C. Emily Feistritzer, *The Making of a Teacher: A Report on Teacher Education and Certification* (Washington, D.C.: The National Center for Education Information, 1984).

13. Ibid.

14. Ray Hull et. al., *Research on Student Teaching: A Question of Transfer* (Eugene, OR: Division of Teacher Education, University of Oregon, Fall, 1981).

15. Frederick J. McDonald, *Beginning Teacher Evaluation Study: Phase II, 1973–1974, Summary Report* (Sacramento, CA: California, State Commission for Teacher Preparation and Licensing, July, 1976); American Education Research Association, B. Othanel Smith, ed., *Research in Teacher Education: A Symposium* (Englewood Cliffs, NJ: Prentice-Hall, Inc., 1971); Gideonse, "The Necessary Revolution in Teacher Education"; F.B. Haisley et al, *A Planning Document;* K. Charlie Lakin and Maynard C. Reynolds, "Curricular Implications of Public Law 94-142 for Teacher Education", *Journal of Teacher Education* 34(2): 13–18 (March-April, 1983).

16. The preparation of elementary and secondary school teachers would differ. Elementary school teachers would focus on learning and development in individuals 4 through 13 years, in a range of subject matter areas including reading, writing, mathematics, and science. Secondary school teachers would focus on learning and development in individuals 9 through 20 years of age, in two complementary subjects such as mathematics and a physical science.

17. Bernard Joyce and Beverly Showers, "The Coaching of Teaching", *Education Leadership* 40(1): 4–10 (October, 1982).

18. Douglas W. Hunt, "Teacher Induction: An Opportunity and a Responsibility", NASSP *Bulletin* 52(330): 130–136 (October, 1968).

19. Dan Lortie, *Schoolteacher* (Chicago: University of Chicago Press, 1975).

20. Patricia Elias and Frederick J. McDonald, *Study of Induction Programs for Beginning Teachers: Executive Summary* (Berkeley, CA: Educational Testing Service, 1982).

21. F.B. Haisley et al, *A Planning Document for Revised Elementary and Secondary Teacher Preparation Programs.*

22. Edna M. Kehl, "The Effects of a First-Year Induction Program on Teacher Competence" (unpublished Ph.D. dissertation), Eugene, OR: College of Education, University of Oregon, 1981.

23. F.B. Haisley et al, *A Planning Document for Revised Elementary and Secondary Teacher Preparation Programs.*

24. Linda Darling-Hammond, *Beyond the Commission Reports: The Coming Crisis in Teaching,* (Santa Monica, CA: Rand Corporation, April 13, 1984).

25. Louis Harris and Associates, *Survey of the American Teacher,* 1984.

26. "A New Design for the K–12 Teaching Profession and Recommended Next Steps", an unpublished paper prepared for the California Roundtable on Educational Opportunity: Asilomar conference July 1–3, 1984, August 30, 1984.

27. Ibid.

28. Ibid.

29. Linda Darling-Hammond, *Beyond the Commission Reports.*

30. Ibid.

31. Louis Harris and Associates, *Survey of the American Teacher,* 1984.

32. "A Closer Look at Teacher Competency Testing", *NEA Reporter* 21(1):4–5 (January–February, 1982).

33. There is a severe shortage of mathematics and science teachers. The Los Angeles Unified School District alone needed 600 math teachers in 1983. See James W. Guthrie and Ami Zusman, *Mathematics and Science Teacher Shortages: What Can California Do?* (Berkeley, CA: Institute of Government Studies, University of California, 1982). Fifty percent of math classes in junior high schools are taught by teachers with less than a minor in mathematics (see Bernard R. Gifford and Glenn Seaborg, "Research Universities and the Improvement of Precollegiate Science and Mathematics Education: Building a New Linkage Between Theory and Practice" (unpublished report), Berkeley, CA: Lawrence Hall of Science, University of California, Berkeley, 1983). This situation is unlikely to improve in the near future. Guthrie and Zusman also reported in *Mathematics and Science Teacher Shortages* that in 1982 the total number of

students enrolled in math and science teacher preparation programs in California was 371. In that same year, they estimate that 2,200 math or science teachers resigned from California schools. In 1981 more than 50 percent of math and science graduates who were qualified to teach chose to go into industry instead. As Guthrie and Zusman point out, the opportunities for career development and high salaries offered to math and science graduates in industry are not matched by those in the teaching profession.

34. California Roundtable on Educational Opportunity, Sandra Smith, Chair, *Improving the Attractiveness of the K–12 Teaching Profession* (Sacramento, CA: Department of Education, 1983).

35. Sarah Lawrence Lightfoot, "The Lives of Teachers"; Gary Sykes and Lee Shulman, eds., *Handbook of Teaching and Policy* (New York, NY: Longmans, 1983); Susan L. Griffiths, "Conditions of Organized Decline: Responses of Experienced Ex-Teachers and Current Teachers" (unpublished Ph.D. dissertation), Palo Alto, CA: School of Education, Stanford University, 1983.

36. Gary Sykes, "Contradictions, Ironies, and Promises Unfulfilled".

37. There is a particular need for math specialists in both elementary and high schools (Gifford and Seaborg, note 33). Currently, no California university offers an advanced specialist credential in the teaching of math. Upgrading the teaching of math requires that math specialist credential programs be instituted and their graduates be appointed to math-specialist teacher positions in elementary and high schools.

12. Robert E. Doherty: "Teacher Bargaining: Teacher Quality, Student Achievement, Public Control"

1. *Chicago Tribune,* March 7, 1977, p. 4.

2. Linda Darling-Hammond, *Beyond the Commission Report: The Coming Crisis in Teaching.* (Santa Monica: Rand Corporation, 1984) p. 2.

3. Ibid., p. 3.

4. Ibid., p. 6.

5. Jonothan Friendly, "Uphill Push for 'Master Teachers,'" *New York Times,* December 18, 1984, C 13.

6. See, for example, a 1984 study by the Association for Supervision and Curriculum Development, *Incentives for Excellence in America's Schools.*

7. *Matter of West Irondequoit Board of Education,* 4 PERB 3727 (1971).

8. Cited in *Government Employee Relations Report,* September 9, 1978, pp. 27–28.

9. Tables H & I, *Labor-Management Relations in State and Local Government, 1980,* Special Studies No. 102, Bureau of Census, Department of Labor, 1981.

10. The Gallup Opinion Index, Report No. 191, (Princeton, N.J.: American Institute of Public Opinion, August, 1981), pp. 7–13.

11. *Ithaca Journal,* February 14, 1978, p. 12.

12. New York State Public Employment Relations Board, *Press Release,* January 9, 1985.

13. *City of Madison Joint School District No. 8 v. Wisconsin Employment Relations Commission,* 429 U.S. 167 (1976).

14. Ibid. at 175.

15. *17 GERR Reference File,* February 8, 1982, p. 4092.

13. Albert Shanker: "Collective Bargaining with Education Standards"

1. Robert J. Braun, *Teachers and Power* (New York, 1972), p. 22.

2. Thomas R. Brooks, *Towards Dignity* (The United Federation of Teachers, 1967), pp. 7–8.

3. Quoted by Ronald Gross, editor, *The Teacher and the Taught* (New York, 1963), p. 178.

4. Sandra Feldman, *The UFT and School Conflict* (The United Federation of Teachers, pamphlet), p. 2.

5. Robert Bendiner, *The Politics of Schools* (New York, 1969), p. 114.

6. Quoted by Chester E. Finn, "Teacher Unions and School Quality: Allies or Inevitable Foes," *Phi Delta Kappan*, Jan., 1985, p. 337.

7. Ibid., p. 333.

8. Cited by Finn, p. 338.

9. A. H. Raskin, "Teachers Now Lions in Political Arena," *New York Times*, Jan. 15, 1975.

10. Finn, p. 334.

11. "Social Promotions Upset Teachers," *The American Teacher*, Feb., 1985, p. 8.

12. Kai L. Erickson, Letter to the Editor, *Phi Delta Kappan*, Feb., 1982, pp. 427–428.

13. Susan Moore Johnson, *Teacher Unions in Schools* (Temple University Press, 1984), p. 33.

14.   Richard Simonds & James Wiebe: "Electronic Technologies and the Learning Process"

1. Alan Jay Weiss, "The Revolution Around Us," *Training* (June, 1983): 42–47.

2. American Academy of Pediatrics, "Doctors to Parents: Cure Kids' TV-itis." *USA Today*. January 24, 1985.

3. T.M. Williams, "How and What Do Children Learn From Television?" *Human Communication Research* 7, no. 2 (1981): 180–192.

4. R.G. Slaby and G.R. Quarfoth, "Effects of Television On the Developing Child," in *Advances in Behavioral Pediatrics* (Greenwich, Connecticut: Johnson Associates, Inc., 1980).

5. Williams, 1981.

6. R. Hornik, "Television Access and the Slowing of Cognitive Growth," *American Educational Research Journal* 15 (1978): 1–15.

7. S. Ball and G.A. Bogatz, *Reading with Television: An Evaluation of the Electronic Company* (Princeton, New Jersey: Educational Testing Service, 1973).

8. D.J. LeRoy, "Who Watches Public Television?" *Journal of Communication* (Summer, 1980): 157–163.

9. G.A. Comstock, *Trends in the Study of Incidental Learning From Television Viewing* (Syracuse, New York: Eric Clearinghouse in Information Resources, 1978).

10. S. Calvert and B. Watkins, "Recall of Television Content as a Function of Content Type and Level of Production Feature Use." Paper presented in a symposium *"Television I"* at the meeting of the Society for Research in Child Development, San Francisco, March 1979.

11. G.C. Chu and W. Schramm, *Learning From Television: What The Research Says* (Washington, D.C.: National Association of Educational Administrators, 1969).

12. D.M. Roberts, "The Impact of Electronic Calculators on Educational Performance." *Review of Educational Research* 50, no.1 (1980): 71–98.

13. "Stumbling into the Computer Age." *Forbes*, August 13, 1984, pp. 35–40.

14. "Master Type" available from Scarborough Systems, 25 N. Broadway, Tarrytown, NY 10591.

15. "CompuPoem" available from Graduate School of Education, University of California, Santa Barbara, CA 93106.

16. For an example of such standards, see the report, State of California, Department of Education, "Guidelines for Educational Software in California Schools." 1985. Taken from a pre-release manuscript dated January, 1985, 8 pages.

17. Franz E. Fauley, "The New Training Technologies: Their Rocky Road to Acceptance," *Training and Development Journal* (December, 1983): 22–25.

18. Kate Barnes, "CBT Gets Good Marks: Studies Show Retention Is High," *PC Week*, March 6, 1984.

19. Greg Kearsley, *Training and Technology: A Handbook for HRD Professionals* (Reading, Massachusetts: Addison-Wesley Publishing Company, 1984), pp. 178–182.

20. Ibid., pp. 95–97.

21. James Hassett, "Computers in the Classroom," *Psychology Today,* September, 1984, pp. 22–28.

22. Greg Kearsley, *Computer-Based-Training: A Guide to Selection and Implementation* (Reading, Massachusetts: Addison-Wesley Publishing Company, 1983), pp. 115–122.

23. Mary Lindquist, et. al., "The Third National Mathematics Assessment: Results and Implications for Elementary and Middle Schools." *Arithmetic Teacher* (December, 1983): 14–19.

24. The National Council of Teachers of Mathematics, *An Agenda For Action: Recommendations for School Mathematics of the 1980s.* (Reston, Virginia: The National Council of Teachers of Mathematics, 1980).

25. Gary G. Bitter and Ruth Camus, *Using a Microcomputer in the Classroom* (Reston, Virginia: Reston), 1984.

16. Glenn Dumke: "A Ministry of Education for the United States? The Problem of Accreditation"

1. J. R. Warren, ed., "Meeting the New Demands for Standards," *New Directions for Higher Education, No. 43* (San Francisco: Jossey-Bass, 1983), p. 9.

2. *The Control of the Campus,* The Carnegie Foundation for the Advancement of Teaching, 1982, p. 76.

3. Ibid, p. 77.

4. Ibid, pp. 77–78.

5. Ibid, pp. 78–81.

6. Ibid, pp. 83–84.

17. Kenneth A. Sirotnik and John I. Goodlad: "The Quest for Reason Amidst the Rhetoric of Reform: Improving Instead of Testing Our Schools"

1. John Dewey, *Democracy and Education* (New York: The Macmillan Company, 1916).

2. National Commission on Excellence in Education, *A Nation at Risk* (Washington, DC: U.S. Government Printing Office, 1983).

3. B. Bloom, *All Our Children Learning* (New York: McGraw-Hill, 1981), and B. Bloom, "The 2 sigma problem: The search for methods of group instruction as effective as one-to-one tutoring," *Educational Researcher,* no. 13 (1984): 4–16.

4. James S. Coleman, et al., *Equality of Educational Opportunity* (Washington, DC: U.S. Government Printing Office, 1966).

5. John I. Goodlad, *A Place Called School: Prospects for the Future* (New York: McGraw-Hill, 1984).

6. R. E. Stake, "The countenance of educational evaluation," *Teachers College Record* 68 (1967): 523–540.

7. John I. Goodlad, & Associates. *Curriculum Inquiry: The Study of Curriculum Practice* (New York: McGraw-Hill, 1979). Lest readers are thinking that we are against the assessment of student learning, we deal briefly with this issue where it matters most—in the context of instructional practice. Assessment includes (but is not limited to) testing, and testing includes (but is not limited to) right-wrong, multiple choice item procedures. Certainly some information is conveyed through an accounting of these item types answered correctly, especially on a test designed for specific course objectives relating to facts and comprehension. But more is

possible and desirable; for example: (1) Exploring error patterns as in answer-until-correct formats for multiple-choice items; (2) Developing testing strategies commensurate with various
learning styles suggested by recent work in cognitive psychology; (3) Thinking of assessment
as formative (vs. summative) and incorporating routines being recently suggested in the areas
of diagnostic testing; (4) Expanding the domains of testing to include attitudes, feelings, im-
pressions, etc., as they relate to the intended curriculum; (5) Expanding response formats
beyond the closed-ended item, e.g., open-ended, short-answer and/or essay-type response; and
(6) Systematically recording and analyzing student work samples.

Creative assessment goes hand in hand with creative teaching. Computer technology makes
much more than conventional multiple choice testing procedures now more feasible and efficient. See the special issue of the *Journal of Educational Measurement* 21, no. 4 (1984).
Moreover, data at individual and class levels can be aggregated up to school and district levels
for evaluative purposes. And in so doing, our hope is that evaluators will be as (or more) concerned with the variance *within* schools as they are with school averages.

8. M. M. Kennedy, *Working Knowledge and Other Essays* (Cambridge, MA: The Huron Institute, 1982).

9. Our work in this area can be traced through these reports and articles: K. A. Sirotnik,
and J. Oakes, Toward a comprehensive educational appraisal system: A contextual perspective, Occasional Paper No. 2, Los Angeles: University of California, Laboratory in School and
Community Education, 1981; K. A. Sirotnik, and J. Oakes, "A Contextual Appraisal System
for Schools: Medicine or Madness?" *Educational Leadership* 39 (1981): 164–173; K. A. Sirotnik, and J. Oakes, Critical Inquiry and School Renewal: A Liberation of Method Within a Critical Theoretical Perspective, Occasional Paper No. 4, Los Angeles: University of California,
Laboratory in School and Community Education, 1983; K. A. Sirotnik, Principles and Practice
of Contextual Appraisal for Schools, Occasional Paper No. 5, Los Angeles: University of
California Laboratory in School and Community Education, 1984; and K. A. Sirotnik, "An
outcome-free conception of schooling: Implications for school-based inquiry and information
systems," *Educational Evaluation and Policy Analysis* 6 (1984): 227–239. Other treatments of
school information systems that are also more comprehensive than test scores alone can be
found in: E. L. Baker, Evaluating educational quality: A rational design. Presented at the conference "Wagging the Dog, Carting the Horse: Testing Vs. Improving California's Schools,"
1984; and L. Burstein, "The use of existing data bases in program evaluation and school improvement," *Educational Evaluation and Policy Analysis* (1984), pp. 307–318.

10. S. B. Sarason, *The Culture of the School and the Problem of Change* (Boston: Allyn and
Bacon, 1971, 1st edition and 1982, revised edition).

This same theme underlies the recent analysis of high schools in T. R. Sizer, *Horace's Compromise: The Dilemma of the American High School.* (New York: Houghton Mifflin, 1984).

11. S. L. Lightfoot, *The Good High School: Portraits of Character and Culture* (New York:
Basic, 1983).

12. B. R. Joyce, *Alternative Models of Elementary Education* (Waltham, Mass.: Blaisdell,
1969).

13. E. Eisner, Using educational evaluation for the improvement of California schools. Presented at the conference "Wagging the Dog, Carting the Horse: Testing Vs. Improving California's Schools," Los Angeles: Laboratory in School and Community Education and Center for
the Study of Evaluation, UCLA, 1984.

14. K. A. Tye, and B. Benham-Tye, "Teacher isolation and school reform," *Phi Delta Kappan*
65 (1984): 319–322.

15. See J.W. Meyer, and B. Rowan, "Then Structure of Educational Organizations," in M.
Mayer, *et al.* (eds) *Studies on Environment and Organization* (San Francisco: Jossey-Bass,
1978).

16. See K.A. Sirotnik, "Responsibility vs. Accountability: Towards a Professional Teaching Profession." Paper presented at the conference of the American Educational Research Association, 1985.

17. J. Naisbitt, *Megatrends* (New York: Warner Books, 1982).

18. T. J. Peters, and R. H. Waterman, *In Search of Excellence* (New York: Harper & Row, 1982).

19. In particular, see pp. 272–279 in Goodlad, 1984.

20. J. I. Goodlad, *What Schools Are For* (Bloomington, IN: Phi Delta Kappa Educational Foundation, 1979).

21. E. Boyer, *High School* (New York: Harper & Row, 1983).

22. R. W. Tyler, *Basic Principles of Curriculum and Instruction* (Chicago: University of Chicago Press, 1949). As an example of what this all might look like, see the list on pp. 51–56 in Goodlad (1984).

23. M.M. Bentzen, *Changing Schools: The Magic Feather Principle* (New York: McGraw-Hill, 1974).

24. Compelling arguments along these lines are offered by D.H. Kerr, "Teaching Competence and Teacher Education in the United States," *Teachers College Record* 84 (1983): 525–592. L. Darling-Hammond, Beyond the Commission Reports: The Coming Crisis in Teaching, (Los Angeles: Rand Corporation, 1984); and T.R. Sizer, High School Reform and the Reform of Teacher Education, (The 1984 De Garmo Lecture, Society of Professors of Education, February 3, 1984.)

25. J. Goodlad, Beyond outcome measures: An agenda for school improvement. Presented at the conference "Wagging the Dog, Carting the Horse: Testing Vs. Improving California's Schools," 1984.

18. Ernest L. Boyer: "America's Schools: The Mission"

1. Lawrence A. Cremin, *The Genius of American Education* (New York: Vintage Books, 1965), p. 6.

2. Adolphe E. Meyer, *An Educational History of the American People,* 2nd ed. (New York: McGraw-Hill, 1967), p. 207.

3. Hechinger, *Growing Up in America,* pp. 114, 115.

4. Ibid.

5. David H. Cohen and Barbara Neufeld, "The Failure of High Schools and the Progress of Education," *Daedalus* 110, no. 10 (Summer, 1981): 72.

6. U.S. Department of Commerce, Bureau of the Census, *Historical Statistics of the United States: Colonial Times to 1970,* Part I, (Washington, D.C.: Government Printing Office, 1975), p. 369.

7. Ibid, pp. 10, 369, and Carnegie Foundation Calculations.

8. A. Harry Passow, *Secondary Education Reform: Retrospect and Prospect,* Julius and Rosa Sachs Memorial Lecture, April 7–8, 1976 (New York: Teachers College, Columbia University, 1976), p. 10.

9. Sol Cohen (ed.), *Education in the United States: A Documentary History,* Vol. E (New York: Random House, 1974), p. 1953. Reprint of Charles W. Eliot, "The Fundamental Assumptions in the Report of the Committee of Ten," *Educational Review,* vol. XXX, 325–43.

10. A. R. Dugmore, "New Citizens for the Republic," *The World's Work* 5, no. 6 (April, 1903): 3323–26.

11. Commission on the Reorganization of Secondary Education, *Cardinal Principles of Education,* Bulletin 1918, no. 35 (Washington, D.C.: Government Printing Office, 1918), p. 9.

12. William James, *Talks to Teachers on Psychology and to Students on Some of Life's Ideals* (New York: W.W. Norton, 1958); William James, *The Principles of Psychology* 3 vols.

(Cambridge: Harvard University Press, 1981); and John Dewey, *The Child and the Curriculum* (Chicago: University of Chicago Press, 1902).

13. John Dewey, *School of Society* (Chicago: University of Chicago Press, 1899), pp. 21–22.

14. Ibid., p. 19.

15. Tyack, *Turning Points in American Educational History,* p. 321.

16. Edward A. Krug, *The Shaping of the American High School,* vol. 2, 1920–1946 (Madison, Wisconsin: University of Wisconsin Press, 1972), pp. 292–293.

17. William Chandler Bagley, *Education and Emergent Man: A Theory of Education with Particular Application to Public Education in the United States* (New York: T. Nelson and Sons, 1934), p. 151.

18. Cohen and Neufeld, "The Failure of High Schools," p. 72.

19. Charles E. Silberman, *Crisis in the Classroom: The Remaking of American Education* (New York: Random House, 1970), p. 168.

20. U.S. Department of Health, Education and Welfare, Office of Education, National Panel on High School and Adolescent Education, *The Education of Adolescents: The Final Report and Recommendations* (Washington, D.C.: Government Printing Office, 1976), pp. 47, 48, 52.

21. For a discussion of communication among nonhuman species, see Carol Grant Gould, "Out of the Mouths of Beasts," *Science 83* (April, 1983): 68–72.

22. See, for example, Herbert H. and Eve V. Clark, *Psychology and Language: An Introduction to Psycholinguistics* (New York: Harcourt Brace Jovanovich, 1977), pp. 554–557, and Roger Brown, *Psycholinguistics: Selected Papers* (New York: Free Press, 1970).

23. John Stewig, *Exploring Language with Children* (Columbus, Ohio: Charles A. Merrill, 1974), pp. 3–21.

24. See, for example, Roach Van Allen and Claryce Allen, *Language Experience Activities* (Boston: Houghton Mifflin Company, 1976).

25. Donald H. Graves, *Balance the Basics: Let Them Write* (New York: Ford Foundation, 1978), p. 7.

26. Arthur H. Applebee, *A Study of Writing in the Secondary School: Final Report* (Urbana, Illinois: National Council of Teachers of English, September, 1980), pp. 140–141.

27. Ibid., p. 54.

28. Jerome Kagan, "The Moral Function of the School," *Daedalus* 110, no. 3 (Summer, 1981): 163–164.

29. Reginald D. Archambault (ed.), *John Dewey on Education: Selected Writings* (New York: Random House, 1964), p. 300.

CONTRIBUTORS

ERNEST L. BOYER is President of the Carnegie Foundation for the Advancement of Teaching, Princeton, New Jersey. Before coming to the Foundation, he was Commissioner of Education, HEW, Washington, D.C., and earlier chancellor of the State University of New York. He is the author or co-author of five books and many professional rticles. His most recent book was *High School* (1983) and he is currently writing a book on the undergraduate experience in America. He is a Senior Fellow at the Woodrow Wilson School, Princeton University; holds memberships on many boards and commissions; and frequently lectures at national meetings, schools, colleges and universities.

GEORGE BUGLIARELLO, President of the Polytechnic Institute of New York, is an engineer with a broad background in research, ranging from computer languages to biomedical engineering to fluid mechanics. He has been chairman of the Board of Science and Technology for International Development (BOSTID) of the National Academy of Science and is the U.S. member of the Science for Stability Steering Group of NATO, as well as chairman of the Advisory Panel for Technology Transfer to the Middle East of the Office of Technology Assessment. He is founder and editor of *Technology in Society—An International Journal,* has authored several hundred papers, and is the author or editor of numerous books, including *Computers and Water Resources, The History and Philosophy of Technology, Bioengineering—An Engineering View,* and *The Impact of Noise Pollution: A Socio-Technological Introduction.*

HOBERT W. BURNS is Academic Vice President Emeritus and Professor of Philosophy at San Jose State University. He served there as Acting President in 1969–1970 and, in 1983–1984, was called out of retirement to serve as President ad interim of Sonoma State University. The author of several books and numerous articles, primarily in philosophy and higher education, he has been an advisor on higher education to the governments of Bolivia, Chile, Israel, Peru, and the United States. He has taught at Stanford, Rutgers, Syracuse, USC, Hofstra, and UCLA.

ROBERT E. DOHERTY is Dean for Academic Affairs at the New York State School of Industrial and Labor Relations at Cornell University. He is the author (with Walter Oberer) of *Teachers, School Boards and Collective Bargaining* and has contributed articles and essays to a number of journals, including the *Yale Law Journal, Teachers College Record,* and *Industrial and Labor Relations Review.* He has also served on several occasions as a mediator, factfinder, or arbitrator in public-sector disputes.

GLENN DUMKE is President of the Institute for Contemporary Studies and Chancellor Emeritus of the 19-campus California State University system, which he headed from 1962–82. Prior to that he was President of San Francisco State. The author of eight books and numerous articles, he is a member of the Western Interstate Commission on Higher Education and of the Advisory Committee on Accreditation of the U.S. Department of Education.

BERNARD R. GIFFORD was appointed Dean of the Graduate School of Education at the University of California, Berkeley, in April 1983. Prior to his appointment, he was Professor of Political Science (Public Policy) and Vice President at the University of Rochester (1981–83). His previous positions were Resident Scholar and Program Officer at the Russell Sage Foundation (1977–81), Deputy Chancellor of the New York City Public Schools (1973–77), and President of the New York City Rand Institute (1972–73).

JOHN I. GOODLAD is Professor of Education, and until June 1983 was Dean, Graduate School of Education, UCLA. In addition to his recent completion of "A Study of Schooling" and the award-winning book *A Place Called School,* Dr. Goodlad's publications include a long list of articles, chapters, and books on curriculum and instruction, teacher education, policy and administration, and educational change and school improvement.

BILL HONIG was elected California State Superintendent of Public Instruction in 1982. His career began in law, serving as a clerk in the Supreme Court of California and as Counsel in the State Department of Finance. He became a teacher and, before being elected State Superintendent, was superintendent of an elementary school district in Marin County (CA), and an active member of the State Board of Education. He is co-author of the *Handbook for Planning an Effective Reading Program.*

MADELINE HUNTER recently left her twenty-year position as principal of the lab school and professor at UCLA to become a full-time professor in administration and teacher education, and an international consultant. She is author of ten books and more than two hundred journal articles, which translate psychological theory into educational practice. Her programs are used in every state and in thirty-five other countries. She is a continuing consultant to the U.S. Department of Defense, Department of State, and to many industries.

WILLIAM J. JOHNSTON was Superintendent of the Los Angeles Unified School District from 1971 to 1981, when he became Manager of Public Affairs for Southern California Gas Company. He is currently Vice Chairman of Blue Shield of California and recently became Vice Chairman of the California State Lottery Commission.

FRANCIS KEPPEL is Senior Lecturer on Education at Harvard University and has been an administrator of educational programs there, Dean of the Harvard Graduate School of Education (1948–62), Commissioner and Assistant Secretary of Education in the federal government (1962–66), and Chairman of General Learning Corporation (1966–74). His teaching activities focus on state and federal policies affecting education, with special interest in federal programs in compensatory education, student financial aid, and desegregation, and in federal-state relations. He serves on several governmental and educational boards, including the Lincoln Center for the Performing Arts in New York.

SALLY B. KILGORE is Assistant Professor of Sociology at Emory University in Atlanta, Georgia. Her various writings in education include co-authored work with James S. Coleman and Thomas Hoffer: *Public and Private Schools* and *High School Achievement.* She recently served as an advisor to a Ford Foundation sponsored study of low-income students in Catholic schools and has presented numerous papers on secondary school achievement in public and private sectors. Her current research interests include tracking practices in middle and secondary schools and the role of school processes on student achievement.

JAMES D. LIKENS is the Morris B. Pendleton Professor of Economics at Pomona College. Among his various writings are *Money and Medicine* (1977), with Joseph LaDou, and two studies he coordinated for the Southern California Research Council, *Our New Interdependence: Mexico and Southern California* (1981) and *Financing Quality Education in Southern California* (1985).

RUTH B. LOVE served as General Superintendent of Chicago Public Schools from 1981–1985. From 1975–1981 she was Superintendent of the Oakland (CA) Unified School District where she was also a teacher from 1954–1959. She has received numerous awards and honors, holds memberships in many professional organizations, and is the author of many books, pamphlets, and articles.

PHILIP N. MARCUS is President of the Institute for Educational Affairs, an educational foundation in New York City. He taught at Kenyon College, after which he became a "fallen away scholar," engaged in public policy work in Washington, D.C., and for the last decade has been a foundation officer, both at the National Endowment for the Humanities and at IEA. He is also founder and publisher of *This World* magazine, and with Peter Berger co-editor of three volumes of essays on modern capitalism (forthcoming).

PAUL M. POSSEMATO is Division Superintendent, Senior High Schools, Los Angeles County, where he oversees the education of 126,000 students. He has also served as a high school teacher, curriculum specialist and administrative coordinator, principal at the junior high school and senior high school levels, and as the Assistant Superintendent in charge of secondary curriculum of the Los Angeles Unified School District. He is the author of several articles and publications in school administration, curriculum development, and teacher and administrator training.

ALBERT SHANKER has been President of the American Federation of Teachers, AFL-CIO, since 1974 and of its New York City local, the United Federation of Teachers, since 1964. He is a Vice President of the AFL-CIO. He has written extensively on education, labor, and human rights matters in "Where We Stand," an advertisement that has appeared every Sunday since late 1970 in the *New York Times*. Over the past two years he has spoken throughout the country and written regularly in magazines and journals on issues pertaining to the education reform movement.

RICHARD SIMONDS is Manager of Learning Systems, Hewlett-Packard. He was on the faculty at the University of California, Berkeley, teaching instructional technology and administering the Educational Technology Labs and Computer Learning Services. He formerly held a similar post at the University of San Francisco. This past year he completed a term as president of the Golden Gate Chapter of the American Society for Training and Development. His most recent publication in the field of electronic technologies was "Computer Graphics in Education and Training," *Computer Graphics World,* 1980. His current research and writing has been about the uses of microcomputers and software in business and education.

KENNETH A. SIROTNIK is a Senior Research Associate in both the Laboratory in School and Community Education and the Center for the Study of Evaluation, Graduate School of Education, UCLA. He participated as a senior member of the research team that conducted "A Study of Schooling." His publications include numerous articles on topics ranging from measurement, statistics, and evaluation, to computer technology, to educational change and school improvement.

TRISH STODDART, an Educational Psychologist, is completing her Ph.D. in educational and developmental psychology at the University of California in Berkeley.

JAMES WIEBE is Associate Professor of Education and Coordinator of Computer Education at California State University, Los Angeles. He teaches a variety of courses related to computer uses in education including BASIC, Logo, and Computer Assisted Instruction. He has published fifteen articles and three books about computer and mathematics education and is a frequent speaker at regional and national conventions.